The Confidence Game
in American Literature

THE
CONFIDENCE
GAME IN
AMERICAN
LITERATURE

Warwick Wadlington

PRINCETON UNIVERSITY PRESS

Library of Congress Cataloging in Publication Data
will be found on the last printed page of this book

Publication of this book has been aided by a
grant from The Andrew W. Mellon Foundation

Chapter 3, Part One, "Godly Gamesomeness: Selftaste in *Moby-Dick*," originally appeared in a
somewhat different version in *ELH* 39 (June 1972),
309–31, copyright © 1972 by The Johns Hopkins
Press. Some of Part Three, "Nathanael West: Trick
or Trash," appeared in "Nathanael West and the
Confidence Game," *Nathanael West: The Cheaters
and the Cheated*, ed. David Madden (DeLand,
Florida: 1974), original copyright © 1974 by
Everett/Edwards, Inc.

Composed in Linotype Baskerville and printed
in the United States of America by Princeton
University Press at Princeton, New Jersey

for ELIZABETH

Contents

Preface

THE traditional function of prefaces is to state what a book does and does not attempt. Usually this is intended more for prolepsis than positive enlightenment: one tries to string barbed-wire against the reader's straying from the work's true path, which still lies in shadow. This preface will follow custom, for an adequate explanation of the book's aims and essential terms must await the sufficient room provided by the first chapter, and indeed the concrete application of method in the book as a whole. Nevertheless, a few general statements are useful here.

This study is concerned with transactions of confidence in the works of three writers—Herman Melville, Mark Twain, and Nathanael West. Specifically, it examines problematic, ambivalent, or deceptive transactions that establish imaginative authority and renew individual identity, in both the world the writer imagines and the relationship he fashions with his reader. The intersection of the two created fictions, imagined world and fabricated relationship, is the center of my interest. The focus on this center is provided by the paradigm of an equivocal game associated with the archetypal Trickster figure—a *confidence game* in which trust is provisionally or fundamentally put into question and reanimated. In traditional terms: this book addresses itself to the complex interplay of rhetoric and theme, broadly conceived. In the language of modern criticism: I wish to contribute to a phenomenology of reading three exemplary writers. The phenomenology I have in mind is much like the community process of renewal analyzed brilliantly by the anthropologist Victor Turner. In Turner's analysis, the process is founded upon a "betwixt-and-between" marginal or equivocal state that summons up the deeply hidden cultural first principles by abrogating everyday life patterns, and so has the power to reactivate a sense of *communitas* that essentially authorizes the quotidian communal structure. The interpersonal, intercommunal behavior of the Trickster, in which the very elements of mutual human faith and cooperation are precariously at stake, is the archetypal analogue of this marginal state.

I take the Trickster archetype, then, as a point of departure, an orienting ideational field that discloses the real and significant coherence of a number of apparent anomalies. Most paradoxical of these perhaps is that the ethically isolating act of cheating can enliven social connections, and inevitably our awareness of reality as opposed to what is counterfeit, by showing how vulnerable and broadly consequential these relations are. This means that I am much less interested in a fictional *type or figure* than in a *mode of fictive experience* in three major writers. The understanding of a type allows us an invaluable introduction to the intrinsically social process that italicizes relationships by a precarious joint imagining; an introduction, that is, to the work's dynamic life, as well as a means of maturing and consolidating our part in it. I stress this distinction to prevent my reader's erring from the path; for the great majority of studies that employ "archetypal approaches" create the widespread preconception, and thus the likely expectation, that such criticism can only be done one way— in my view, much too often a mechanical and simplistic way false to human experience, imaginative or otherwise.

"Archetypal" studies usually establish an all-inclusive categorization of the selected type as it appears in an author's works, and survey a number of writers to show some more or less linear development in the historical "use" of the figure. It thus often happens that the particular creations and writers become subordinated to the powerful symbol they are said to manifest, and we are provided a matching exercise that follows, like a crossword puzzle, some putative mythic story-design. Another kind of investigation might stress the national inheritance more strongly. For example, I might have shown how certain motifs repeatedly allied to the confidence game—regeneration, purification, and contagion—are given a particular native accent by a preoccupation with these matters continuing from the Puritans through Thoreau's *Walden* to the modern age. Instead of proceeding along either of these lines, I have employed the Trickster figure with its related model of persuasion as a tool for examining the detailed working and action of discrete texts, as well as the larger, overarching text these form throughout each writer's career. Not that I am uninterested in, or unaware of, the wider native currents evident in such terms as *Yankee, operator, flimflam man,* and *shingle-man*; in numerous forms of popular culture or more lasting achievements like Faulkner's Snopes trilogy; in our political habit of taking the pulse of "public confidence"; and, perhaps, even in the sobriquet we have given a President. For, if we look at the three writers I have chosen, the hundred-year period covered by careers and fictions apparently so disparate by itself suggests that whatever vision is held in common is a deeply shared, sustained imaginative possession in American experience. Yet today we do not need to be told that tricksters and trickery are an important part of our literary, and general cultural, heritage; for some time now writers, critics, and scholars have been contributing this information to the public domain. What remains, I believe, is to grasp in the works of key seminal writers what this form of communal imagination genuinely consists in—to see what, in the vivid presence of a few crucial works of art, we really possess; and what possesses us in the living act, the vital *trans-action,* of reading them.

In being attentive to this joint act of "crossing over," we will have as our patron the archetypal keeper and dissolver of boundaries. Why use an archetypal schema at all? The answer lies in my conviction that the several studies during the past decade treating deceptive fictions and artists have been largely too parochial, and thus too monotonic (usually despairing), to explain the rich uses of equivocation. Even when most valuable, they have lacked the sort of generous, coherent frame for comprehending important but obscure relationships that the Trickster myths and their cultural functioning can provide. In short, I have wanted an approach that is not overly schematic and is yet sufficiently informed to disclose the broadly encompassing issues and elusive but precise attitudes underlying the contradictions of equivocal art.

While equivocality has its place in the scheme of things, it is a pleasure to acknowledge as unambiguously as I can the help I have had from a number of people. Donald Pizer, Richard P. Adams, and Earl N. Harbert gave this study encouragement in its earliest stages. The University Research Institute of The University of Texas at Austin awarded a grant that helped me to complete the work. R. J. Kaufmann, John A. Walter, William R. Keast, and Barbara Babcock-Abrahams provided support and assistance in various ways. I have been especially fortunate in the friends kind enough to read the manuscript. Max Westbrook, Roger Abrahams, Joseph Doherty, and, again, R. J. Kaufmann contributed suggestions and criticism that for careful, thorough incisiveness went much beyond what one can fairly ask of colleagues. I hope my book may reflect in some small measure the advantage offered me in the broad, ardent intelligence of Joe Doherty, whose tragic death has deprived his friends and the profession at large of a comradeship and a talent we could not afford to lose.

Above all, I am grateful to my wife Elizabeth, who aided me through a period of research and composition that we began to measure in geological ages. It is appropriate that the last layer of composition be my dedication of the book to her.

The Confidence Game
in American Literature

1

Akin to Genesis

I desire to speak somewhere without *bounds; like a man in a waking moment, to men in their waking moments. . . . The volatile truth of our words should continually betray the inadequacy of the residual statement. Their truth is instantly* translated; *its literal monument alone remains.*

Thoreau, *Walden*

LET us start at the beginning of things, with a solicited visionary act: "the original character, essentially such, is like a revolving Drummond light, raying away from itself all round it—everything is lit by it, everything starts up to it (mark how it is with Hamlet), so that, in certain minds, there follows upon the adequate conception of such a character, an effect, in its way, akin to that which in Genesis attends upon the beginning of things."[1] These words, frequently cited in scholarship of recent years, seem to me inexhaustibly remarkable as a challenge to understand a phenomenon by envisioning its effect in the mind. This is Melville's later dominant rhetoric, which with cogent purpose suggestively makes demands on the reader's imagination rather than rushing to meet it, as in the earlier writing. Here critical perception must begin by answering the challenge to "certain minds," unreservedly yielding itself, as best it can, to an invited moment of astonished expanding consciousness. The waking moment, to borrow Thoreau's language, will be pertinent to everything I have to say in this book.

The effect that attends upon the beginning is the sense of circumambient dark and silence out of which comes, in

[1] Herman Melville, *The Confidence-Man*, ed. Hershel Parker (New York: W. W. Norton, 1971), p. 205.

3

a simple tremendous act, a moving light and breath. From the magma of potencies everything starts up to the omni-directional force, each thing declaring itself according to contracting bounds of shape and function and kind, and so foreswearing other alignments and other bounds. The effect is an awesome total contingency coordinate with the necessary exclusions of particular form: the revealed in-stant of mute chaos, with its infinite potentials, even as light and breath emerge to blot them out and create the world that is from all the worlds that are not.

In a recent book that is already a classic, Frank Kermode starts with the ends of things to demonstrate eloquently how our sense of an ending molds the human fictions that shape our lives. On behalf of a proper sense of fictive ordering, he urges us to distinguish between myths and fictions: "Myth operates within the diagrams of ritual, which presupposes total and adequate explanations of things as they are and were; it is a sequence of radically unchangeable gestures. Fictions are for finding things out, and they change as the needs of sense-making change. Myths are the agents of stability, fictions the agents of change. Myths call for absolute, fictions for conditional assent. Myths make sense in terms of a lost order of time, *illud tempus* as Eliade calls it; fictions, if successful, make sense of the here and now, *hoc tempus*."[2] I would add, not so much in outright disagreement as awareness of other em-phases latent in Kermode's rich book, that it is difficult to see many myths as agents of stability *in contradistinction to* fiction; nor indeed do myths and fictions admit of being categorically opposed regarding belief. There are myths, and there are myths; and how can one separate any of them from the fictive uses to which they may be put in a given culture? Some myths treat not only origins but the origina-

[2] *The Sense of an Ending* (New York: Oxford, 1967), p. 39. For a useful contrasting view of myth that includes a discussion of the Trickster, see Victor W. Turner, "Myth and Symbol," *International Encyclopedia of the Social Sciences* (New York: Macmillan, 1968).

4

tive; not so much a Genesis that once was as a genesis that is here and now, its boundaries still fluid and the unrealized plenum once more at hand. They enact the re-genesis "in certain minds" that makes for ongoing process and keeps in exercised readiness the cultural capacity for experiencing, producing, or surviving novelty. They seem to have a function much like the one Kermode proposes for fiction: they modify, not social ordinations or the order of practical thought, but attitudes toward both of these and the way they can function in serving, and not wholly dictating to, human life.

The Trickster, whom ethnologists tell us is among the most archaic of mythical generators, is of this type. And I will be concerned with writers—Melville, Twain, and West—who are committed to the genius of origin to the degree that their works resist termination, resolution, and above all the apocalypse that influential criticism has attributed to them. Impatient of the fictive, skeptical of *telos*, and prodigal of originative energy, Melville and Twain are preoccupied not with ends that shape but with recovered beginnings situated somehow outside fiction even if quickly enfolded by it in our narratives of time. Not without recurrent despair at the circular endlessness of human effort, they look for the radically unshaped but protean force enacting all processual change. With Nathanael West, the modern in whom apocalyptic resistance almost collapses, they are committed to the Trickster, for them the true *arche*-type, the creative and determining first moment from which all moments develop. This entails, moreover, a commitment to the persuasions that dissolve customary boundaries and re-create new alignments from heretofore excluded potentials. In a word, it involves a particular rhetoric.

Sophisticated modern study of the art of persuasion has gone far beyond the traditional circumscription of rhetoric as the arousal of conviction through artfully deployed language on a given occasion, to a more inclusive notion of man as a persuasive or persuading animal. Men seek and create the grounds of confidence, which is to say, mutual faith, as much to validate themselves as to control the wills of others. This conception has led Kenneth Burke through rhetoric to provocative issues of psychosocial motivation in life and art; and it underlies Wayne Booth's complementary investigation of authorial responsibility in *The Rhetoric of Fiction*. These two coordinates of study define the area of my interest in fictions where an "irresponsible," protean figure in varying degrees stands for the elusive, impelling artist.

The archetype, the persuasive Trickster, appears in variants ranging from the demonic to the messianic; he thus represents the ready transformation of a basic motivation into a set of social deportments, like cunning and stupidity, that to common view seem mutually exclusive. It is the Trickster's genius to recombine the exclusive to put us in touch again with a power akin to Genesis, like that emerging, startling light in the mind Melville describes. For if we investigate motives underlying the confidence trickster's deceptions, we see that all his roles and ideas are merely convenient counters used to express a powerful psychic energy and at the same time to elicit repeatedly the confidence in his existence that he needs to exist, to begin again. In fact, the highly symbiotic relationship between trickster and tricked evidences a mutual exigency hinted at in Tertullian's *credo quia absurdum*, a statement that for modern men seems itself to have come out of a familiar dark and silent disorder.

This interdependency and the persuasive art that supports it offers a model for exploring the rhetorical craft binding author and reader in a creative partnership. Once we understand that the Trickster archetypically "presides over" change and the accompanying social renegotiations of cooperation and belief—over change and exchange—we need only remember the history of approximately the last century and a half to begin to see why the idea of a confidence game is central to the world view and craft of Melville, Twain, and West. This is the period in which change, not only as experience but as governing idea, comes to dominate the occidental life-world. I refer of course to more than the extraordinary rapidity of social and technological disruptions and innovations; the complementary fact is that change becomes a primary, instead of a secondary, category in modern Western ontology. The mutability of things "beneath the moon" is an ancient, enduring commonplace. But if decisive, even cataclysmic, transformations have frequently marked the Christian era of occidental history, yet they took place, as it were, before a presumptive great fixed backdrop of fundamental reality that, when the smoke and dust cleared, was still static. If now *viewed* differently, still it in itself was not thought *to be* in motion, in continuing process. But during the period in question, particularly in the seismic consciousness of artists and thinkers, the cosmos itself increasingly began to seem protean: change was a fundamental constituent of reality. So began that mixture of nostalgia and futurism that set the tone for Western philosophy, historiography, and literature. An entire multi-national culture moved into a "between-two-worlds," "betwixt-and-between" state of permanent transition. For this kind of state Victor Turner has proposed the term *liminoid* to distinguish it from the systematically planned *liminal* stage of "primitive" ritual process in which community is temporarily disrupted or transfigured so as to be renewed. But whether haphazard and unending, or ritualized and closed, the protean condition of marginality dramatizes the profound and vulnerable communal confidence that we are permitted to assume unthinkingly at other times.

What I want to examine in this book is not at the level of such world-historical generalizations regarding communal contingency as I am making now, but instead at the microcosmic level of mirroring transactions in which the writer-reader "community" takes shape. The variety of this partnership, and consequently of literary imagination, is clearly demonstrated in the careers of our three authors. For aside from the writers' intrinsic importance and the rather obvious bearing of the subject matter I have so far sketched on such works as *The Confidence-Man, Huckleberry Finn,* and *Miss Lonelyhearts,* Melville, Twain, and West demand study because their artistry preeminently represents chief "moments" in the development of the relationship between artist and audience. That is, the different rhetorical relationships with an audience established by these seminal writers at intervals over a period of national historical development (c. 1840–1940), correspond closely to the crucial stages of negotiated confidence between artist and reader in the individual reading experience: a problematic distance, a problematic authority, and a problematic "familiarity." And each writer's *oeuvre,* though particularly characterized by one of these typical moments, manifests in an urgent form the whole interlocked pattern of the historical/individual process.

For these reasons the writers I have named are especially rewarding and suggestive for the process-centered rhetorical criticism contemplated here, a criticism responsive to both individual stages and whole patterns of change as well as to the originative motive it enacts.

Unfortunately, however, there is annual evidence that such models as the one I envision, though they aspire to powerful comprehensiveness, are disastrously reductive if they are not carefully scrutinized and in some manner adapted specifically to the artists in question. Two amplifying contextualizations are therefore essential to specify the contribution I intend. Though both these orientations deal with what is profoundly original, they claim a minimal originality in viewpoint. In them, I wish to organize several commonplaces of debate taken from various disciplines as a means of cross-illuminating, and cross-examining, concepts I will employ. The first orientation develops further my view of the Trickster and related concepts assumed in

8

the later analyses. (Since my analytical use of this material will be much less taxonomic than is the rule when criticism calls upon an archetype, at this point the reader may be well advised to heed the Preface's admonition. The Trickster will be, in the manner of Melville's Bulkington, a "sleeping partner"—initially advanced to present a constellation of important themes, but in what follows remaining comparatively "invisible.") Then, rather like the stabilizing ritual of which Kermode writes, the critical preliminary evokes the guardian axioms allowing access to the texts at hand and attempts to coordinate, if not cast out, certain diabolisms the works intrinsically tempt. After a critic completes these tool-sharpening enterprises, he can only hope that he will escape the dangers he has pointed out. If he also escapes in some measure his own blindness to others, it will be by a virtue borrowed from his materials.

THE TRICKSTER AND HIS DOMESTICATION

American song, then, in its melodies affirms the nostalgia for the old, even while in its words it often expresses a deliberate and stubborn paradox, a denial of trust in love, a denial of a need for trust. It thus becomes a more intimate declaration of independence.

Erik H. Erikson, *Childhood and Society*

Americans have always been, in one sense or another, confidence men. This is why, now that an existential failure of confidence cuts at the very quick of our experience, we have discovered the Melville of *The Confidence-Man*, have overvalued the later writings of Mark Twain, and have put a proper value on the novels of Nathanael West. At the outset it will be helpful to remember the American iconography that serves as the basic vocabulary of their fiction.[3]

[3] For the principal resources the following discussion is distilled from, see the selected bibliography. Books that appeared too late for me to profit from here are Richard B. Hauck, *A Cheerful Nihilism: Confidence and 'the Absurd' in American Humorous Fiction* (Bloomington: Indiana

9

In the national iconography, Americans are peddlers of assurance. The iconography was shaped early by the historical uniqueness of the experience open to the nation, by the new Romantic faith in the self, and by the competitive energies of capitalism. The mood that is central to the nineteenth-century love of tall talk and of patriotic oratory in a particular "spread-eagle style" is also fundamental to the advocacy of confidence by Franklin as well as Emerson, the self-reliance that in its various forms was *The Way to Wealth*, to wholeness of spirit, and to the Oversoul. The vibrant national mood vivified, if it did not alone create, the loftiest metaphor of Protestant America's dream—the identification of America as the land of promise, the New Jerusalem trustfully awaiting its secular and transcendent Redeemer. At a more immediate level, the matrix of robust confidence produced a figure who was the most popular national type from the Revolution to the Civil War—the Yankee. *Yankee* became a synonym for both *American*, a man of confidence, and *New Englander*, a confidence man. In the first versions of the comic type, the "Jonathan," the bumptious certitude often scornfully attributed to Americans by foreigners was picked up by the fledgling culture as a nose-thumbing badge of identification. As the Yankee appeared on the stage and in the literature and sub-literature of the century, he increasingly reflected the deprecation of everything sophisticated and the exaltation of a shrewd, peasant common sense that was thought to be a native gift. The primary manifestation of the Yankee was the Peddler, whose lonely, wandering life-style, true to the promptings

University Press, 1971); and Susan Kuhlmann, *Knave, Fool, and Genius: The Confidence Man as He Appears in Nineteenth Century American Writing* (Chapel Hill: University of North Carolina Press, 1973). As irony would have it, Wayne Booth's *The Rhetoric of Irony* (Chicago: University of Chicago Press, 1974) appeared while my book was in press. I have resisted the temptation to modify my present quasi-dialogue with *The Rhetoric of Fiction* in light of this latest statement from Booth. I will say only that the recent work does not seem to be anywhere near as satisfactory as Booth's first *Rhetoric*.

of democratic patriotism, Romanticism, and free enterprise, was the icon of self-confidence above all.

In the familiar mythology, America, disembarrassed of the weight of European institutions and traditions, placed all its trust in the untrammeled self. The song of the open road was the native "Song of Myself," and the only weight to be reckoned with was the Peddler's bag of "Yankee notions," borne willingly because it was his own, because what he was marketing was chiefly himself.

Insofar as the Yankee Peddler was seen as upholding the American virtues, he was a benign figure, like Sam Slick, whose slyness in trading was the harmlessly comic consequence of the national game of merchant self-reliance versus customer self-reliance. The benign Peddler was our cracker barrel mentor, a Romantic rustic given to apothegms on trust in oneself, in one's fellow man, and in the benevolence of "Natur." The wise cunning of a Sam Slick was an amusing lesson in the necessary game of confidence involved not only in a money economy but especially in an expanding capitalist system. In 1849 the *Merchant's Ledger*, as might be expected, found comfort in the exploits of a swindler who achieved a great notoriety in the newspapers of the time as "The Original Confidence Man": "That one poor swindler, like the one under arrest, should have been able to drive so considerable a trade on an appeal to so simple a quality as the confidence of man in man, shows that all virtue and humanity of nature is not entirely extinct in the nineteenth century. It is a good thing . . . that . . . men *can be swindled*." The *Merchant's Ledger* article was quoted approvingly in the *Literary World* (our writers would have smiled knowingly at the literary angle), which added, "It is not the worst thing that may be said of a country that it gives birth to a confidence man."[4] The con

[4] In Paul Smith, "The Confidence-Man and the Literary World of New York," *Nineteenth Century Fiction*, 16 (1962), p. 334. See also Johannes Dietrich Bergmann, "The Original Confidence Man," *American Quarterly*, 21 (1969), 560–77; and Michael S. Reynolds, "The Prototype for Melville's Confidence Man," *PMLA*, 86 (1971), 1009–1013.

man's game was to ask ingenuously that the intended dupe display his trust in the trickster by a loan or a purchase. The formula was the quintessentially American mode of Romantic capitalism: an ingenuous pose concealing a private, secret self confident of its powers, confident especially of its power to elicit trust in the pose. The stronger one's feeling of secure selfhood, the more successful the persona; and the more successful the mask, the surer one's private sense of self, confidence breeding confidence.

The Peddler, "The Original Confidence Man," and another famous bunco artist, P. T. Barnum, excited the American imagination as iconic marginal figures, existing on the periphery of "ordinary life" yet embodying values central to the dominant culture. Like all marginal figures, however, the Yankee trickster could also represent the dangerous side of cultural values. When the focus shifted to the exploitation of trust, as in accounts like Timothy Dwight's *Travels* (1821), the Peddler was regarded with moral distaste. Especially in the humor of the Old Southwest (for example, the Sut Lovingood and Davy Crockett stories), the Peddler with his wares was a detested image of Northern mercantilist attitudes. Still another widely popular figure, the frontier picaro of the Old Southwest, further exemplified the deceitful abuse of confidence. Though there is a comic relish in the frontier trickster's duplicity, there is also a recognition of the more grotesque impulses of the confidence game, often combined, as in the Simon Suggs tales, with a satire of Jacksonian faith in the common man and rugged individualism.

The great writer, as we are accustomed to say, takes imaginative currents, widely circulating but relatively shallow in popular culture, and by following them to their recessed sources in human experience, makes what is wide also deep. When the "imitated" cultural reality itself offers analogues to artistic invention and its enticement of a peculiar kind of belief, there is a redoubled process of recognition and research by means of fictive thinking, within the literary act with its necessitated conceptual vividness and deepening narrative progression. Familiar national habits and unthinkingly reasserted concerns are made elements of the writer's own cognate obsessions; and the local influence, the native genius loci, therefore takes on a decisive increment of imaginative complexity that connects it to multiple creative reserves surpassing the local—precisely, to the archetypal sense. "In certain minds" the recognition is mutual between popular culture and its transformation in masterworks.

Noting the scarcity of the true *picaro*—the marginal wanderer, the "half-outsider"—in nineteenth century European fiction, Claudio Guillén writes:

There were picaresque echoes in Dickens's child-man— the vehicle of social criticism not limited to observation. By and large, however, it was the moment of the full outsider, the dreamer and the bohemian, the revolutionary and the ideologist, the rebel against man and God. The *picaro* could not very well act the part of Prometheus or of Robespierre. In America, the land of pioneering and wide spaces, . . . Mark Twain did not forget him. . . . William Dean Howells thought that the picaresque novel was the form of the future for America. He wrote in *My Literary Passions* (New York, 1895), p. 143: "each man's life among us is a romance of the Spanish model; it is the life of man [sic] who has risen, as we nearly all have, with many ups and downs." (Concerning *Lazarillo*.)[5]

Mark Twain's popular career-long rendition of the trickster's craft, with a strong grounding in Old Southwest

[5] Claudio Guillén, "Toward a Definition of the Picaresque," *Proceedings of the Third Congress of the International Comparative Literature Association* (The Hague: Mouton and Company, 1962), pp. 265–66, 266n.

13

humor but an inherent insight that went to its archetypal base, is well-known. Melville too, scholarship has shown, was influenced by this vigorous, rakish material and its Yankee counterpart. And his recognition as a kindred spirit is indicated by the several excerpts from his works printed and warmly advocated in William O. Porter's *The Spirit of the Times*, the reigning journal of frontier humor, even after Melville's welcome had ended elsewhere. To mention West in this connection is to recall *A Cool Million*, which alone would reveal his debt to the national rediscovery of Melville's and Twain's native heritage during the 1920s and '30s, both in pop culture and in such widely accessible and respectable scholars as Constance Rourke and Bernard De Voto.[6]

Original confidence man the American swindler may have been, in one sense, since *confidence man* and *confidence game* are indigenous terms, but the thing clearly was, long before a national preoccupation with trust gave it a name. As our money advertises, in God we Yankees profess to trust. We make a similar profession regarding man as well, although our popular forms give contradictory testimony in denying the autonomous person's need to rely or to confederate except in the safely distant approaches of nostalgia—with results that Erik Erikson and others have shown. Around the national professions of confidence, which protested too much their achieved reality, was a penumbra that some of our most exemplary fictions could readily body forth: fraudulent excitements, secret aliena-

---

6 John T. Flanagan, "*The Spirit of the Times* Reviews Melville," *JEGP*, 64 (1965), 57–64. See also, for example: Constance Rourke, *American Humor: A Study of the National Character* (New York: Harcourt, 1931); F. O. Matthiessen, *American Renaissance* (New York: Oxford, 1941); Edward H. Rosenberry, *Melville and the Comic Spirit* (Cambridge: Harvard University Press, 1955); Kenneth S. Lynn, *Mark Twain and Southwestern Humor* (Boston: Little, Brown, 1960); Daniel G. Hoffman, *Form and Fable in American Fiction* (New York: Oxford, 1961); James F. Light, *Nathanael West: An Interpretive Study*, 2nd ed. (1961; rpt. Evanston, Ill.: Northwestern University Press, 1971), pp. 140–41.

tions, broken promises. (It is worth mentioning in this regard, that Melville's Ahab, who curses mortal interindebtedness, identifies himself as a peddler carrying a crushing pack.) But besides the "original" native *daemon*, with whom we keep countenance as best we can, or whom we propitiate with names and stunted lives, many ways lead to the true arch-principal, the Trickster.

And as with confidence itself, all of the ways have to do with interfaces, mediations, incongruous affiliations; or with boundaries, divisions, contradictory juxtapositions—the entire set of relational ideas surveyed when we observe that a line both partitions and joins. The Trickster is the epitome of this marginality, so that, while the emphasis in a given myth may fall on dividing or conjoining, the Trickster always incarnates both. Even when he appears as wholly different from the human, as with the god Hermes, he is messenger, mediator, and psychopomp, "the hoverer-between-worlds who dwells in a world of his own,"[7] who even with the prevailing Olympian moral standards is singled out as the thief god—and who applies his artifice also to making the lyre we call Apollo's. To name some of his avatars: in Eddic lore, the Trickster is Loki; in Polynesian, Maui; in Yoruba (West Africa), Eshu-Elegba; in Zande (Central Africa), Ture; in Hindu, Krishna; in North American Indian, Coyote, Raven, Hare, and Wakdjunkaga (i.e., Trickster); in South American, Daiiru, O'oimbre, and Tikarau.

The Trickster, thus straddling oppositions, embodies two antithetical, nonrational experiences of man with the natural world, his society, and his own psyche: on the one hand, a force of treacherous disorder that outrages and disrupts, and on the other hand, an unanticipated, usually unintentional benevolence in which trickery is at the expense of inimical forces and for the benefit of mankind.

[7] Karl Kerényi, "The Trickster in Relation to Greek Mythology," in Paul Radin, *The Trickster: A Study in American Indian Mythology* (1956; rpt. New York: Schocken, 1972), p. 189.

Operating at those extremes of human experience that are almost impossible to recognize outside fictions and intellectually puzzling within them, the Trickster may appear as an anarchic creature, at once transhuman, transanimal, and transdeific, who seeks self-gratification by japes played at the level of the insane or the infantile, yet whose unaltruistic appetites establish social order and create its elemental instruments. At once bestial and divine, fool and deceiver, the archetypal Trickster spans the entire range of shadowy, baffling worlds beyond the ordinary man's control, from the superhuman to the subhuman, from the supersubtle to the subconscious. Whether he is seen, according to social and historical circumstances, as demiurge, culture hero, savior-god, devil, shaman, or comic rogue, the Trickster has a profound fascination, abrogating as he does in his tricks and self-deceptions all restrictions, rules, and taboos, manipulating the untouchable, and freely tapping the unchecked powers of the unconscious or the afterworld by means of illusion and metamorphosis.

Such cultural contravention as the Trickster represents—variously treated under names like counteractive patterns, ritual reversals, ritual rebellions, symbolic inversion, and deviance—is the subject of much recent attention in anthropology and sociology, with the dominant aim of understanding the phenomenon in frameworks other than the single, traditional cathartic rationale borrowed from Freud and Aristotle (the traditional explanation, that is, of the periodic or institutional saturnalia as a catharsis or steam-valve that, in the interests of stability, gives disruptive forces a way of dissipating). The attempt is to supply a variety of additional explanations sufficient to deal with the disparate cultural functions of the illegal, the completely antinomian, or the unaccountable—all the elements that seem obstinate to acculturation and yet constantly pertinent to it. Indeed, as with the extra-formalist movement in literary criticism, the important efforts of the social scientists seem to comport nicely with the equally important efforts they are studying, as they contravene the bearers of modern tradition, Freud with Piaget, Malinowski with Leach, Durkheim with Goffman.

For what do men do but establish two opposing concepts to bracket reality and discover that they need a third; then find that the triangulation of the world, because of some crucial contradiction issuing in time and human fate, also will not suffice. And in the inexorable continuances of time and human fate, men suspect repeatedly, at some deep level, that a whole developed network of crosschecks and rationales still allows reality to fly through the openings. In our various "primitive" or modern vocabularies, we can call these holes heavenly mysteries, the locus of the gods alone, or some equivalent, and thereby bring them to consciousness and satisfactorily make even the openings in the grid support the structure. But more disturbingly and perhaps more excitingly, we also suspect that along the network's connections, but somehow not of them, there exist things that we cannot see—except out of the corners of our eyes—since they are not made visible, positively or negatively, by our covering concepts and their linkages. In "primitive" societies, and modern as well, men experience these elusive presences by myths of abrogation, or tales featuring the iconography of the peripheral, or by taboos that give these presences the odd status of cultural non-persons or nonthings. Here, in conceptual crevices and perceptual blindspots, dwells the trickster Spider of several mythologies, or the invisible man, as Ralph Ellison called him, or many of the infiltrating, in-between entities that we call dirt, or impurities, as Mary Douglas has explained in her interesting book, *Purity and Danger*. It is the repulsive but strangely fertile realm of silence, of darkness, and that darkness just sufficiently visible to be called chaos.

To invert Kermode's formula, myths that deal with this anomalous realm seem to be, not for finding things out, but for being found out *actively* by things. They comprise a way of focusing attention on, or as near as human conceptualization will allow, the reality that is what it is, and does what it does, no matter what we may contrive to say about it. They furnish the possibility for an instantaneous analogue to genesis, creating not a new objective grid for reality but an enlivened subjective experience of what the present one means, what its exclusions and precise exactions are. John Crowe Ransom, in an essay addressed to Kenneth Burke to which I will return shortly, is concerned with a parallel, less seemingly exotic, experience:

> . . . I cannot help thinking that laughter is one of the profoundest of human actions, betokening ontological sense, and, specifically, that of the substantival existents as opposed to the better advertised rational forms. . . . Like the dialectic, [humor] is critical of programs. But not "constructively," to make them workable; nor does it try to furnish the frail . . . structure with some decent imagery in order to make it "ontologically" presentable. It sweeps the whole thing away with laughter; which, though wise, is primitive and organic rather than vocal, but, if it could be articulate, would be found reiterating, Substance, Substance.[8]

This humorous apprehension of things, as we fleetingly sense them through the conflict and helplessness of our articulate categories, is very close to the animating sense imparted by the Trickster's marginal antics, which, depending on their pitch, swerve our response either toward the pleasantly vertiginous or the uncomfortably disoriented.

Ransom's comment on dialectic notwithstanding, we can complete our survey by making summational connections, observing the functional similarities between dialectic, play, and the Trickster. The starting point for these connections is a further examination of the concept of marginality,

8 "An Address to Kenneth Burke," in *Critical Responses to Kenneth Burke: 1924–1966*, ed. William H. Rueckert (Minneapolis: University of Minnesota Press, 1969), p. 157. Reprinted from *The Kenyon Review*, 4 (1942), 219–37.

which can be understood as a fertile idea of "neither-both." That is, the Trickster is a means of identifying, and more importantly, experiencing, an elusive fullness that is not "either-or" (as, either good or evil; either cunning or stupid) nor exactly "both-and," but a margin that is in a sense both the sectors it lies between yet truly, completely, neither.

Dialectic, as a method and habit of mind, gives us one way of understanding this idea, if dialectic is not reduced to the mechanical three-step, as Walter Kaufmann has called it, of thesis-antithesis-synthesis.[9] The Trickster's marginal nature does not so much synthesize oppositions, as serve as a referent for them: it is what oppositions seek to capture. If we remember Socrates in "The Symposium," not merely as a master dialectician reconciling opposites, but as the ironic, grotesque, yet internally beautiful and always elusive object, the Silenus as he is called, of several opposing loves, then we have a "trickster" analogue for locating a reality by many vectors. Or we might imagine a magic wheel whose "contradictory" spokes could not reach the hub, but could point toward it. For dialectic is that refining operation of thought that continually seeks to accommodate the opposite of a proposition or object. As method, it may seek a standpoint from which contradictions are seen as part of a common ground or process. The standpoint may be formulable discursively, as a "both-and" (Melville's "The tortoise is both bright and dark"); or implicitly and aphoristically (Twain's "True irreverence is disrespect for another man's god"); or metaphorically-philosophically (Hegel's *Geist*).

Or dialectic, as an element of mental temper evasive of every workable program, may be an achieved confident hesitancy, a maintained internal space for the love of wisdom, that avoids overhasty antinomies and recognizes the numberless filaments between categories for thinking, judging, and acting (Nietzsche's notorious "beyond good and evil," in one of its many significances). The viewpoint that

[9] *Hegel: A Reinterpretation* (Garden City, N.Y.: Doubleday, 1965).

19

the notion of a combined social-ontological marginality allows us to see most sharply is one in which a putatively extra-social reality—the "Cartesian" world of Nature—cannot be understood apart from those very filaments of concrete social intercourse. Moreover, as with myth, there are dialectics, and dialectics. Erich Auerbach, in his magisterial study, *Mimesis*, cites Rabelais' inspiration by the famous Silenus figure of Socrates; and the hint discloses the link between Rabelais' play with dialectic and a humorous sense of realism. Thus Auerbach describes Rabelais' rhetoric: "Rabelais' entire effort is directed toward playing with things and with the multiplicity of their possible aspects. ... The revolutionary thing about his way of thinking is not his opposition to Christianity, but the freedom of vision, feeling, and thought which his perpetual playing with things produces, and which invites the reader to deal directly with the world and its wealth of phenomena."[10]

Though Auerbach does not say so, Rabelais' dominant imagery of gigantic ingestion and elimination can be seen as a typically comic-transvalued figure for dialectical process (related to the beautiful god concealed in Silenus' grotesque belly). This would be Rabelais' grossly exaggerated version of a dialectic repeatedly incorporating the "other" and yet establishing a distinction from it. The figure not only reminds us again of the appetitive and catabolic nature of the Trickster, but permits us to preview the interconnections between significant actions and metaphors that we will encounter: Melville's pervasive benign and malevolent images of consumption, combined with his portrayal of self-definition by the dangerous approach toward boundaries of identity; Huckleberry Finn's fluid marginality, epitomized in his love of cooking in which "the juice swaps around," combined with Twain's bent for making contrasted distinctions; and the inert cultural waste that West envisions as the counterpart of radically abridged interpersonal distances

---

[10] *Mimesis* (Princeton: Princeton University Press, 1968), pp. 275–76.

and obliterated distinctions between the human and non-human.

But we need not go to Rabelais alone. The American phrase, confidence *game*, is a shrewd recognition of the trickster's attempt to establish a "neither-both" autonomy. Play, too, is immediately devious, "frivolously" unresponsive, with regard to official practical effort, but is psychologically serious as a revelation and germination of fundamental cultural attitudes and psychosocial conflicts. In short, it exists in a marginal area, where one may act out a normally prohibited behavior, or a ritually fastidious heightening of order and its consequences. To meditate on the idea of *game* is to see that it specifically pinpoints a trickster's actions and transactions of confidence. For example, Til Eulenspiegel vengefully places a sleeping woman in a bed of hot coals, and Sut Lovingood sends a bee-stung bull crashing into an unsuspecting party; but these pranks do not require that the victims exercise their confidence. In contrast, the confidence trickster not only requires the consent of his victims, but, like a creator, demands belief. Magpie-fashion, the con man collects and adopts all available conventions of thought, action, and language because the confidence game is essentially a ritualization of human intercourse—the transfer of goods or trust between individuals. According to the theory of games, "the cheat's dishonesty does not destroy the game," which is to the contrary "ruined by the nihilist who denounces the rules as absurd and conventional, who refuses to play because the game is meaningless."[11] In this sense, the confidence game, like art, excludes the utter nihilist, although paradoxically the game may be operated by one who believes in nothing outside of its circle. The game in its autonomy becomes a determining and creative instrument for the con man that

[11] Roger Caillois, *Man, Play, and Games*, trans. Meyer Barash (Glencoe, Ill.; Free Press, 1961), p. 102. Cf. Johan Huizinga, *Homo Ludens: A Study of the Play Element in Culture* (Boston: Beacon, 1955), p. 11.

may substitute for his own lack of belief an organized set of responses built on the glorification of faith as well as its covert negation. But *negation* does not necessarily mean *destruction*. Believing in nothing outside his game, he fashions belief, and he is believed in. This ritualization is made possible solely by the trickster's use of stereotyped masking and hyperbolic illusions, which for him are literally a *make-believe*. Corresponding to the characteristics of play that Caillois calls mimicry and *ilinx* (vertigo), masking and illusion tender immediate play-pleasures to the dupe that also encourage him to experience the primary satisfaction of trustful belief.

For the audience that observes these machinations in fiction or myth, the play area offers freedom from the debased coinages of the everyday, precisely because we see vacuous deceptiveness so much at home there, in the stale habit and unconsciously engrained deceptions by which we devalue ourselves and others. In the combined fictive and ludic charmed area, there is potential liberation from the cowardice that inevitable consequence breeds in us all; and the means are, paradoxically, pattern and consequentiality, but seen in a doubled frame of *make-believe* that allows us to be unflinchingly attentive to them.

From the largest perspective on the Trickster's incitement to belief, perhaps we can recognize, within the archetypal absolute, a very real type of social "carrier" or catalyst who promotes fundamental experiences of confederation precisely by not participating in them except in the completely mediate rituals of arousal and self-arousal. Religious hucksters are only the most obvious examples of what I mean. It does not take an exceptionally skeptical mind to wonder how long a culture of any moderately complex sort would survive without the widespread existence of such self-privileged, totally focused energies, licensed by what Clifford Geertz has called a culture's deep play,[12] and exercised by

[12] "Deep Play: Notes on the Balinese Cockfight," *Daedalus* (Winter 1972): *Myth, Symbol, and Culture*, 1–38.

men who would never think to distinguish whether the manipulations of confederation or its substance commanded their essential allegiance. And how long, too, would a culture survive without a profoundly accepting, yet self-protective anamnesis of its costly, oddly sourced, unaltruistic manipulative energies. The question, in sum, *is* survival, regenerating continuance in process, which is for any species —and any art—the question antecedent to all others. Without such an honest amoral grounding as the Trickster provides, no genuinely humane choice can be made concerning how, in what form, and with what order we wish to survive, if we do so desire.

CRITICAL PRELIMINARY: RANSOM AND BURKE

> *Consciousness is in the first place not a matter of "I think that" but of "I can."*
>
> Maurice Merleau-Ponty,
> *The Phenomenology of Perception*

I am primarily concerned with critical practice, not theory. At their best, however, critical and fictive thinking are not divergent, but convergent, so that perhaps the principal critical modes I want to look at are classifiable with a second assistance from Auerbach's *Mimesis*, which distinguishes between one fictive realism that is primarily sensory and concrete, and another that is mainly figural. For our purposes, it will be most useful to remember that Auerbach shows how these contraries are productively combined. A retrieval of competing critical methods and terminologies will allow a more exact treatment of the creative tensions surrounding the idea of originative persuasions. As we review theory, we are implicitly beginning to discern dialectically conflicting central interests in the fiction. In short, allowing our writers to suggest the method used to approach them, I have sought out Kenneth Burke, Wayne Booth, and John Crowe Ransom because in their very disagreements they furnish the most direct admission I know of, to such fruitfully countervalent tendencies. Booth's *The Rhetoric of Fiction* is a widely familiar landmark, so I take the previous brief reference to be a sufficient indication of my shared concern with authorial responsibility in persuasive creations.

Burke and Ransom, older and more deeply influential practitioners, are something else again. Ransom's New Criticism has so rehabilitated and dominated the field for the last thirty years in a number of versions and perversions, that it will be helpful to recollect some of his unmodified inaugurating concepts. Burke's critical method, to which Ransom gave strong but respectful opposition during the crucial development period for both critics in the early forties, seems to be coming openly into its own during the current disenchantment with Ransom's critical legacy. We can begin a binocular focus on the two systems through the idea of purification. Burke's concern is with purification as a central activity in human life, art, and language (for Burke these approach equivalence), as in his motto to *A Grammar of Motives: ad bellum purificandum.* This activity can be described as a process of dialectical idealization. Stated in the briefest terms, Burke's aim is to work through mankind's deadly, guilty conflicts and oppositions to discover a shared basic idea, a common linguistic symbol, on which community can be founded. In contrast, Ransom's attempt is to purify literature and criticism of every form of "practical," "logicomathematical" thought that obscures poetry's concrete, inutile, imaginative recapturing of the world's body. Thus, of poetry's "ontological" relationship to the world's fullness, Ransom writes:

> The true poetry has no great interest in improving or idealizing the world, which does well enough. It only wants to realize the world, to see it better. Poetry is the kind of knowledge by which we must know what we have arranged that we shall not know otherwise. We have elected to know the world through our science,

24

and we know a great deal, but science is only the cognitive department of our animal life, and by it we know the world only as a scheme of abstract conveniences. What we cannot know constitutionally as scientists is the world which is made of whole and indefeasible objects, and this is the world which poetry recovers for us. Men become poets, or at least they read poets, in order to atone for having been hard practical men and hard theoretical scientists.[13]

Ransom's attempt to banish from essential poesis everything but (certain kinds of proper) lyric threatens a brilliant, because brilliantly generaled, Pyrrhic victory over literature's bounty. Such lust for purity tends to be triumphantly self-defeating. Burke is just as lustful; however, his is a wide-ranging, Don Juan lust that locates ethical purity in all the body's dregs. Ransom sees poetry as *cognitive* purification directly the opposite of idealization; Burke sees it as an *act* of ethical purification, epitomizing language's general effort to idealize, or in some measure transcend the brute facts. Consequently, Burke is methodically intolerant of any heterogeneity unaccountable by human language; he threatens, if not to erase Ransom's substantival world, to make it fade into a distant backdrop.

So, to use terms favored by each, we have Ransom's *ontological* purification versus Burke's *logological*—both difficult to put into practice, as witness the subtle heresies of much exegesis written under the New Critical banner; and the widespread, sometimes furtive, piecemeal borrowing of Burke's copious ideas. Is it a matter of you pays your money and you takes your purification? I think not. My own approach will try to be conscientiously heretical to both, but under the primary aegis of Burke's own systematic apostasies. We need not, in fact, abandon the world's body and its incorporation in a work's texture, nor the most

13 *The World's Body* (1938; rpt. Baton Rouge: Louisiana State University Press, 1968), pp. x–xi.

abstracting dialectics. Certainly for our writers, I believe a poised double-flanking maneuver will be at once the best critical ontology and the best dialectics. Let me forestall a possible misunderstanding. I desire no colorless all-color, no undeviating via media between criticisms. Rather, it is a question of an ideal heuristic: each kind of critical purification to sensitize us to its corresponding modes in the fiction; and one purity to correct the other, as in the artists at hand. Thereby we should be able to register accurately the recalcitrant wisdom and craft with which each author, while responding to the urgencies of purgation, yet resists obliterating all ontological considerations in favor of the ethical, and vice versa. In this view, the world's body and its verbal ethical transcendence become attractive poles of absolute purification between which the creative imagination anxiously, and productively, moves. Thus, *Moby-Dick* will be seen as a fictive world where mute ontological seduction, consuming all in a pure whiteness of being, is a hazardous necessity; and *The Confidence-Man*, as an environment overwhelmed with an all-obscuring human language that is equally hazardous and necessary.

Both Ransom's *The New Criticism* and Burke's *The Philosophy of Literary Form* appeared as new, ambitious titles in 1941. Soon after, in a remarkable, lengthy reply to Burke, Ransom asserted that the other critic's speculations, in their general tendency, did not comprise a true poetic theory because "he is no lover of nature. In the last resort we shall not be talking intelligently about art unless we can pronounce with warmth two terms . . . : Love, and Nature" ("An Address to Kenneth Burke," p. 153). This is not the last time that we shall have occasion to see one man's form of love being unacceptable or unreal to another. Nevertheless, in principle I take Ransom's admonition seriously. Ransom wants to love the substantival, and he sees this as a privileged way of knowing. Burke wants love to conquer in the social, practical life of men, and he looks for its hidden operations as a way of knowing that life. We need not discount either Ransom's imaginatively direct ontological *caritas* nor Burke's tracing of human persuasion to motives of ideal identification and hierarchy. On the contrary, we will need to keep these terms of Burke's and Ransom's in mind, and with warmth, too, as we proceed.

But Burke's conceptions are most in keeping with this study because his researches into the Word are also a revealing self-exploration—and he is himself a trickster. It should be clear that my use of the concept carries no necessary negative connotation. Far from it. I mean that Burke is an elusive, intellectually playful boundary-dissolver, freeing up the orderings of civilized consciousness by a calculated irreverence toward our intellectual and cultural pieties, in the service of a larger reverence, a larger community. If one may "Burke" his own motto by a shifting of stress, his aim is not only the *purification* of war, but the purification of *war*. He practices a Nietzschean cruelty of thought, urbanely pressing against the nerves of our deepest civilized habits, our civility in its fullest meaning. He comes down from his verbal "mountings" not to smash but to manipulate away our golden calves and establish in their place the unengraved but all-engraving logos. He, too, is pious, he, too, acts in the name of what for him is the true "god-term"—the name of Naming. For Burke, that is, man is the Symbol-User, and this means linguistic shape-shifting. Men use persuasive symbolic transformations to erase or pool their guilt as ethical creatures, and thereby achieve community. This is the presiding motive for everything that Burke is concerned with. And he is, as he is concerned with, the genius of the negative—the eradicating, prohibiting, but also purifying—in language. Hence, conjoined to the high intelligence of his writing, the emphasis on sly irony toward his own verbalism, the punning pratfalls, and the digressions at the expense of the argument's dignity. Hence also, amid Burke's restless energy, the general tonal effect of a certain shadeless light, or a trickster's deadpan, for Burke is intimating on behalf of his advocated comic spirit: "see? it 'doesn't hurt' " (even as he exactingly points out in our civilized wounds the places from which pain springs).

The record of Burke's career shows the "invention" of structuralism from within the premises of his system as they fully develop. With this realization, it is the better part of valor to hesitate for a moment, since any system that sets out to explain everything must inevitably secure the requisite efficiency by slighting whatever is distant from the conceptual center. My argument must anticipate an emphasis to follow later: the structuralist and antistructuralist modalities in several key texts. I have in mind the way, as in *The Confidence-Man* and *Huckleberry Finn*, a fiction unmasks verbal manipulations analogous to those it performs, defines what such transmutations can do, and rejoices or laments at what they cannot. Readers of various dispositions usually see one or perhaps two of these three interlocked symbolic acts. For the rigorous structuralist like Lévi-Strauss, and to a large degree for Burke, the limit of transformation is generally not an issue. Rightly describing man as the symbol-user, they often give insufficient attention to him as therefore the symbol-*maker*, in mythopoeic wrestlings with the obdurate concrete world. (Ransom, too, tends to see the poet as too passive in this respect; but see E. H. Gombrich's brilliant *Art and Illusion*, and his treatment of "schema and correction.") These recommencing struggles and the partiality and tenuousness of whatever artistic or mythic conquests may result, tend to be whisked away in structuralist presuppositions about a consubstantial world in which real trees, rocks, and people disappear into the interchangeable fictions that incorporate them. This objection, or a similar one, is frequently made against structuralist practice; it is not a superstition, but identifies an important drawback to the method's effectiveness. (Lévi-Strauss would reply, of course, that the individual creative subject is an invention of Western men.) It is revealing that at one point Burke should shrewdly take hold of Cleopatra's protest in *Antony and Cleopatra*, "he words me," without fully recognizing its implication for his own logology. But

28

while Lévi-Strauss usually elides history and its processes as well, Burke is always devising strategies of style and substance to rescue it.

Part of the excitement in reading Burke is exactly the communicated sense of process when his thinking is most abstract, although sometimes his critical readings seem statically preordained by the purgation scheme. His single most stimulating examination of processual ordination is directly relevant to understanding the Trickster, his invitations to confidence, and the rupturing and reordering of boundaries that ensues. As is usual with Burke, several related terms telescope into and out of each other and approach equivalence as he pursues them in the dialectical round—rounding them out, as he says. Beginning with the attributes of language, Burke wishes to understand how social and metaphysical orders are generated; and concomitantly, how what he calls variously the courtly principle, the hierarchic principle, or else the courtly or hierarchic psychosis involves a fundamental motivation of *homo dialecticus.* Two linguistic properties, Burke says, account for these realities. One is the inherent tendency of language (that is, for Burke, the human mind) to transcend brute matter by moving to levels of ever-higher, more broadly encompassing ideational terms. The other explanation given is far more significant for my purposes. Since language, and therefore, man, is basically persuasive, men establish a courtship relation with others wherein the courted object is placed on a higher level, and courtly rituals establish self-imposed constraints. For the persuasion that succeeds completely in abolishing all interpersonal distances can be persuasion no more. From this line of reasoning, which is of course drastically foreshortened for this summary, Burke traces the establishment of "mystery" between social classes and the ingenuities of hierarchic discriminations. In turn, hierarchy, as the objectification of man's persuasive urges, itself becomes persuasive and motivational. What Burke stresses is the idea that language and language-related realities, although ultimately grounded in the nonlinguistic (or more-than-linguistic) world, themselves provide sources of human motivation going beyond it. Hierarchy, a creation of the idealizing and persuading properties of language, becomes a strong motive instigating both linguistic and translinguistic behavior. (I will have more to say about this motive in my discussion of Twain, and especially *Huckleberry Finn*.) Finally, Burke sees the culmination of this many-named motivation in pure persuasion, that which is done for its own sake. This is a cardinal instance of Burke's frequently emphasized observation that, in human life, means repeatedly tend to become ends in themselves, an axiom surely essential not only in critical theory but in detailed practice. Although existing nowhere in the absolute sense, pure persuasion is to be discerned in the self-interfering elaborations of courtliness, and is closely approximated in prayer, for which the ideal focus is God, the supremely unreachable transcendent title. At this point, Burke had better speak for himself:

> Here, in this conclusion of dialectic, one should look for the ultimate rhetorical motive of *homo dialecticus*. Human effort would thus be grounded not in the search for "advantage," and in the mere "sublimating" of that search by "rationalizations" and "moralizations." Rather, it would be grounded in a *form*, in the persuasiveness of the hierarchic order itself. And considered dialectically, prayer, as pure beseechment, would be addressed not to an *object* (which might "answer" the prayer by providing booty) but to the hierarchic principle itself, where the answer is implicit in the address.[14]

With the term *courtship* and its punning resources, realized in Burke's discussions of Castiglione's *The Book of the Courtier* and Kafka's *The Castle*, we come to a fork in the road of motivations. The divergence I envision here is, strictly speaking, my own notion, not Burke's, but it comes directly from his usages. Its consequences are of the first

[14] *A Rhetoric of Motives* (Berkeley: University of California Press, 1969), p. 276.

importance, for along one branch Melville, and along the other, Twain, can be most accurately placed. This bifurcation from one conceptual source is further significant because each writer uses the complementary motive as a stalking horse, so that between the two there is a complete reversal of masks and meanings. From the idea of courtship, one branch leads to the persuasions of love, including that "godly love" celebrated in the last section of Castiglione's work and climaxing in a vision of origination dramatically outside the previously inward-gazing fictive circle: "all stars voided, saving only the sweet Governess of heaven, Venus which keepeth the bounds of the night and day, from which appeared to blow a sweet blast, that filling the air with a biting cold, began to quicken the tunable notes of the pretty birds, among the hushing woods of the hills." On this avenue there is the promise of an end to hierarchy in an ideally consummated identification with that which "keepeth the bounds." On the other motivational branch there is the perpetuation of hierarchy, if only *faut de mieux*. This divergence leads to the courtier's pursuits as an end in themselves: the fascination with authority's "mystery" as seen in its discriminations of rank and value, and courtly play with attitudes of negligent effortlessness—*sprezzatura*. To speak in common oppositions: on one branch, love; on the other, power; and what the foregoing Burkean exercise has shown us is a common ground of psychosocial, persuasive motivation for divergent human acts. In short, this is the dialectical counterpart of the Trickster's archetypal revelations by means of "contradictory" behavior.

Let me now complete the orientation of intentions in a more polemical fashion, hoping to show what is wanted by increasing the stress on what is not.

Too often criticism only comprehends one-half of the total dialectic; it boils down a text to rational doctrine only to boil away the volatile truth Thoreau speaks of in our epigraph. Instructed by New Criticism and Formalism to be alert to irony, it is good at seeing ironic corrosions, but without seeing, often, that irony can dissolve and not dissolve everything; can dissolve in order to purify an essential of its accidents, to test and prove some irreducible human fact. Too many times criticism does not see the connection established and maintained between author and reader, which therefore with our joint, newly tested insight re-creates the presented world that apparently went up in the smoke of a self-consuming artifact. Criticism such as this sees de-creation and not its rhetorically stimulated complement of re-creation—the tough, ebullient resilience that *Moby-Dick* calls "godly gamesomeness," and *Huckleberry Finn* exercises in "troubles" and "adventures." The work may collapse or reverse both the structuralist's synchronic and diachronic axes of understanding, yet what remains is not only a zero point, but a point of departure.

The failure to comprehend that an intellectual zero point may be another sort of point as well is largely traceable to the widespread habit of freezing a work of art that is in. motion, and thus ignoring the motivating drive itself. (Or else motivation is understood only as a Freudian biographical given, and not as something created and dynamic in the text.) Critics with such a propensity, and they are legion, can tell us of art that savages itself or savages something else without ever telling us what moves this savagery. To take a discovery eternally rediscovered, intellectual disillusionment by itself is not a drive but the sapping of all force. Looking for an intellectual contract between the artist and his work, critics fail to recognize the *force majeure*: the writer's exploration of what moves such savaging and what remains after the assault is over. This is at any rate the major effort for the artists we have at hand. For what moves in every sense is the essential origin and subject and end of our authors, all strikingly characterized by that restless traversing between the varieties of belief and unbelief that Hawthorne noticed in Melville, and Howells in Twain.

To think of art in stasis is assuredly proper as an initial

tactic; it is immensely valuable as a propaedeutic for further discussion or an encouragement for more alert reading. To say what is obvious, it is absolutely essential, and some of the most admirable critics do this work marvelously well. Preliminary labor in the intellectual sense is far from humble, and in the widest view it is never once-for-all, but must be periodically reachieved. What is wrong-headed is the pretense to total adequacy in a first act, the delusion that this one step in a long journey of inquiry has brought us triumphantly to our destination.

To make such disparaging statements is to risk being at once presumptuous and trite. But even a cursory review of actual critical practice seems to demand their repetition from time to time. We can never totally capture the artistic motion and motive, of course; but we can try to identify how the real artistic thing moves and what its vital truth of motive is as it exists volatilely before us in the text. The ideal is to catch literature in the act, as it words itself out. If we can understand, especially from criticism and literature of the last two centuries, an art that takes itself as its subject, can we not also see, at least in the artists before us, that the subject is further specified as the creative process per se? It consequently demands a processual critical method, one alert to drives and counter-resistances, the moment-by-moment activity that betrays the processual force as contrails do an aircraft at high altitude. Our criticism in practice has tended too much to look at the fixed design of the artistic contrails, or recently, against Formalism and New Criticism, insisted on how that breathless coherence fades under scrutiny. In both cases, it has typically ignored the moving craft itself and the wonder that it moves at all, and continues to do so despite fixity or fading.

Here, as Whitman says, on the verge of a usual mistake, I have another advocacy particularly occasioned by Richard Poirier's recent study, *The Performing Self*. It is that we do not, as critics like Poirier sometimes tend to, take creative process in too narrow a sense. A moment's thought should show that this will only double us back to a critical romantic solipsism in which everything disappears but the straining nerve of the artist's performing self. The brilliant truth of a view like Poirier's, recalling something we forget at our peril, also is conducive to a drastic demotion of everything else, so that we are left with Truth: self-performance is what it's really all about. But no matter if the writer himself thinks that his desperate verbal theatrics are all there is—and Melville, Twain, and West look solipsism steadily in its narcissistic face—for the critic to receive this as the import of their wisdom is a radical impoverishment in every respect.

The burden of a work's wisdom is its total way of acting toward the world and the reader it at once envisions and creates. It is, to rephrase, the entire motivational thrust that identifies itself in dialectical parts whose mutual debate acts out the motive in behavior, or whose lyric expression unfolding during the time of reading, image by rhythm, dances the motive's successive moments. Fiction (poetry, drama) is essentially about behavior, whole-bodied stances taken toward the world's body. Into these attitudes conventionally abstractable notions enter more or less as one constituent in a complex. Ransom is correct, and so is Burke: the poet suffers direct knowledge, but he also acts it. To use a common analogy comparing great things to small: in art, knowledge and act are finally as inseparable as in riding a bicycle; in any deeply skilled performance, one knows by doing, in the doing, and one does by knowing, in the knowing. Yet I would add that in regard to the whole universe of imaginative writing, though Burke is not "more correct," assuredly his view is logically prior to Ransom's. Literature, seen as a whole, concentrates on what happens when men act in a situation, and often on how the knowledge and confidence that they manifest is distinguishable from what they think they know and believe; or how the total situation constrains them to perform in direct opposition to what they truly know in any sense of the word. In terms of the present study, this may be restated: literature is founded not only on faith, but *con-fidens*—"having faith-with" a present context for such manifestation. Burke's view demonstrates that in literature there is nothing unless there is a "posture" toward something. In literature, the field of incipient action is the precondition for percept, concept, and precept. *Drama* in the root sense ("to do") is the general case, and lyric *cogito* is the special.

For the writers with whom we are concerned, this means that fiction is about acting in Burke's dramatistic sense, which equivocates productively between the philosophical and the theatrical meanings of *to act*. Here Burke makes another distinction extremely useful for gaining access to imaginative writing. Burke reserves the term *act*, in general usage, for humanly chosen and willed deeds, in contradistinction to the mere unconscious *motions* of the nonhuman world, to which he claims scientists simplistically ascribe human behavior. In more subtle usage, human behavior too may be contrastable as act and motion. Now the latter term (in my employment, equivalent to "mere deed" or some such locution) designates physical, mental, or social tropisms, or what Bergson would call "mechanical encrustations on the living," as against the unfrustrated, authentic investment of individual human motive that comprises an act. With the Trickster, the two concepts can be combined: as for instance, his overt motions may conceal and yet furtively express a covert act; indeed, in a given fictive world, these duplicitous deeds may be the sole means of safely and purely enacting a genuine motive.

Finally, the creative process that is revealed to us straining and failing and rising again against its stubborn environment and the inner contagions of bad faith, is a process-in-the-world—it is ours. The specific fashion each writer has of seeing this process, the particular name with which he metaphorically names its deep texturizing motive, is the domain of wisdom he can rhetorically offer us concerning our literary and nonliterary process, the risks it actually takes and feeds from, and the end, or beginning, to which it actually moves. And further, this disclosure is not abstractive: even where, in Twain, a certain kind of authorial transcendence is sought, it is rhetorically evoked in our imagination, done as a negotiation of consent between us and the narrative consciousness, while in the text motive remains immanent, illuminating a world and a behavior solidly *there*. The author's textual performance lights up the performance of his world and rhetorically connects us to its reemerging genesis: in the words of our writers, to "the living act"; to the manner that will "chain the reader's interest"; to the "game we want to play and we need you to play it."[15]

[15] In order, the quotations are from *Moby-Dick*, ed. Harrison Hayford and Hershel Parker (New York: W. W. Norton, 1967), p. 144; *Mark Twain's Letters*, ed. Albert Bigelow Paine (New York: Harper, 1917), II, 737 (and cf. *Mark Twain's Travels with Mr. Brown*, ed. Franklin Walker and G. Ezra Dane [New York: Knopf, 1940], pp. 174–75); and *The Complete Works of Nathanael West* (New York: Farrar, Straus & Cudahy, 1957), p. 312.

PART ONE

Herman Melville:
In Trust Nevertheless

Nur wer sich wandelt, bleibt mit mir verwandt.

Nietzsche, "Aftersong,"
Beyond Good and Evil

. . . the magical effect of the admission into man's inmost spirit of a before unexperienced and wholly inexplicable element, which like electricity suddenly received into any sultry atmosphere of the dark, in all directions splits itself into nimble lances of purifying light; which at one and the same instant discharge all the air of sluggishness and inform it with an illuminating property; so that objects which before, in the uncertainty of the dark, assumed shadowy and romantic outlines, now are lighted up in their substantial realities; so that in these flashing revelations of grief's wonderful fire, we see all things as they are; and though, when the electric element is gone, the shadows once more descend, and the false outlines of objects again return; yet not with their former power to deceive. . . .

Pierre

Introduction

WE come to Melville, as a rule, by way of an initiation in *Moby-Dick*. We meet him, usually, in an academic environment and see him, whatever our individual inclination, from the perspective of a distinctly positivistic century. Each of us is instructed more or less thoroughly by a body of Melville criticism that responds skillfully to our mystification at *Moby-Dick* and at successive encounters, most typically, with the enigmatic "Bartleby" and *Billy Budd*. Our initial acquaintance remains with us as a strong imprint while we extend our knowledge of his works and the extent of human experience they command. Melville, we see from the vantage of our perspective, our environment, and our instruction, is characteristically interested in bold, difficult ideas resulting from an imaginatively intense scrutiny of existence.

Two statements will afford the profile of our encounter—the more sharply because each critic modifies with a valuable special interest the outlook we hold in common. A Melville scholar and student of the English and American literature of the period writes, "[Melville] thinks it his business to provide a spacious and undivided wisdom, and he makes no clear distinction between art and teaching, representation and statement. He partly shares in the general nineteenth-century distrust of plot and external action, and he is fond of apologue and parable." Another commentator, whose illuminating study of Melville's style is only secondarily concerned with thematic ideas, summarizes Melville's artistic virtue as "the insistent thrust forward [his prose] develops toward an entire explicitness, an unstinting exactness. . . . 'Thrust toward explication' might be more exact: he will lay it all open and he will get it all said. Like so many of the major Americans he is an explainer. . . . His art, not always under control, is in keeping this will-to-explain in the service of his prime narrative objects. . . ."[1]

These critical assessments, I believe, are admirably accurate. They also indicate the ground we stand on when we encounter Melville and the habits we bring to the meeting. Melville is one of ours, an explainer that we with our exegetic bent can explain in turn, for even his explicitness is challenging. Coupled with his will-to-explain is his representation of an existence-to-be-explained. Indeed, a modern reader feels that somehow the spacious wisdom is provided for him alone in its integrity, the puzzle and its explanation being a secret between him and the volume, "Herman Melville: A Problem." However the reader's humility may remonstrate, if Melville is "for him" at all, he feels about the writer rather as he may feel about James Joyce: the intellectual test has the exclusiveness of a chess game played expertly in a back parlor. Melville as well as Hawthorne, we recall, had a good deal to say about the exclusive (in the extreme, isolating) quality of intellectual puzzling; more specifically, Melville's famous "Mosses" review describes exactly the decoding appeal that is likely to draw a modern reader.

But perhaps we endanger our appreciation of Melville's achievement above all because our bias so well matches his; or to put it less pejoratively, because we can see certain important attributes so clearly, we risk blindness about others that are there less intensely or less consciously for us. This tends to be true whether our critical interest be with ideas per se, with the form that the explicatory drive subserves, or with the rhetorical consequences sketched in the

[1] Richard Harter Fogle, *Melville's Shorter Tales* (Norman: University of Oklahoma Press, 1960), p. 4; Warner Berthoff, *The Example of Melville* (1962; rpt. New York: W. W. Norton, 1972), p. 208. I am much indebted to Berthoff's outstanding book; my difference with it may be indicated by observing that his Melville seems to me rather too staid, neither sufficiently agonized or playful.

preceding paragraph. Were it even desirable, which I deny, it would be impossible to ignore the engrained bias we share with Melville. My discussion will certainly attempt in part to explain the wisdom Melville is explaining. The primary aim, however, will be to expand the rhetorical sketch given above into a more adequate description of the artistic effectiveness of Melville's writing. The description will be more adequate insofar as it enlarges the defining conditions of our encounter with Melville so that they are somewhat less limiting conditions. More simply: what is Melville's full persuasive appeal, and how does that appeal coexist with and in the embodied concerns—the wisdom—of a given work?

The rare feeling Melville solicits is of a bond in full possession of its consequences; and it is by no means to be dissociated from understanding his recurrent representation of human ties and human bondage, or from the irresistible impact of mind, heart, and will he typically explicates and enacts. Neither an intellectual riddle, nor an imaginative energy driving toward explication, nor the power of blackness itself can fix and fascinate us in quite the way Melville does. To produce the rare tonic response to which many Melville readers have given testimony, there must be something immediately at stake in the live circuit between author and reader. There must be something at hazard— and not merely an interpretation to be won—for the work at hand to be more than a created entity, for it to make us "start up," as Melville says everything does in the presence of an original generative source. And further, Melville must show us that what is jeopardized between author and reader is of crucial value, that its loss or gain significantly matters. Only this fully achieved connection by hazard will be, in Melville's words again, to create the creative. Like the whale he sports with, Melville is to be vitally found out only in the heart of quickest perils.

2

Picaresque and Picturesque:
Omoo, Typee, Mardi

...you hero of rogues, Count Fathom!
—what a debt do we owe you!

Omoo

"Delegate your power, you leagued mortals
must. The hazard you must stand."

Mardi

I

Typee and *Omoo* are minor works. What is more important
for my purpose, they are successful, both historically and
abstractly considered, as rhetoric, as engagements of a public. They reveal an accomplished tact that seems to rule out
our viewing them as providential biographical expressions
with little to tell us about Melville's mature art. Genuine
tact, whether literary or social, is the very opposite of ego-
centricity; but I will propose that in an important sense
Melville's work is obsessed with self to an extraordinary
degree. This tact, in Melville, is an acute awareness of an
audience as a presence to be reckoned with, an awareness
that is inseparable from the strong sensation of self.

As Gordon Roper has noted of *Omoo*, in the experience
of writing and publishing *Typee*, Melville learned to trim
his craft somewhat to the requirements of audience; that is,
of the popular travel library his publisher John Murray
was producing.[1] Yet Melville also renewed his attack on

[1] "Historical Note," *Omoo*, ed. Harrison Hayford, Hershel Parker,
and G. Thomas Tanselle (Evanston, Ill.: Northwestern University
Press, 1968), p. 327. Unless otherwise indicated, where they are available the Northwestern-Newberry editions of *The Writings of Herman
Melville* hereafter will be cited, in the text.

missionaries and the general depredations of Western civilization in an even more polemical vein. Incorporating these opposing tensions, *Omoo*'s rhetoric is in some ways more instructive than that of *Typee* concerning his developing skill. Before directly treating the first novel, then, I begin with *Omoo* by citing a long quotation of a kind not often used for cutting in.

At the beginning of chapter 2 (the first chapter being primarily a transition from the end of *Typee*), the description of the ship *Julia* inaugurates the book's picaresque creative transactions:

> First and foremost, I must give some account of the Julia herself: or "Little Jule," as the sailors familiarly styled her.
>
> She was a small barque of a beautiful model, something more than two hundred tons, Yankee-built and very old. Fitted for a privateer out of a New England port during the war of 1812, she had been captured at sea by a British cruiser, and, after seeing all sorts of service, was at last employed as a government packet in the Australian seas. Being condemned, however, about two years previous, she was purchased at auction by a house in Sydney, who, after some slight repairs, dispatched her on the present voyage.
>
> Notwithstanding the repairs, she was still in a miserable plight. The lower masts were said to be unsound; the standing rigging was much worn; and, in some places, even the bulwarks were quite rotten. Still, she was tolerably tight, and but little more than the ordinary pumping of a morning served to keep her free.
>
> But all this had nothing to do with her sailing; at that, brave Little Jule, plump Little Jule, was a witch.

For an interesting further discussion of the nature of Melville's audience and his relationship with it, see *The Profession of Authorship in America: The Papers of William Charvat*, ed. Matthew J. Bruccoli (Columbus: Ohio State University Press, 1968).

Blow high, or blow low, she was always ready for the breeze; and when she dashed the waves from her prow, and pranced, and pawed the sea, you never thought of her patched sails and blistered hull. How the fleet creature would fly before the wind! rolling, now and then, to be sure, but in very playfulness. Sailing to windward, no gale could bow her over: with spars erect, she looked right up into the wind's eye, and so she went.

But after all, Little Jule was not to be confided in. Lively enough, and playful she was, but on that very account the more to be distrusted. Who knew, but that like some vivacious old mortal all at once sinking into a decline, she might, some dark night, spring a leak and carry us all to the bottom. However, she played us no such ugly trick, and therefore, I wrong Little Jule in supposing it. (pp. 9–10)

Confidence is the unifying topic; confidence in something that is old and disreputable, whose playful behavior nonetheless indicates spirited energies in reserve, yet whose very liveliness is seen as grounds for distrust. But the final assertion goes beyond considerations of appearance, behavior, and philosophical generalization to declare that, in the event, the entire supposition thus far is unjust. To employ the narrator's own frequent pragmatic bluntness, what then is the use of the supposition and the line of thought leading to it? The narrator's admiration for brave exuberance rising above a mere dogged adequacy to the situation, yet the sagacious recognition that this admiration must result in his adverse judgment—what do these count for when the judgment is at once proclaimed unfair? This question is perhaps in a sense foolish: we impatiently assume that we at least intuitively follow the fictional train of thought. After all, the tone is lightly comic, the object described relatively unimportant; and clearly the function of this quotation here at the beginning of the *Omoo* story proper is to characterize the narrator by rendering his reaction to his ship. But this observation does not eliminate the question; it moves it to another level of analysis. It is precisely this kind of passage—with numerous counterparts in *Mardi, White-Jacket, Moby-Dick,* and *The Confidence-Man*—that can repay patient curiosity about how to take Melville on his own terms. The dialectical quality of the passage perhaps offers a provisional warrant for Socratic questioning of the "obvious"—playing the fool in a sensible way, as Melville's later Socratic Confidence-Man will advise.

At stake is not only the narrator's experience with the ship, but also the reader's experience with both. What is at hazard is a vital confidence on the part of both reader and narrator. Melville's contemporary readers, on their own terms, were conscious of the wager. A representative review of the early books noted the new writer's "arch manner"; and several years later a reviewer of *The Confidence-Man* found the unusual protagonist familiar after all: "His hero, like Mr. Melville in his earlier works, asks confidence of everybody under different masks of mendicancy. . . ."[2]

Melville indeed gave his public the cue that they took in debating the veracity of his adventures; the preface of *Typee* concludes his implicit exhortation by openly "trusting that his anxious desire to speak the unvarnished truth will gain for him the confidence of his readers." One of Melville's deepest creative instincts surfaces here: what he would win, he first must risk. This intuition is already evident in *Typee*'s novel combination of tonal effects: first, the mendicancy of the mild preface; second, a general freedom of view Hawthorne cited in defending Melville's approach to sacrosanct topics; and third, a colorful heightening that exceeds the "unvarnished truth" the author repeatedly claims. Melville's inclination was corroborated and sharpened by an audience

[2] The early review is attributed to Margaret Fuller, New York *Tribune,* 4 April 1846, in *The Recognition of Herman Melville,* ed. Hershel Parker (Ann Arbor: University of Michigan Press, 1967), p. 3; the later is in the *Westminster Review,* 1 July 1857; in Parker, pp. 98–99.

response covering all shades of incredulity, delighted in many cases and in just as many, morally disapproving. The exotic polemical material alone, and particularly coming from such a polished stylist who alleged himself a sailor before the mast, had much to do with Melville's appearing before his public as a deponent. The truth remains that his audience's response, both anticipated and actual, made its strong impression on his art over his entire career; and his typical stylistic gestures are part of the wager for confidence.

This is not at once apparent in the present passage from *Omoo*. Melville's characteristic narrative presence might be demonstrated more obviously, for example in the opening paragraphs of *Typee*: "Six months at sea! Yes, reader, as I live. . . . Oh! ye state-room sailors . . . what would ye say to our six months out of sight of land?" But this stylistic device, at this intensity, cannot be kept up for long. The passage from *Omoo* provides a compact opportunity to examine a more representative, unobtruding relationship of subject matter and constitutive rhetoric. Raised to a higher intensity and even greater thematic pertinence, the rhetoric of this second novel later contributes largely to the success of one kind of masterwork including *Moby-Dick* and *The Confidence-Man*.

Speaking aloud, as it were, of the ship *Julia*, the narrator's voice is *addressed*.[3] The effect is not that of thinking overheard, nor is the narrator's attention consumed by a subject-object relation. The consciousness is reflective, intent on its object, but it is not retired to a point where the reader assumes the character of a privileged, unseen eavesdropper. The typical manner of taking thought seems to be that of taking speech. And while the communication is clearly meant to be heard, not overheard, it is not addressed to a world-in-general, as a declamation would be. It is much more exactly vocative, so that audience-awareness is a con-

[3] Cf. the problem of interiority and communication F. O. Matthiessen discusses in "Consciousness" and "Eloquence" in *American Renaissance*, pp. 5–24.

structive part of the whole consciousness, woven into its basic dialectical process. Barely a sentence rapidly passes, before we are given another "notwithstanding," "but," "to be sure," or "however." We follow the workings of a consciousness engaged before our eyes in fashioning a detailed judgment adequate to every element of the case. There are many ways to reflect a mental process; this dramatized consciousness, to repeat, is dialectic: it is a mimicry in small of public discourse, implying participation by several voices. An addressed voice in itself increases the participatory sense; the present manner of address—the zestful pace, the breezily familiar tone ("plump Little Jule") and awareness of sailor familiarity—is a positive encouragement to adopt unconsciously the succession of discursive postures.

This mind is a theatre, or better, a symposium as dramatistic in its make-up as the original; and it is one in which we are silent but not passive partners. This is genuine dialectic in that none of the positions stated is really abandoned, and this vocative trait establishes another incentive for ready involvement in each of them. Each declaration is warranted from its own perspective, yet every one is a modification of a previous statement and in turn originates another. None of the positions, even the "final" one, can be understood adequately outside the sequence leading up to and away from it. In the last paragraph, "But after all" sounds like the concluding note. The straightforward conclusion is, "Little Jule was not to be confided in." The culminating reasons follow; then as if reluctant to let any one statement be conclusive, the narrator shifts completely out of the narrative present to a "However" and "therefore" that show the previous conclusion to be penultimate. The terminal now seems to be, "therefore, I wrong Little Jule in supposing it."

But in a fundamental respect this last statement is only as true as any other in the entire sequence, and is only intermediate after all. In briefly pronouncing the imputation wrong, it throws us back upon the consequentiality of the predicate. If we do not literally go back and re-read the whole passage, the contradiction serves to italicize the authority of its attractive presentation: the supposition plainly stands, though it wrongs. We are surely meant to share the narrator's admiration for the behavior of the gamesome personification. And we are surely not intended to dissent from the cryptic, knowing logic that sees lively playfulness as a basis for distrust, and cleverly ratifies its reasoning in the submerged self-contradictory pun, "vivacious . . . mortal." (Such a pun, as criticism has shown, is representative of Melville's juggling word connotations and roots; compare "sinister dexterity" in *Billy Budd*, for example.) The whole suppositional process is compounded of the narrator's affectionate bond with a being that is ardently game as well as his lack of confidence in the precariously maintained exaltation. He will deny neither precariousness nor spirit, and he joins in the latter by mock-gallantly—and not mockingly—attributing the old vessel's rolling motion to its "very playfulness." No simple schematic statement will quite do justice, then, to the narrator's confidence. The observation that the ship "was not to be confided in" is a categorical assertion transcending the immediate need for a description of his mere response at the time; nonetheless, he also declares categorically that in supposing *Julia* would play the murderous "ugly trick," he wrongs her. For all the logically fluid style, there is an uninsistent, casual paralogism existing in suspension in the quotation.

If one word could sum up the enacted narrative posture, and also permit a generalization about Melville's works, it would be "Nevertheless." The attitude mediates between spirited affiliation and disabused intellect; between impossibility and necessity. This dialectic of consciousness, playing off its audience's desire for concord with the narrative master of ceremonies, recurs in nearly every conceivable variety of comic, pathetic, and tragic nuance throughout Melville's career. It is, I believe, central to his genius; as a necessarily invitational and elusive stance, it is intimately bound up with the question of confidence.

As to the reader's confidence in *Omoo*'s narrator, it is obviously not challenged here to the extent that it is in the sections criticizing the missionaries, or those showing the narrator's assistance in mutiny. No such drama is present here. But there is the beginning of a subtle pressure, a modest wager of trust, which as the book progresses, performs the minute-by-minute evocative tasks without which the novel would be only the repository for a few histrionic moments. First, although the invitational address of the passage has been stressed up to now, it is also significant that the description provides the reader no *single* reliable statement, since each discrete observation refers to the dialectic in its circular entirety. This might not be so noteworthy, except that Melville's characteristic explicatory thrust prompts the reader's unwitting desire for explicit conclusiveness. When someone directly addresses us from an overall explanatory posture, to some degree whatever our sophistication and whatever the subtlety of the presentation, we expect explanation—thorough to be sure, but the more conclusive the better. This is especially so when the thing to be elucidated seems fairly simple. Melville's most famous narrator later directly answers the expectation when he interjects an attack and counterattack into his analysis of a whale-spout: "But why pester one with all this reasoning on the subject? Speak out! You have seen him spout; then declare what the spout is; can you not tell water from air? My dear sir, in this world it is not so easy to settle these plain things. I have ever found your plain things the knottiest of all."[4]

In the present passage, though the reader's confidence is solicited, it is also kept hovering by the minute contradictory signals of almost blandly easy address, explanatory posture,

[4] *Moby-Dick*, ed. Harrison Hayford and Hershel Parker (New York: W. W. Norton, 1967), p. 312. Hereafter cited in the text.

and elusive holistic process. We can repose confidence only by shifting its focus away from the imitated reality, the ship and its behavior, to the entire dialectic process—that is, to the narrative consciousness itself—just as only the whole process can do justice to the narrator's "contradictory" response to his world. What is more, the first signal named above alone makes a slight but unmistakable contribution to affronting confidence. The narrator runs some risk, as he does throughout the book, of assuming too much, of being too negligently confidential. We quickly discern the narrator's general admiration, indeed, for the "lounging" and the "offhand."

Melville's contemporaries felt this, of course, much more strongly than the modern reader is likely to. His audience was used to having its literary dignity not only respected but fostered. On the scale of prevalent assumptions, they registered a tremor at the "free and easy style"[5] (as one reviewer disapprovingly called it) that tacitly questioned the conventions of the author-reader relationship almost as much as it did those regarding missionaries, religion, and sex. It is one thing to be asked to suspend one's disbelief in reading avowed fiction. It is another "to be confided in," in the full meaning of the term, on short acquaintance within the opening pages of a travel-adventure book purporting to literal truth. Thus the narrator remarkably interrupts an exclamation, "How the fleet creature would fly before the wind!" by turning to his putative audience with: "rolling, now and then, to be sure, but in very playfulness." This is play-judiciousness, with the commas marking off the publicly thoughtful strophes; it expresses the narrator's gallantly sportive will much more than it accounts for a literal nautical motion. But the reader, thus approached, is liable to decline the invitation to play, especially when his prudence is echoed by the narrator's own suspicion of play in the next paragraph.

None of this is meant to imply that Melville was system-

[5] In Parker, *Recognition*, p. 4.

atically alienating his public in his first two books; that he won quick popularity is well known. His point was, of course, to win what was risked. But his fame was also a notoriety, and he was from the first instinctively operating on margin. This was partly because of the man he was, and partly because his public's Anglo-American Christian assumptions about personal interchanges had to be renovated if readers were to understand, as if from within, his rough-and-ready experiences as a whaler, Typeean captive, and South Sea wanderer. Again, Melville's prefaces show his conscious aim. *Typee's* inclusive creative illusion of unmediated involvement is given this formulation: "There are some things related in the narrative which will be sure to appear strange, or perhaps entirely incomprehensible, to the reader; but they cannot appear more so to him than they did to the author at the time. He has stated such matters just as they occurred, and leaves every one to form his own opinion concerning them. . . ." *Omoo's* preface, having spoken of the reckless, lawless sailor life, declares that "it is, partly, the object of this work to convey some idea of the kind of life to which allusion is made. . . . Another object proposed, is to give a *familiar* account of the present condition of the converted Polynesians. . . ." And Melville sums up the illusion he seeks: "In a familiar way [the author] has merely described what he has seen; and if reflections are occasionally indulged in, they are spontaneous, and such as would, very probably, suggest themselves to the most casual observer." In order to be renovated, his audience's *familiar* premises must be activated in the largely unconscious negotiations of rhetoric; they must be exercised in a way analogous to the narrator's experiences.

Melville's use of the play-analogue, in metaphor and in tone, is symptomatic of his general practice. The mass of men, as Melville might put it in a favorite phrase, lose their playfulness at an early age; all the more reason to value (*and* to distrust) it in a "vivacious old mortal." *Omoo's* beachcomber's motto is this: appreciate whatever of value is found, wherever it is found. The equivocal *Julia* is a synecdoche for the book's hard, comic, shabby picaresque world, and here the value of the ship's survival is unquestionable.

In classical rhetorical terms, the principal basis of Melville's appeal here and in all the early books is that of ethos. His narrative presence, relatively unobtrusive but strongly inflected, wins a jeopardized confidence as the encompassing voucher for truth. N. P. Willis struck the right note in reassuring the public: "Herman Melville, with his cigar and his Spanish eyes, *talks Typee* and *Omoo*, just as you find the flow of his delightful mind on paper. Those who have only read his books know the man—those who have only seen the man have a fair idea of his books."[6] Persona matches ethos, the public is told: the man is true, and this is what matters. One reviewer of *Omoo* spoke for many when he guessed that the author must be "exceedingly good company."[7] The Romantic doctrine that the author is greater than his creation enters here (as in Melville's discussion of Shakespeare in the *Mosses* review), but Melville's individual stamp is fixed by the inventive rhetoric in which ethos as problematic appeal converges with ethos as problematic theme. Examination of the later work will reveal this convergence most fully, but for now we can concur again with the reviewer who compared the early Mr. Melville to the Confidence-Man; above all, as the Confidence-Man says, what is desired is "confidence in *me*." Beyond belief in his abstract views or in his achieved expression, and even beyond belief pure and simple, *Omoo*'s narrator insinuates that all depends on a confiding relationship with *him*. In the more forthright strategy of *Typee*, ethos is frankly avouched: "I may here state, and on my faith as an honest man . . ." (p. 23). In *Mardi*, the third book, through the transparent guise of the fictitious author Lombardo, Mel-

6 *The Home Journal*, 13 Oct. 1848, in *The Melville Log*, ed. Jay Leyda (New York: Harcourt, 1951), I, 320.
7 In "Historical Note," *Omoo*, p. 335.

ville proudly asks indulgence for the book's failures on the ground of personal genius, with its unformulably profound ideas. Neither this habit nor Melville's frequently voiced desire for frank, open, unmediated expression means that rhetorical study must yield to biography. I mean to argue that Melville's greatest successes and failures run similar risks, and that in *Moby-Dick* and *The Confidence-Man* he succeeds in transposing the *merely* rhetorical-personal into the superpersonal by the sheerest and most durable of margins.

A curious evidence of the revulsion felt by some early readers is one denunciation of *Omoo*'s "perfect want of heart."[8] The oddity is that Melville's customary assessments of people involve compounds of "heart," as in the following initial encounter and final leave-taking: "I could not help loving the free-hearted captain. . . ."; and, "About nightfall, we broke away from the generous-hearted household . . ." (pp. 314, 316). In typically responding with very personal tones to the Melville ethos, as well as ethic in the modern sense, each reviewer revealed the texture of his confidence, which is to say, the qualities of character that engage his instinctive commitment. The reviewer last quoted found what he called Melville's "reckless spirit" and "cool, sneering wit" incompatible with heart. He clearly would be unable to share the narrator's feeling for the ship *Julia* or the large range of phenomena her portrait stands for. The genius of the ship, and of the novel, is the picaro Dr. Long Ghost. The narrator's companionable wanderings with the woman-chasing, work-dodging prankster is the test case for confidence at the level of immediate human encounter, as against the generalized collisions of practical Christianity and sensual, languid Polynesia.

Omoo's theme of friendship, continued from *Typee* and carried prominently through *Moby-Dick*, looks squarely at the hazardous and indispensable immediate human connection that the rhetoric obliquely enacts. In twin keystone

8 *Ibid.*, p. 336.

chapters ending the first and beginning the second half of
Omoo, the narrator marvels at both the spiritual generosity
of Polynesians and the extreme affectation they evince:
"The really curious way in which all the Polynesians are in
the habit of making bosom friends at the shortest possible
notice, is deserving of remark. Although, among a people
like the Tahitians, vitiated as they are by sophisticating
influences, this custom has in most cases degenerated into a
mere mercenary relation, it nevertheless had its origin in a
fine, and in some instances, heroic sentiment, formerly
entertained by their fathers. . . . Filled with love and admiration for the first whites who came among them, the
Polynesians could not testify the warmth of their emotions
more strongly, than by instantaneously making their abrupt
proffer of friendship" (p. 152). In the first of the two
chapters, Poky is a trustworthy friend prefiguring Queequeg
(complete with black pocket-idol), and in the second,
Kooloo is the degenerated Polynesian hypocrite who abuses
the narrator's comradely confidence.

The combination of such mutually antagonistic attributes
in one person, as to a largely benign degree in the picaro
doctor, provokes the narrator's greatest curiosity and inventive skill. One of the raciest scenes concerns a Tahitian
girl who, in answer to the narrator's grave question about
her Christian belief, seriously replies by touching her mouth,
eyes, and hands and saying she is indeed converted there.
Then "her whole air changed in an instant; and she gave
me to understand, by unmistakable gestures, that in certain
other respects she was not exactly a [Christian]" (p. 178).
Seen in the context of the whole novel, Melville's comic
point is not primarily to question the sincerity of her
Christian spiritual gestures any more than her carnal ones,
for Tahitian "hypocrisy in matters of religion" is shown to
extend to ancient pagan practice as well as present Christian.
Rather, the theatricality of the girl's performance, which
ends in laughter all around, is of a piece with the general
self-dramatization repeatedly demonstrated in Polynesians,

sailors, missionaries, and civil functionaries alike: the bois-
terous or sly pranks of gentlemanly Long Ghost; the high
theater of the fake mutiny "trial" and the church services;
the gaudily sensual reign of the Tahitian Queen Pomaree.
From naively unconscious desire for dramatic effect to fully
conscious, planned duplicity, the incongruities of human
behavior exist as modulations along one continuous psychosocial scale of motivation. *Omoo* everywhere suggests the
deep-seated social dramatistic motive within the individual
psyche, in the picaresque world and narrative consciousness
alike. The novel's picaresque premise is that the individual's every private action is in an important respect social,
played before an internal as well as an external audience.
But since *every* action is also inherently an "act," whether
performed by true friend or hypocrite, the social motive of
generous amity is no less a valuable "fine, and in some
instances, heroic sentiment" than meanly hypocritical self-
seeking is despicable. For the individual psychic theater may
have a greater or lesser purview of what its audience comprises and what it is owed.

My preceding paragraph is not a statement of the book's
doctrinal theory but rather an analysis of the fictional
premise underlying character, scene, and action as an all but
conscious incipient idea. In the next book, *Mardi*, and in
Moby-Dick and especially *Pierre*, similar premises become
much more overt in examinations of human motive that are
"frank" and "unguarded" (*Pierre*, v, vii). Only in *Moby-
Dick*, however, does this not cause a fatal mutual lesion between abstract statement and fictive embodiment. In *Omoo*
one implicit presumption subtends both picaresque characterization and earnest polemical attack on cultural hypoc-
risies, so that Melville can move from one extreme of the
tonal curve to the other undistracted by "pretensions to
philosophic research" (as the preface puts it) and without
relinquishing his light, firm rhetorical hold.

Omoo's rambling diversity is sustained by a narrative presence shepherding the reader's imagination. In relative

contrast, *Typee*'s focus is tighter, its rhetorical charm more open, with the additional claim of a capture-and-escape suspense plot. The book exemplifies the convention of picturesque charm that Melville began with, and to which his "major phase" of the fifties recurs. This convention, bent to Melville's own purposes, allowed him to come at the question of confidence from a familiar angle, to provide the crosslights he sought on every subject.[9]

II

perspective, *the basic condition of all life.* . . .

. . . *it is high time to replace the Kantian question, "How are synthetic judgments a* priori *possible?" by another question, "Why is belief in such judgments* necessary?"—*and to comprehend that such judgments must be* believed *to be true, for the sake of the preservation of creatures like ourselves.* . . . *Or to speak more clearly and coarsely: synthetic judgments a* priori *should not "be possible" at all.* . . . *Only, of course, the belief in their truth is necessary, as a foreground belief and visual evidence belonging to the perspective optics of life.*

Nietzsche, *Beyond Good and Evil*

Picturesque charm dominates *Typee* not only because conventional pictorial descriptions set a marked rhetorical

---

9 The reviews of Melville's works through *Moby-Dick* were agreed in noting his "Picturesque" descriptions, his "pretty and spirited pictures," and his "cabinet pictures," forms of praise Melville was to turn on their heads in *Pierre*'s treatment of "the povertiresque." Melville first published "The Encantadas" under the sardonic pen name Salvator R. Tarnmoor—in reference, of course, to one of the most famous practitioners of picturesque, Salvator Rossa, commonly known simply as Salvator. Melville also featured himself in the thin, sour disguise of the landscape painter, B. Hobbema Brown, in the late sketch, "The Marquis de Grandvin." Useful modern discussions of picturesque are found in the following: Mario Praz, *The Romantic Agony*, 2nd ed. (1933; rpt. London: Oxford, 1967), pp. 19–22; E. H. Gombrich, *Art and Illusion* (Princeton: Princeton University Press, 1961), pp. 181–202; Samuel H. Monk, *The Sublime: A Study of Critical Theories in XVIII-Century England* (Ann Arbor: University of Michigan Press, 1960); J. H. Van den Berg, *The Changing Nature of Man (Metabletica)* (New York: W. W. Norton, 1961). See also William Gilpin, *Three Essays on Picturesque Beauty; on Picturesque Travels; and on Sketching Landscape* (London, 1808).

example but because the book's overall narrative progress widens and deepens the implications of the picturesque. The progress of the story can be called movement into the picture. This is a special case of the device Melville later employs widely, in which the protagonist moves from genteel appreciative observation to troubled involvement. It could be described approximately as a movement from the aesthetic to the ethical view, with the originally static pictorial scene coming to ethical life as the observer's perspective shifts from distance to immediate proximity. It could be so described, except that this implies a simplistic distinction between the two categories; the narrative progress really articulates a mutual toughening of the tempers of composed appreciation and troubled active choice. From the standpoint of narrative technique, the picturesque sense of nearness-with-distance is maintained throughout *Typee*, as in the early works in general, above all by the persistent nostalgia that sets experiences before the reader as being "aesthetically" distant or gone forever even at the moment they are supposed to exist as attractive immediate phenomena in the fictional present.

At the beginning of the book, while the narrative voice vibrantly denounces the injustices done the Polynesians, the young Tommo whimsically views a particular encounter between a beribboned French admiral and a tattooed savage from the angle of conventional notation and picturesque contrast: "At what an immeasurable distance, thought I, are these two beings from each other. . . . 'Yet, after all,' quoth I to myself, '. . . may not the savage be the happier man of the two?' Such were the thoughts that arose in my mind as I gazed upon the novel spectacle before me. . . . I can recall even now with vivid distinctness every feature of the scene. The umbrageous shades where the interview took place . . . the picturesque grouping of the mingled throng of soldiery and natives—and even the golden-hued bunch of bananas that I held in my hand at the time, and of which I occasionally partook while making the aforesaid philosophical reflections." Two pages later, Tommo figures again in an attitude of self-assured, appreciative consumption as he reveals that a principal attraction in the idea of desertion is scenic: "how delightful it would be to look down upon the detested old vessel from the height of some thousand feet, and contrast the verdant scenery about me with the recollection of her narrow decks and gloomy forecastle! . . . I straightway fell to picturing myself seated beneath a coconut tree . . . with a cluster of plantains within easy reach, criticizing her nautical evolutions as she was working her way out of the harbor" (pp. 29, 31). This is the very spirit of picturesque, in which the artist-viewer's attitude of gentlemanly offhandedness is an integral part of the effect of charmingly easy indulgence. Without insisting too much on it, we can note the link between this coolly lounging posture and that of the aristocratic rogue Long Ghost in *Omoo*; further, the connection between picturesque and picaresque in the gentlemanly *sprezzatura* that eschews vulgar labor and does its work in a quick, cunning stroke, without being morally or aesthetically finical. *Omoo*'s outlook, in other words, is *Typee*'s translated into a different fictional idiom under the influence of Smollett's typical combination of aristocratic-picturesque outlook and gentlemanly rogue-hero: ". . . you hero of rogues, Count Fathom!—what a debt do we owe you!" (*Omoo*, p. 293).

Typee's several set-piece descriptions in their conscious conventionality ("until from gently rolling hillsides . . . it sensibly swells into lofty and majestic heights, whose blue outlines . . . close in the view") accurately reflect Tommo's initial mentality. At the same time, the encompassing narrative nostalgia is the tonal counterpart of picturesque execution. In the famous Edenic view of the Typee valley that dramatically ends chapter 7 ("I chanced to push aside a branch, and by so doing suddenly disclosed to my view a scene which even now I can recall. . . ."), the formula "peculiar charm" occurs to summarize the blended viewpoint of protagonist and narrative consciousness. This coincidence of focus, along with the contrasted denunciatory humanistic concern of the "older" narrative presence, encourages us to be receptive to picturesque charm while noticing without censoriousness that Tommo's initial manner of enjoying it is callow. Because of this blending on the one hand, and reassuring contrast on the other, the picturesque descriptions can be as naively pleasurable for us as they are to Tommo, and yet have an extra dimension not present to him.

Metaphorically speaking, the piercing of Tommo's static picture plane is accomplished by the perilous descent into the valley down the steep picturesque perspectives, and by his sudden mysterious leg ailment. Both of these means suggest that old distanced valuations no longer apply, as the recurring pains and successive vertiginous surprises of the descent keep pace with the increasingly difficult tests of cool assurance. When finally, after five days of fatigue and hunger, the valley floor is reached and the companions gaze back up toward their initial prospect, a significant change has taken place in the narrator's stance from that of idling consumer of sights and fruit: "we both stood with no limbs broken" (p. 65). Picturesque conventional scenes and descriptive techniques continue to be deployed throughout the book, but the picturesque tone progressively becomes more sympathetic and humane as the Typees strike Tommo less as "beautiful" curiosities and more as individual persons. By the last third of the book, the Typee landscape is fully animated as a place of contingent, reciprocal ethical choices; and when the narrator does look askance at Typee curiosities, as in the discussion of belief in chapter 24, his tone is a friendly echo of the Typees' own represented playful disposition.

Thus Tommo's fundamental propensity is not abandoned but matured in his experience of changing visual and cultural perspectives. This maturation pattern, slight and relatively unsystematic as it is, helps to give *Typee* the sense of closure that frames its picturesque charm, and yet makes it more than incidentally "charming." This effect is related to the book's total rhetorical coherence in ways that demand closer attention to the structure outlined so far.

The ethical maturation of aesthetic outlook is keyed to a succession of choices that expose the deepest assurances on which individual and social life rest. If the *Omoo* narrator is more maturely knowing about what to expect from men as social creatures, the *Typee* narrator is equally on the outlook for a confidant. When he plans to desert ship in Nukuheva, he immediately seeks a companion in desertion whom he can trust among the "parcel of dastardly and mean-spirited wretches" aboard (p. 21). On a sudden congenial impulse, he enlists Toby, a "big-hearted shipmate" whose "fearless confidence was contagious" (pp. 32, 58). As *Typee* inclines much more than *Omoo* toward an initiation motif, the dilemma the young narrator is repeatedly brought to might be simply stated, What is reliable?

The novel first sets Tommo's personal problem within the context of intercultural betrayal. Before the desertion takes place there is an exposition of the ironic conversion the Christians really effect in the Polynesians: the "Unsophisticated and confiding" islanders are debauched and swindled, with the result that the proto-Christian "instinctive feeling of love within their breasts is soon converted into the bitterest hate." Christian nations, the narrator goes on to say, have created the very savages that they name, by wanton abuse of naive trust and love freely given (pp. 15, 26–27). Toward the end of the book it is argued that behind this betrayal is the culpable license Western civilization gives its missionary vanguard: "An unwarranted confidence in the sanctity of its apostles—a proneness to regard them as incapable of guile . . ." (p. 198). Even in such generalizations, filled with bitterness, Melville contextually maintains his major reference points of untutored

human reliances. These run the gamut from the unpre-
meditated demands of personal courage during the descent
("dreading to lose all confidence in myself, if I remained
meditating upon the step . . .") to the untorn Edenic network between men and wild creatures in the Typee Valley
("confidence in the kindliness of man"). Concordantly, the
novel's action is largely the see-saw of trust in the hero's
closest relations, as when Tommo first reposes "full confidence in [Fayaway's] candor and intelligence" in reassuring him about Toby's mysterious disappearance, then
promptly feels betrayed by the suspected "perfidy" of Toby
(pp. 108-09).

As each choice of trust suspensefully arises—Typee versus
Happar, Typeean cannibalism versus Typeean benignity,
betrayal by Toby or not—it becomes increasingly evident
that knowledge can only be gained, if at all, by venturing
confidence and then observing the result. The entire adventure sequence forces the issue, as does the adventurous but
clear-sighted Toby. The narrator's part in the complementary character scheme is invested in one phrase: "I reminded [Toby] that it was impossible for either of us to
know anything with certainty . . ." (p. 51). For his part,
Toby leads the way in descending the cliffs by performing
literal leaps of confidence onto flimsy supports; and he wag-
gishly answers one impossibility with another, on the basis
of a picturesque morality: "It is impossible that the in-
habitants of such a lovely place . . . can be anything else
but good fellows" (p. 56). Both impossibilities are in one
sense real, and in another false. In this situation, every life
or death choice of vision, movement, or speech constitutes
an effective act of trust whatever one's conscious reservations
or outright disbelief. Confidence must be placed in things
flimsier than trees and vines—in verbal sounds selected on
intuitive impulse before an inscrutable, half-naked audience. When the runaways face the unidentified natives of
the valley, they must at once decide, in response to a
peremptory question, whether they will declare allegiance

61

to the supposedly fierce Typees or gentle Happars. Tommo's blurted reply, " 'Typee mortarkee!' " is formed of "talismanic syllables" (p. 71) that produce an instantaneous transition to delighted friendliness in the audience. The incongruous, exotic magic, coming from the erstwhile picturesque connoisseur, more effectively than a dissertation highlights the precariousness of human interchange and choice. Perhaps for the first time we begin to see vividly what Melville represents all along in the book. Our deeply impulsive, automatic commitments of quotidian enmity and civility seem, precisely, *alien* when brought to consciousness, as in this absurd, vital verbal act done on a tiny barbarian island engrossed in its parochial warfare.

The subtly re-visionary persuasiveness of *Typee*, although not fully achieved, adumbrates *The Confidence-Man*, which consciously and systematically articulates the first novel's more inchoate dramatization of acts of faith in the widest sense. *Typee*'s device of cultural contrast has an intrinsic basis of persuasion because culture, like rhetoric, is consensus of the profoundest sort, in the same way operating as a pervasively motivating, unconscious datum of consciousness. In both cases, the most revealingly differentiating consensus can often be found in the unspectacular incidentals and the small "free unstudied actions" (p. 15) that Tommo notices admiringly in the Polynesians. As with the best travel fiction, *Typee* establishes imaginative perspectives back upon the basic subintentional reflexes to which we need not and normally cannot attend. Inquisitive of the minutest details of the Typees' everyday life, it allows us to observe the inherently unfamiliar in the subliminally familiar. By this momentary flash of estrangement we can be startled into seeing the usually invisible automatisms that in our experience comprise an *ur*-confidence far below willed choice. These are the synthetic processes of Nietzschean foreground belief on which daily survival depends —whether, as in *Typee*, at the level of domestic life or more immediately impressive adventurous dilemma. Merely to see the invisibly familiar, as if for the first time, is to begin to be persuaded of the vision. And the descriptive counterpart of this effect is provided by the picturesque, which is in general based upon the domestication of the exotic (as in seeing the striking Typee Valley in the familiar frame of Eden), and more importantly upon the pleasing alienation effect arising when the hitherto unremarkable is seen as an aesthetic stimulus.

In Tommo's grimmer moods, he envisions in the slightest acts the "fearful death which, under all these smiling appearances, might yet menace us" (p. 97). But when he experiences a healthful "elasticity of mind" (p. 123) the young Calvinist gentleman-sailor is above all struck by the Typees' combination of playfulness and "an inherent principle of honesty and charity toward each other" (p. 201), a sportive "fraternal feeling" (p. 203) pervading the most ordinary collective enterprises: "To tell the truth, they were somewhat inclined to be lazy, but a perfect tumult of hilarity prevailed; and they worked together so unitedly, and seemed actuated by such an instinct of friendliness that it was truly beautiful to behold" (pp. 203–04). By contrast, a prevision of *The Confidence-Man* satirizes the genteelly corrosive Christian version of sociability and charity: "certain tea party excitements, under the influence of which benevolent-looking gentlemen in white cravats solicit alms . . . toward the creation of a fund . . . whose end has almost invariably been to accomplish [the Polynesians'] temporal destruction!" (p. 195). The irony, in brief, is that the Polynesians already have superlatively the cardinal virtue that the Western civilization complacently imposes on them nominally and disastrously.

Typee makes clear—what is centrally important in understanding Melville—that for him Charity is not at all the rather chilly theological notion that it tends to be for us as for his orthodox contemporaries. The concord, the *caritas*, that moves the narrator is the same "vital mode of being, not an incident" that Melville will recall in *Mardi*'s allegorical Serena from the represented Typee example. In the smallest occupations the narrator marvels at the "buoyant sense of a healthful physical existence," a "general hilarity" that sets the whole population playing in the "great popgun war," and infuses the unstrained social fabric of affection, as if among "one household, whose members were bound together. . . . The love of kindred I did not so much perceive, for it seemed blended in the general love . . ." (pp. 127, 204–05). Offset by corrupting strenuous Christian evangelism, the Typees' casual motives, portrayed in the daily "vital mode" of playful existence, accomplish on a large consensual scale what the "talismanic syllables" do on a small: an illumination of human possibilities for grace as well as absurd cruelty. The mystery is the genuine coexistence of both in one social consensus and one individual.

To maintain the credibility of the suspenseful plot and of his attack on Western exploitation, the narrator must square the Typees' Charity with their cannibalism and with Tommo's lurking distrust of their intentions toward him. As in all Melville's works, and *The Confidence-Man* most significantly, inconsistencies within the unitary psyche must be accounted for explicitly, incorporated in truthful characterization, or both. In *Omoo*, the self-dramatizing psychosocial premise supported picaresque comedy and serious polemics. In *Typee*, the fundamental psychosocial motive among the natives is reflected in Charity, which here exists in the specific form of a collectivist unanimity making almost no distinction between the inner and the public experience. From the narrator's cultural viewpoint, the malign side of this motive is the tattooing ritual, which he fears as an obliteration of individual identity in its own way akin to consuming another human being. Lacking, except in a very diffuse way, the additional theatrical, picaresque premise of *Omoo*, *Typee* has no characterization principle inherently allowing for incongruity. Yet the whole effect of the book demands that incongruity be both present and credible.

In this first book, then, the slightly more naive narrative presence first makes the claim that "these apparent discrepancies are easily reconciled," next admits he "cannot so confidently speak" of the origin of intertribal hatred, then directly faces the basic rhetorical issue: "The reader will . . . perhaps charge me with admiring a people against whom so odious a crime [as cannibalism] is chargeable." For the contradictory Typeean character to be credible as fact, for the reader not to suppose that the narrator has "overdrawn this picture," ultimately the rhetorical ethos must be credited. The basic reconciliation is that of reader and narrative consciousness; it is the primary condition of the other harmonization, that between contradictions. In the immediate context, aside from a few plausible palliations for cannibalism, the narrator resolves on a final wise saying and a flat reassertion of personal testimony: "But here Truth, who loves to be centrally located, is again found between the two extremes; . . . fearful as this custom is . . . still I assert that those who indulge in it are in other respects humane and virtuous" (pp. 204–05).

This forthright approach alone, however, cannot secure the conviction needed. It obviously will not sustain the imaginative hold that the book in fact has, but itself needs support and extension. If human contradiction cannot be credibly explicated, it can be rhetorically placed in a coherent viewpoint. The book's aim, we are now in a position to see, is to subsume the rhetorical risks it takes and its combination of fictive and journalistic stances under the rubric of picturesque charm. This communicated temper establishes the permissible boundaries of our response and so gives the novel its fundamental rhetorical foundation. The charm (there is no more accurate term here than Melville's old-fashioned one) is that of indulged wonder commingled with indulged suspicion, and both without issue in analytical conclusion. This effect in large part serves the important end just noticed, that of establishing the narrator's good faith, on the Romantic principle of "Thus I have felt." The ethos of intense, and maturing, sensibility underwrites accuracy of judgment and angry polemic. As regards the story proper, the commingled emotions exist in and for themselves, to reflect, as the preface indicates, the rounded experience at the time as if the reader were undergoing it. But we have noticed another force at work besides that of immediacy. Every edge of anxiety and admiration is buffered by distancing nostalgic motifs ("Were I to live a hundred years, I should never forget. . . .") and a recurrent condescending note toward the childlike Typees, so that the conjoined distrust and wonder are converted into a pleasurable form, to provide pleasure. The Typeean portrait retains to the last the picturesque *sprezzatura*. The "negligent" lack of finish refuses to bear the weight of explanation, or intellectual speculation, that it halfway invites. Particularly the refusal to resolve the story's most important motivational ambiguity—why the Typees so urgently wish Tommo to remain with them—prevents the book from falling into the moral reductionism that the hero's (understandable) desire for certainty sometimes threatens to produce. A negative capability is maintained by the narrative technique, if not by the narrator as occasionally foolhardy hero. In fact, Tommo's outbursts of impatience for a solution, in establishing a periodic threat to the book's charming mysteriousness, contribute toward heightening the sense of pleasurable irresolution.

A final illustration should help to make the point clearer. The narrator recognizes that his detention by the Typees seems to have religious significance, somehow connected with their desire that he be tattooed. His curiosity about their belief is therefore not merely casual, but might be expected to be thoroughgoing. In chapter 24, a direct treatment of the Typee religion, a picturesque scene demonstrates the governing focus of feeling. The narrator says that a famous chief's canoe-mausoleum

> had a peculiar charm for me; I hardly know why; but
> so it was. As I . . . watched the play of the feathery

headdress, stirred by the ... breeze ... I loved to yield myself up to the fanciful superstition of the islanders, and could almost believe that the grim warrior was bound heavenward. In this mood ... I bade him "God speed. ..." Aye, paddle away, brave chieftain. ... To the material eye thou makest but little progress; but with the eye of faith, I see thy canoe cleaving the bright waves, which die away on those dimly looming shores of Paradise.

This strange superstition affords another evidence of the fact, that however ignorant man may be, he still feels within him his immortal spirit yearning after the unknown future. (p. 173)

The passage concerns a misty vision with an indefinite horizon, quickly and boldly suggested by a few strokes—the play of feathers, the bright waves, the dimly looming shores. But the attitude espoused toward this vision is not anything like profound speculation; the description has "peculiar charm" in its rendition of wistful feeling and of the aesthetically permissive eye of faith that could almost believe. The concluding moral statement attempts no more than conventional intelligence; and it unmistakably closes off the reader's horizon to anything but the hero's nostalgic yielding to fancy, which is valued for its own sake as a reflection of human yearning.

The context provided by the whole chapter is an enlargement and variation of this response, as the narrator's attitude, *mutatis mutandis*, has its Typee counterpart. When Tommo attempts to fathom a public ceremony in which the high priest converses with and buffets the chief deity, a ten-inch wooden god, Tommo can only conclude that the Typees "appeared merely to seek a sort of childish amusement," and that "The whole of these proceedings were like those of a parcel of children playing with dolls and baby houses." Of the daily religious rituals surrounding him, he says, "I saw everything, but could comprehend

67

nothing" (pp. 174–77); but the portentous quality of this statement out of context is belied by the general amused, teasing narrative viewpoint of the chapter, which responds to play by making indulgent play of Tommo's puzzlement. Admittedly, the Typeean language barrier makes it unlikely that the hero's suspicion or curiosity will be finally satisfied. But while this consideration realistically "explains" the situation, it does not explain it away; the effect remains, and it is fully exploited by Melville.

I am saying in passing that *Typee*'s mysteries are not to be read as we read those of *Moby-Dick* (although this has been tried). But though *Typee*'s artistry and its picaresque analogue in *Omoo* seem at a considerable distance from Melville's sixth book, or even his third, *Mardi*, in some respects the distance is more apparent than real. It can be spanned by a further examination of the fictional approaches discerned thus far, which result both in an instructive failure, for us as for Melville, and in his greatest art.

III

The public's rebuff of Melville's confiding impulse in the middle period of *Mardi*, *Redburn*, and *White-Jacket* was bitterly felt, even though the last-named book was relatively well received: "What a madness & anguish it is," Melville wrote to Evert Duyckinck, "that an author can never—under no conceivable circumstances—be at all frank with his readers."[10] Melville is not exaggerating. *Mardi* risks everything, and probably because the next book, *Redburn,* risked comparatively little, he unfairly thought it to be beggarly. *Mardi* represents Melville's attempt to be altogether open, to confide in his audience on the basis of a generally shared nostalgia that was one of the increasingly pronounced feelings of the century, keeping pace with the discovery and despoliation of the primitive nature Melville had set forth in the first two works. As a rhetorical act the book also

[10] *The Letters of Herman Melville,* ed. Merrell R. Davis and William H. Gilman (New Haven: Yale University Press, 1960), p. 96.

represents—as the quest-and-pursuit plot signifies—a defiant bad conscience at seeking an unheard-of intimacy beyond the normal bounds. The narrator's composition is treated in the same overwrought terms of being driven and feeling guilt as his quest: "My cheek blanches white while I write, I start at the scratch of my pen, my own brood of eagles devours me, fain would I unsay this audacity, but an iron-mailed hand clenches mine in a vice and prints down every letter in my spite. Fain would I hurl off this Dionysius that rides me. . . ." And the passage immediately following views the search for full sympathy, in the root sense, as ironically ending in isolation: " 'And if doubts distract you, in vain will you seek sympathy from your fellow men. For upon this one theme, not a few of you free-minded mortals . . . are the least frank and friendly' " (pp. 368–69). The protagonist's driving force, like Pierre's later, turns out to be a yearning for human union at an inhuman, "Dionysian" level of intensity and for naked, trustful complicity of doubt, and concurrently a broodingly touchy impatience with what normally passes for social responsibility and closeness. This is the dark truth incorporated most significantly in the allegory of Hautia's association with and covert substitution for the quest-object, Yillah. The protagonist, as hero and as narrative presence, ultimately wants commitment without civility. For *Mardi* lacks primarily the commitment to fictional form that it seems to want to make; it fails in this elementary rhetorical civility necessary for garnering our imaginative commitment.

Melville's is a twofold formal effort that in effect turns out to be contradictory: first, to be much more daringly explicit than before; second, to win the public's confidence in him as a maker of fiction, not simply as a sailor who wrote *Typee* because he talked it. The wistful nostalgia that was diffusely present in the first two books is transformed into obsession, abruptly expanded to heroic dimensions one-third way into the novel. This is not merely a risk such as we have seen; at the crucial juncture Melville seems scarcely concerned with taking the reader with him at all—or rather, he wants to take the reader with *him* and the imperious disembodied dynamics of feeling and idea, since it soon becomes apparent that the quest story itself does not gamble on any conceivable sort of credence. In fact, although the picaresque initial chapters are very well written, the emotional imperative is presented nakedly from the first, only very weakly excused by references to an unsympathetic ship captain and undesirable destination, and in a preliminary realistic embodiment not to be credited: desertion in a whaleboat a thousand miles from land.

The ruling disposition of the novel is first sounded by the brief preface, which does not seek the reader's confidence but instead challenges it with a rhetorical rationale that flirts with arrogance: "Not long ago, having published two narratives of voyages in the Pacific which in many quarters were received with incredulity, the thought occurred to me of indeed writing a romance of Polynesian adventure and publishing it as such to see whether the fiction might not, possibly, be received for a verity. . . ." This is a preface impatient of prefaces as well as bargaining for trust, and so is an appropriate introduction into *Mardi*'s general failure of patience. The book's traveling symposium has only intermittent room for the reader. In making into a systematic story device the dialectical interchanges implicit in *Omoo*'s narrative consciousness, Melville too often substitutes fictively unsupported "frank" declamation for the more intimately enacted connections he had been mastering.

Melville's failure of patience is to be distinguished from the book's formal failure, but the two are mutually exacerbating. In the last chapters of the book his obvious impatience with his medium, his means of intercourse with his audience, shows up in the destruction of limiting bonds imposed by his allegory of successive cultural perspectives: "On we sailed, as when we first embarked; the air was bracing as before. More isles we visited; thrice encountered the avengers, but unharmed . . ." and so on in a reckless predicate litany that parodies action. This is an authorial act of isolation from audience and infidelity to chosen form equivalent to Taji's lonely symbolic suicide despite his earlier declaration that "the only true infidelity is for a live man to vote himself dead" (p. 39).

A qualification must be made promptly. Melville toward the end of the novel invites us strongly to identify ourselves with the badgered author more than with the quest story or its defiant hero, who ceases to be a credible character almost as soon as he is (falsely) named. Again, as in the earlier passage, the driven quality of the writing-voyaging is stressed in extenuation; the suffering of the author as he candidly exposes the "world of mind" claims primacy over the pathos of the story. The address is at first modest: "Oh reader, list! I've chartless voyaged. . . . And though essaying but a sportive sail, I was driven from my course by a blast resistless, and ill-provided, young, and bowed to the brunt of things before my prime, still fly before the gale. . . ." But then as if angry at having been forced toward sentimental special pleading, the narrator veers away from self-depreca-tion into defiance: "yet . . . better to sink in boundless deeps than float on vulgar shoals; and give me, ye gods, an utter wreck, if wreck I do" (pp. 556–57). The ambivalence of this exculpation of creative willfulness—the "blast resistless"— is continued in the engrossing dialogue in which Lombardo (-Melville), the profound author who must hurry forth his admittedly faulty work, consumes his very real defiance of public response in a proud apologia. Through a sympa-thetic character who admires the author, the reader is signaled, and not very covertly, to become part of an audi-ence self-selected from the uncomprehending multitude. Long before Melville named it in *Billy Budd,* one kind of "inside narrative" is exhibited in *Mardi*; part of its appeal is to the reader's inclination to number himself among the cognoscenti Melville is plainly seeking.

So Melville's very infidelity to fictional civility and his nearly naked offering of authorial ethos, especially when seen in the context of his whole career, can be rather engaging, and there is a relish in granting a great writer his *Mardi* and *Pierre*. For all their undeniable great interest, they are painful to read; but we are glad to *have read* them. In the later works, Melville's command of orthodox forms is shown in "Bartleby" and *Israel Potter*. But his infidel impatience with his public and the formal limits it constrained helps to shape the brilliant experimental rhetoric of *Moby-Dick*, "Benito Cereno," and *The Confidence-Man*.

Melville's increasing ambivalence toward his readers and his growing sense of the effect they had on his role as a serious writer become evident beginning with *Mardi*. In *White-Jacket*, the conceit of Lemsford's poems' being blown out of the cannon seems invented solely to express the aggression that *Mardi* to an extent represented:

> [Jack Chase:] "That's the way to publish . . . *hull* the blockheads, whether they will or no. . . ."
> [Lemsford:] "I [recently] published a volume of poems, very aggressive on the world. . . . Heaven knows what it cost me. . . . [A]s for the addle-pated mob and rabble, they thought they had found out a fool. Blast them . . . what they call the public is a monster. . . ."

But in his fair-minded way, Melville makes a distinction in his audience and, more broadly, among mankind, that he tries to make good in the rhetoric of *Moby-Dick*: " 'The public is one thing . . . and the people another. . . . Let us hate the one and cleave to the other' " (p. 192).

Lombardo's announcement in *Mardi* that he has "created the creative" (p. 595) is perhaps easy to pass over as Romantic ecstasy, but it is as good a gloss on Melville's highest aesthetic reach as any single statement is likely to be. *Moby-Dick* is an all-out effort to create a work that in turn vitally shapes those who encounter it. Its design is no less than to fashion, out of the "the public," "the people" to whom an author can cleave.

3

Godly Gamesomeness:
Selftaste in *Moby-Dick*

"The art itself is nature."

The Winter's Tale

THE power of *Moby-Dick*—what D. H. Lawrence praised as
"the sheer naked slidings of the elements"—has long been a
subject of critical attention over and above the usual interpretive interest in such notoriously "difficult" novels.
Though one may assume that the final secret of that power
will always be safe, hermeneutic probings at the mystery
over the last several years have shown clearly that Melville's
masterpiece is not just *about* the world. To an unusual
degree the book is an attempt at sharing in the life of the
world: the fiction exists not so much to mirror life as to be
in itself vitalizing. I believe that one principal source of
this animating energy is the peculiar sense of self dramatized
both thematically and rhetorically—that is, by the issues
on which the novel focuses and by an enactment of those
issues that intimately involves the reader and the narrator
Ishmael in a creative act of "godly gamesomeness."

The phrase originates in Ishmael's own gamesome as-
signment of a family of porpoises—"Huzza" is the name he
invents for the breed—as a subcategory of the whale species.
The name is appropriate, Ishmael says in the audience-
oriented voice typical of his playful rhetoric, because if
the reader can resist three cheers at the sight of the vivacity
of the fish, "the spirit of godly gamesomeness is not in ye"
(p. 126). Gamesomeness can be taken as the generic term
for a significant constellation of ludic motifs in the novel.[1]

[1] By my count, the novel contains twenty-two references to play,
games, etc., including the word "juggle" and its variations—"be-

73

The trait helps to establish the porpoises' kinship with their larger cousins, the Hump-Back whales, who are "the most gamesome and lighthearted of all the whales" (p. 123), and with the entire "sporty, gamy, jesty, joky" (p. 413) cetological catalogue. If the whale is a joker, as Stubb sings out, he is also by grace of Ishmael's whimsy a book in himself (the Hump-Back is book I, folio, chapter IV in Ishmael's bibliographical system; *The Whale* is the subtitle of Ishmael's novel). The Whale is, moreover, the chief masquerader obsessing a captain who rails that the masked gods are "'cricket-players . . . pugilists'" (p. 147), who mutters "'Here some one thrusts these cards into these old hands of mine; swears that I must play them, and no others,'" and of whom Stubb says admiringly, "'And damn me, Ahab, but thou actest right; live in the game, and die in it!'" (p. 413). Ishmael comes to a comparable conclusion when he "takes this whole universe for a vast practical joke" at his own expense and consequently regards the whaling quest and its object with a "free and easy sort of genial, desperado philosophy" (pp. 195–96). This is Ishmael's central and saving mood, the most typical ludic combination of his psychic extremes—on the one hand the black despair of alienation and on the other a genial expansive delight in fellowship with humankind and with the All. Ishmael can "take" the vast practical joke; Ahab refuses to.

All this is godly gamesomeness indeed, and prefigures the jests of the player-deity of *The Confidence-Man*. But the argument runs ahead of itself. First, as Ishmael would say, a few preliminaries are required.

I

The power of *Moby-Dick* is ascribable not alone to its mythopoeic creative force, although that of course is con-

juggled and destroyed," e.g., p. 448. The terms cover a wide range of responses to the world, from "merry's the play" (p. 408) shouted out by the *Bachelor*'s captain to Ahab's cries for "fair play" (pp. 144, 415).

siderable. Congruent with this power is that arising from an unrelenting rhetorical exercise that establishes as an almost tactile presence the tormenting, mild images of personal identity and vitality. This is "the ungraspable phantom of life" itself, and it is, as Ishmael plainly says, "the key to it all" (p. 14). The operative words in the preceding sentences are *almost* and *ungraspable*: the Narcissus image of the self may be apprehended at an overwhelming pitch of concrete force or at a low, nearly imperceptible level; yet in either case it is tormenting in its elusiveness from cognitive processes and mild hint at the formless, unspeakable terror of essential being.

Perhaps the closest one can come to naming the sense of oneself that is meant here is Gerard Manley Hopkins' coinage, "selftaste": "my selfbeing, my consciousness and feeling of myself, that taste of myself, of *I* and *me* above and in all things, which is more distinctive than the taste of alum, more distinctive than the smell of walnutleaf or camphor, and is incommunicable by any means to another man. . . ."[2] Intimately precious and ineffable, beyond the reach of the descriptive words of public reality, the taste of self paradoxically combines the feeling of electric connectedness with everything and yet isolation from all others. Although it cannot be directly communicated, this reflexive sense is capable of stimulation both in oneself and others.

[2] *The Sermons and Devotional Writings of Gerard Manley Hopkins*, ed. Christopher Devlin (London, 1959), p. 123. Cited in J. Hillis Miller, *The Disappearance of God* (New York: Schocken, 1965), p. 271. By adopting Hopkins' term, I do not mean to imply any further similarity on his part with Ishmael or Melville; as Miller notes, "Hopkins does not want to melt into the totality, to expand into vagueness, or to lose the sharp taste of himself in possession of the 'all' " (p. 286).

The propriety of the metaphor for Melville is suggested by his habitual gustatory images; for example: Dr. Long Ghost's singing "in a voice so round and racy, the real juice of sound" (*Omoo*, p. 12); Isabel's desire "to feel myself drank up into the pervading spirit animating all things" (*Pierre*, p. 119); the Confidence-Man's many hints about "that good dish man"; and of course the numerous images of consumption in *Moby-Dick*, like the smacking sharks that are comically sermonized by the cook.

Indeed, for Melville—and here, perhaps, he is most centrally in the Romantic tradition—the savor of one's private being is a primary register of reality, and the heightening of self-taste a necessity for existence.

For Melville the matter is even more urgent than for most writers in the tradition. Selftaste is unformulable not only because it is purely private feeling but because at the deepest, barely imaginable level of being, the self seems to be inherently without form, without properties, purely "white." Floating quietly before man the water-gazer, the self's mild reflection is the image of full life; but it is also, for Narcissistic man, potentially as fatal as the white *Requin* shark with its "ghostliness of repose" and "mild deadliness" (p. 164). The attempt to grasp the self directly means a destructive plunge to the primal fluid level of complete formlessness, where boundaries are confused, and gentleness and ferocity flow inseparably into one another, as they do in the White Whale. As the description of Ahab's "eternal, living principle" indicates, the profoundest self is "form-less . . . being, a ray of living light, to be sure, but . . . a blankness in itself" (p. 175). It is the basis for all the "linked analogies" (p. 264) between nature and man: the amorphous, blank lifestuff within resonates in a sympathy of fascination and horror with the universal whiteness that "by its indefiniteness . . . shadows forth the heartless voids and immensities of the universe" (p. 164). *Shadows forth* these voids, it should be noted, not *is equivalent* to nothing-ness, nonbeing. On the contrary, in regard to both the individual and the visible world, whiteness and indefinite-ness in general are the most important metaphors for the pure life principle, like the tingeless "great principle of light" (p. 170) and the shapeless white squid: "an unearthly, formless, chance-like apparition of life" (p. 237).

Though totally without qualities in itself, this life prin-ciple furnishes the necessary *stoff* for the individuating process of earthly existence. As Ishmael says, "Nothing exists in itself"; distinctive qualities exist merely "by contrast" (p. 55). In order to beget the experiential world, the principle of being combines with the nonbeing, the total void, that it horrifyingly adumbrates, just as in the Bower in the Arsacides the grim old god Death "wived with youthful Life" (p. 375) to beget the diverse colors and shapes of the beautiful scene. The crucial, nearly unthinkable paradox of the metaphysical marriage of opposites is that the union of an amorphous entity and nothingness produces the individual forms of life. Whiteness is what Ishmael would characteristically call the "corresponding contrast" to void, as life is to death (p. 185).

In short, at the profoundest level of his unanimistic being, a man is not indelibly marked by the fixed, unique stamp of individuality. If the world is a ludic construct in which all counters of reality are merely virtual, dialectically contingent, the cultivation of selftaste is not a decadent exercise; it is of literally vital importance because it means taking on properties, defining an indefiniteness, and thus creating one's individual life. Self-being results from an endless cycle of activity pitting one's sense of separateness against its opposite—the obliteration of personal separateness either by a "pantheistic" merging with others or by death, real or metaphorical. Another way of putting this is to say that one's will to distinctive form is, and must be, recurrently hedged about by the antagonistic but tempting absences of form in both life and death—the undifferentiated, pure white lifestuff that all beings share and the dark void of nonbeing. Though perilous, these antithetical conditions are seductive because they are essential to intensifying selftaste. They are "taking terrors." The Ishmael who takes to sea as a substitute for pistol and ball and never quite falls out of love with death is the obverse image of the Ishmael who is fond of pantheistic reveries at sea. Symbolically, whiteness and blackness are equally horrors and equally necessities, and one must, like Ishmael, learn to be "social" with "a horror"—with the "unspeakably unsocial" (pp. 16, 235).

77

Individuality is a willful fiction in perilous balance between cosmic nothingness and undifferentiated plenitude. Repeated confrontation with these opposed principles conjures up "by contrast" a selfhood that consists of a heightened sense of one's differentiation and individuality, sharply defined yet as elusively visceral as a physical taste and accompanied by a wide range of emotions. Ishmael in the wintry darkness sharing bed and covers with Queequeg yields completely to the cozy, delicious feeling of oneself hugged close: "no one can ever feel his own identity aright except his eyes be closed; as if darkness were indeed the proper element of our essences, though light be more congenial to our clayey part" (p. 55). But when Ishmael opens his eyes to emerge from "my own pleasant and self-created darkness into the imposed and coarse outer gloom" and feels a sharp revulsion, we see the master pattern of his experience, a design that is carried out in the masthead and try-works scenes and in the other halcyon or tortured moments when Ishmael awakes from a visionary state with a shock. At one extreme of feeling is the reassuring selftaste of the "one insular Tahiti" deep down within, where he can "disport in mute calm . . . [and] mildness of joy" amid an "appalling ocean" of storms (pp. 236, 326). But the self-image is transmogrified when seen in the perspective of isolated inadequacy that is presented to the castaway Pip: "The intense concentration of self in the middle of such a heartless immensity, my God! who can tell it?" (p. 347). Each captivating mood, each "enchanted" apprehension of self, has its truth (but "who can tell it?"); and each succeeds the other in an endless sequence.

One of the basic structural and rhetorical patternings of *Moby-Dick* is the repetition of these enchantmentlike captivations or commitments and the subsequent releases from them, a cycle that establishes Ishmael's self-being as both character and narrative consciousness. If one looks at the structure of action in the novel from Ishmael's standpoint, the pattern emerges clearly. Insofar as a cycle may be said to begin anywhere, the pattern of Ishmael's experience first entails a psychic state (for example, the famous "November of the soul") plus an external event or phenomenon that corresponds to it. Ishmael becomes—to use two of his favorite words—*entranced* by the *spell* of this state or, equivalently, indulges in a self-forgetting commitment to a vision of life embodied in the mood-phenomenon. In this phase of commitment there is a vibrant feeling of being electrically alive: "you . . . only exist in a delirious throb" (p. 323), as when Ishmael is towed furiously toward the "enchanted calm" (p. 324) of the encircling Grand Armada of whales, or when Ishmael with the rest of the crew raises delirious shouts of vengeance while mesmerized by Ahab's quarter-deck rituals. But as personal autonomy is dissolved into the intensely immediate global experience and Ishmael descends to the level of undifferentiated existence or approaches self-destruction and void, a recoiling movement is initiated. This second phase, whether triggered by a fortuitous shock or a saving epiphany, usually involves a sudden terror or feeling of estrangement from the experience. This is followed by the third phase of reflection and conscious awareness of separate identity, often accompanied by comic dismay or an ironic tone that helps to complete Ishmael's liberation from the bondage of his visionary commitment.

But this phase is no more stable or permanent than any other, for although there may be a relief from threatened loss of separate identity, there is also a residual stark, "drizzly November," a postpartum mood of the soul, after one has ceased to live at the highly charged level of un-self-conscious psychic impulses. Self-aware, but also with a lurking sense of being empty, meaningless, and abandoned, one is again vulnerable to the next "spell" that seems brimming with full life, that seems an absolute condition and not a momentary one; and the cycle is repeated.

For Ishmael, a man's whole life shows this circular pattern: "infancy's unconscious spell, boyhood's thoughtless

79

faith, adolescence' doubt (the common doom), then skepticism, then disbelief, resting at last in manhood's pondering repose of If. But once gone through, we trace the round again; and are infants, boys, and men, and Ifs eternally" (p. 406).[3] *Ifs*—the word communicates the almost unbearably contingent nature of identity throughout the cycle, as one moves away from and then back toward the "unconscious spell" of an illusionistic world.

Time and again Ishmael comes to himself in a dangerous, enchanted circle where he is given the heightened self-savoring that in effect makes him Ishmael. Conceived in the broadest terms, the novel shows Ishmael gradually coming under the influence of Ahab's quest; identifying himself completely with it in the enchantment weaved on the quarterdeck; recoiling in horror from the hypnotic vision of the try-works and, symbolically, from Ahab's spell; and finally circling down to and being "liberated" from the "vital centre" (p. 470) of the destructive vortex that engulfs the *Pequod*. Every destructive vortex in the novel has a vital center. The story may be envisioned as a great spiral of repeating cycles leading to the final paradigmatic image of Ishmael captured and released, along with the coffin that symbolizes the potentially life-giving confrontation with the formless or void. It is of course possible to see Ishmael's sole survival at the end as replete with moral implications, as many commentators have; but, to repeat, the final action is fundamentally a paradigm of the recurrently generated individual existence that is at stake at every turn of the book.

[3] Although Hayford and Parker retain the usual attribution of this passage in their edition, they note the possibility that the speech should be Ahab's (I am indebted to Hershel Parker for having reminded me of this note, p. 494). In that case, the words would be largely ironic in regard to Ahab's determination to break out of this cycle by an epistemologically final act, but they would still reflect the universal pattern Ishmael portrays most vividly.

In the notes to his edition, Charles Feidelson, Jr., also frequently points out the importance of a cyclic pattern (Indianapolis: Bobbs-Merrill, 1964).

Just as knowledge of the living whale can be attained "Only in the heart of quickest perils" (p. 378), Truth itself is inherently perilous; only "salamander giants" can glimpse it and survive. Endless voyaging is necessary not because Final Truth is attainable short of self-destruction—repeatedly the book tells us it is not—but because the quest entails the seductive and dreadful confrontations that engender identity. On the one hand, one must be able to escape the soul's emptiness by enthusiastic commitment to an experience through a warmhearted capacity for wonder and sympathy; on the other, one must be able to disengage oneself from the exclusive demands of the moment's mood and its partial vision of truth. The ideal combination of resources requires the unique double-consciousness, the "equal eye," of a master player. For him the ludic reality is for the time being universal, utterly absorbing, an "undoubted deed," a "living act" expressing his innermost needs; and yet it is an ultimately limited structuring of total reality, with a term, a boundary at which the experience must come to an end, the illusion of completeness abandoned.

So a man's identity is to be conceived as diachronic, a process in time consisting of psychic phases and corresponding partial visions of truth that necessarily contradict earlier and later stages. Even within a brief space of time, as the mercurial Ishmael demonstrates most dramatically (see especially chapters like "The Chapel," fashioned out of Ishmael's quick turns and counterturns from confidence to doubt, somberness to jocularity), a man is a sequence of quick changes that seem, from a synchronous view of selfhood, mere inconsistencies. Later, in *The Confidence-Man*, Melville covertly and overtly makes sport of those who attempt to act as if identity were static in time and who thus balk at a fictional "inconsistent" character that is "to common view incongruous in its parts, as the flying-squirrel, and, *at different periods, as much at variance with itself as the caterpillar is with the butterfly into which it changes.*

81

. . ."[4] In *Moby-Dick*, Ishmael along with the diddling game-player Stubb can admire the unrelenting passional commitment that attempts to extend a moment's visionary rage into a whole life: "live in the game and die in it!" But Ishmael's goal is to live *through* the game by daring and then escaping the deadly tyranny of the moment's view. Like the mate who, amid "gamesome talk" in the unsteady boat, balances his lance like a "juggler" before casting it (pp. 309–10), and like the whale who reveals "his power in his play" and hurls whaleboats in the air "as an Indian juggler tosses his balls" (pp. 316, 317), Ishmael endeavors to play the cycle of his being with balance, vivacity, and suppleness on the very edge of destruction.

If we turn now toward the book's heroic figures—heroic in the sense that they each in some way reach beyond the ordinary human, temporal state—we see that they embody alternative modes of being that are unavailable or unacceptable to Ishmael, however intriguing they may be. To be Ishmael means in part to be intrigued by these particular alternatives but not to choose them.

There is Bulkington, whose self-reliant and nearly uninterrupted commitment to "shoreless, indefinite" landlessness, to the fluid principle itself, entails an inevitable "ocean-perishing" but also an apotheosis beyond the endless circularity of personal existence (pp. 97–98). That is, the apotheosis that Ishmael confers on Bulkington is a tribute to the massive strength of Bulkington's identity achieved by confrontation with the Formless as well as an admiring and tragic acknowledgment that not to recoil finally from this confrontation, not to return to the solid, circumscribed

---

[4] *The Confidence-Man*, ed. Hershel Parker (New York: W. W. Norton, 1971), p. 58; my italics. Hereafter cited in the text.

Cf. Melville's well-known statement to Hawthorne: "This 'all' feeling . . . there is some truth in it. . . . But what plays the mischief with the truth is that men will insist upon the universal application of a temporary feeling or opinion." *Letters*, p. 131.

"land," means ceasing to exist within the cyclic pattern of ordinary life. Bulkington with his coffer-dam chest is, like the whale, a lodestar of Ishmael's search for a profound interior life secure against the threats that it must face: "the rare virtue of a strong individual vitality, and the rare virtue of interior spaciousness. Oh, man! admire and model thyself after the whale!" But at once Ishmael adds to this outburst of desire the punning, skeptical qualification that ironically disengages him, and us, from the enthusiastic vision and so completes one of the many cyclic sketches of his own being: "But how easy and how hopeless to teach these fine things! Of erections, how few are domed like St. Peter's! of creatures, how few vast as the whale!" (p. 261).

There is also, at the opposite extreme, the religious hero praised by Father Mapple as one who "stands forth his own inexorable self" precisely because he has abjured Bulkington's kind of autonomously directed effort in favor of complete commitment to God's will. If Bulkington's heroic identity is created by his purely private commitment to a sea that is "indefinite as God," the religious hero, who has submitted wholly to the ultimate indefinite Other, can perhaps even more strongly taste his vital "inexorable self" with "delight and deliciousness," as Father Mapple says (p. 51). Ishmael's notable failure to comment directly after reporting Father Mapple's sermon and the immediate juxtaposition of the worship scene involving Queequeg's idol indicate the narrator's final skeptical unwillingness to commit himself to Father Mapple's Presbyterian deity or in fact to any such religious self-definition through literal self-denial—"this disobeying ourselves," in the minister's words (p. 45).

To be Ishmael means to be neither the rare Bulkington nor the equally rare religious hero; but to be Ahab means to be a tragic combination of both; utterly dominated by a commitment that is ambiguously located somewhere between Bulkington's purely private drive toward apotheosis and the religious hero's achievement of identity by a willed abnegation of self. Ahab desires to set himself alone against gods and men, divested of all "mortal inter-indebtedness" (p. 392). And at some moments his thinking is a solipsistic parody of Ishmael's pantheistic reveries: "all are Ahab" (p. 359); other men are merely mechanical extensions, "my arms and my legs" (p. 465). Yet Ahab also clearly conceives of himself as "under orders" (p. 459) by a higher will, a "sire" itself ignorant of its own "beginning"; and pledges his worship-by-defiance to this spirit he glimpses in the flames burning in the ship's rigging (p. 417). Ahab is both defined and torn apart by the destructive split between his two visions of himself—as the autonomous hero who shouts, " 'In the midst of the personified impersonal, a personality stands here' " (p. 417); and also as the divinely obsessed self-doubter who wonders, " 'Is Ahab, Ahab? Is it I, God, or who that lifts this arm?' " (p. 445). Whereas Bulkington's end is recorded as an apotheosis leaping up from his sea-death, Ahab's fitting close is rendered in his epitaphic words, " 'let me then tow to pieces' " (p. 468).

Two other characters complete the book's pantheon of heroic being. Ishmael turns away without comment from Father Mapple's description of the religious hero, and the subsequent chapter significantly focuses on the "calm self-collectedness" of Queequeg. The pagan savage, not the God-driven man, elicits the narrator's approving commentary on the serene integrity of one who is "always equal to himself." Perhaps, Ishmael says, "to be true philosophers, we mortals should not be conscious of so living or so striving" (p. 52). Queequeg represents the life of primitive, unreflective self-possession; but again, although Ishmael admires this form of being, it is beyond the grasp of the ordinary man, or ordinary Westerner at least. Queequeg is capable of intense, full commitment, as witness his youthful inauguration of wandering by clinging to a visiting whaling ship despite threats of being hacked to pieces, and his two life-saving exploits involving the greenhorn and Tashtego. The single-minded life-or-death resolve of Queequeg might be seen as roughly paralleling Ishmael's commitment to the sea at the novel's beginning; even though the pagan's mode of engagement is intense, however, it is not tortured by the self-consciousness of a Westerner such as Ishmael, Ahab, or even the brooding Bulkington. Similarly, Queequeg's abandonment of a resolve, as in his sudden, apparently superhuman decision not to die of fever, is made on the same flat, calm plane of self-collectedness—at no time does he threaten, Ishmael-fashion, to "lose" himself or return to himself with horror. Queequeg the exotic pagan hero is also outside the pale of those ordinary souls who are infants, boys, men, and "Ifs" eternally.

Similarly outside the pale and helping to delimit its boundaries is the "fool" Pip, whose "insanity is heaven's sense" (p. 347). The price of Pip's immersion in the depths of the indefinite sea, the locus of this wisdom, is the loss of a sane identity. Neither split asunder like the tragic Ahab nor apotheosized like the willful Bulkington, Pip is left to mourn his former possession of identity—" 'Where's Pip?' " he cries—with plentiful insight to see its inadequacy: " 'Pip, he died a coward!' " (p. 398). Willy-nilly, he has been brought to a condition comparable in one important respect to that of Father Mapple's religious hero: a "heaven's sense" that embodies ontological reality, a lack of definition congruent with the basic nature of things. The equation pointed to by Pip's fate—loss of autonomous self-definition equals heaven's wisdom—is seen benignly in the religious view and agonizingly in Ahab's. Pip is accidentally victimized by, and Ahab tragically acts out, the human original sin: the acute consciousness of a tenuous personal identity surrounded by an infinite, amorphous "heartless immensity."

However, for the vast majority of men, even as they watergaze, the troubled awareness of this disparity only exists at the edges of consciousness, if at all. Men unwittingly seek in the world the image of themselves, and it is this heightened subliminal sense of their own being that Ahab symbolically offers his crew when he holds out to them the promised doubloon. The round coin is not only a talisman of the Whale, it is a talisman of the self, of the self's perfected wholeness, and of the never-ending circle of experience that generates identity. As Ahab knows, like the ocean the silent crowds stare into, and like "the round globe itself," the doubloon "to each and every man in turn but mirrors back his own mysterious self" (p. 359). But Ahab's offer of selfhood to the crew is in the most important sense false because he pledges them to an unremitting "linear" mood, a prolongation of one delirious moment on the quarter-deck of communally shared anger, fear, and hatred (and these directed at the very symbol of the self's elusiveness). There is to be no disengagement from this spell that merges them into one overriding mood, a sinister version of Ishmael's visionary "melting" with his mates as they squeeze case.

The quarter-deck scene follows immediately upon Ishmael's masthead reverie dramatizing nature's inherent potential for swallowing up individual identity; in the ritual event, as elsewhere, Ahab mimics the same natural fact that outrages him. Instead of genuinely offering the crew members a viable selfhood, Ahab attempts to swallow up their separate personalities into his own to the degree that Starbuck eventually fears that "all of us are Ahabs" (p. 422). Even before they plunge into the indefinite sea, they have become an undifferentiated entity—"one man, not thirty. For . . . all varieties were welded into oneness, and were all directed to that fatal goal which Ahab their one lord and keel did point to" (pp. 454–55).

II

My next point has perhaps already been anticipated: that Ishmael in truth offers his readers, insofar as possible within the limits of an aesthetic experience, what Ahab purports to offer to his "audience"—selfhood; that a primary effect of Ishmael's rhetoric is to stimulate what I, following Hopkins, have called selftaste. There is a sense in which this statement about the rhetorical effect of *Moby-Dick* might be thought applicable to every successful book. We may cite Henry James, as Wayne Booth does in *The Rhetoric of Fiction*: "The author makes his readers, just as he makes his characters."[5] However, the preceding discussion has been intended to show that the making of individual identity is of primary thematic importance in *Moby-Dick*. Does a universe whose manifestations of individuality seem to be only pasteboard masks, whose life principle seems as terrifyingly characterless as nonbeing itself, offer any sanction for the human desire for selfhood? Or does this universe indeed "stab us from behind with the thought of annihilation" (p. 169)? To borrow Melville's phrase, what "ontological heroics"[6] are required to achieve genuine individual being in such a cosmos? This is precisely the issue at stake for Ishmael's hero, Ahab; and it is above all crucial for the younger voyager Ishmael who embarked on the *Pequod* as well as the older Ishmael whom we experience as the book's narrative consciousness. When the achievement of every existence hangs precariously in the balance, then necessarily, if the book is to be honest with itself, fictive rhetoric also becomes problematic. Narrative and reader consciousness are jointly put into question, and they must discover some means of reestablishing their right to exist vis-à-vis one another. In *Moby-Dick*, they are open to a skeptical inquisition that entertains the problematics of their relationship, and they are jointly reinvigorated by a tenacious exercise in experiential resilience. Rhetorical effect is knit organically into structure and theme—it is peculiarly true of Ishmael that he "makes his readers as he makes his characters," including himself. What remains to be seen is the way the processes of making fit into each other.

The famous first sentence of the narrative assigns an

---

[5] Chicago: University of Chicago Press, 1961; epigraph to part I.
[6] *Letters*, p. 133.

identity that is less a statement of individuality than it is a relationship initiated between author and reader. The narrator's first creative act begins to establish the dependency of identity and of the creative act upon just such a relationship. No one in the novel *calls* the narrator Ishmael;[7] only the reader is told to do so for patently symbolic reasons, as a convention of storytelling. Nevertheless, the narrator is as firmly impressed on the reader's mind as a real presence as if his name had been Huck Finn or Jake Barnes instead of one with such starkly portentous biblical overtones. The name tendered us is a synonym for alienation and animosity between the name-bearer and all other men. Yet despite these forbidding connotations and the impression that the reader has been ironically fended off by a convention behind which the "real" narrator has retreated, a counter effect is produced by the device of literary allusion, which in itself rests upon an appeal to shared experience, an implicit assumption that writer and audience possess a common knowledge. Thus, even though the narrator's tone may be chilly, the reader is permitted, if not invited, to align himself, however slightly, with the writer and the writer's irony. Other slight tonalities of Ishmael's first words reinforce this latter effect: we are presented a "first" name, not a last, and there is an agreeable bluffness implied in the narrator's willingness to assign himself such an apparently forbidding identity.

The combination of cool distance and sophisticated willingness to allow the reader to approach up to a point is the dominant note of the voice that we begin to learn how to hear in the book's opening sentences. If the narrator is capable of telling us to "never mind how long [ago] precisely" (p. 12) the story is set, we are still reassured by the fact that he applies the same offhand deprecation to himself and to his own adventures (". . . I thought I would sail about a little and see the watery part of the world. It is a

[7] With one minor exception, when he and Queequeg are signing aboard the *Pequod*.

way I have of driving off the spleen, and regulating the circulation"). Having apparently given notice at the outset that a certain unspoken distance between audience and narrator is part of the aesthetic decorum to be observed in this story, Ishmael becomes more expansive and intimate. But the reader is still kept at a little distance from Ishmael's private feelings of grim depression by such devices as the air of ironically calculated exaggeration (Ishmael speaks of "involuntarily pausing before coffin warehouses," "bringing up the rear of every funeral," and wanting to knock people's hats off) and the sophisticated collocation of Ishmael's own commitment to sea as a "substitute for pistol and ball" with Cato's committing suicide "with a philosophical flourish" (p. 12). At the same time that we are being made privy to the dreary November of the narrator's soul and to his suicidal mood, the studiedly unruffled tone as well as the open exhortation urges on us a man-of-the-world response of *nil admirari*: "There is nothing surprising in this. If they but knew it, almost all men in their degree, some time or other, cherish very nearly the same feelings toward the ocean with me."

But now, having identified the personal feeling with mankind's common experience and thus held us off from the *narrator's* deepest privacy, the narrative voice uses this same association as a transition to direct attention away from itself and to begin directly implicating the reader in the dynamics of the mood: "There is now your insular city. . . . Right and left, the streets take you waterward. . . . Look at the crowds of water-gazers there. Circumambulate the city. . . . What do you see? . . . How then is this? . . . But look!" (pp. 12–13). Ishmael is no longer talking merely about his experience, but about the reader's, and that of all men. In the powerful evocation of the enchanting effect of water that follows, this association is emphasized and re-emphasized until all human and natural barriers seem dissolved in what *Pierre* will call the "universal subject world." At the ocean's edge "all unite" (p. 13) in reverie, drawn by the dreamy allurement of water. Ishmael's very assertions of fact are founded on the common sharing of outlook that he is depicting: "Yes, as every one knows, meditation and water are wedded for ever" (p. 13).

The watery world at its most spellbinding is linked to aesthetic experience, and the beholder's share is not neglected: "[The artist] desires to paint you the dreamiest . . . most enchanting bit of romantic landscape." The picture that Ishmael describes underscores the same universal quiescence in communal subjectivity that the water-gazing crowds represent: "here sleeps his meadow, and there sleep his cattle . . . and though this pine-tree shakes down its sighs like leaves upon this shepherd's head, yet all were vain, unless the shepherd's eye were fixed upon the magic stream before him" (p. 13). The rhetorical questions Ishmael has employed since the third paragraph as a means of implicating the reader begin to come one after another, in a long, insistent sequence: "Why is almost every robust healthy boy . . . crazy to go to sea? Why upon your first voyage as a passenger, did you yourself feel such a mystical vibration . . . ? Why did the old Persians hold the sea holy?" (pp. 13–14). The insistent repetitions and rhythms of the prose—note for example the repeated "ol" sound in the third sentence—and the suggestive indefiniteness of the questions all reflect and reinforce Ishmael's depiction of the sea's influence; and so the reader too is drawn increasingly into something very much like the oceanic feeling and self-forgetting meditation of the water-gazers.

It is at this point, immediately after having surrounded the sea and the dreaminess it begets with attractive connotations—aesthetic pleasure, youthfulness, holiness—that Ishmael abruptly sums up the allurement of water and reminds us in the same breath of its horror by alluding to the story of Narcissus and his drowning. Though the reader, caught up in the intensity of the experience, has probably forgotten why he initially began to consider the phenomenon of the sea's allure, he has full warrant now to recall that the sea was first referred to as a desperate surrogate for self-destruction. We are brought up short as we come to the heart of the mystery with the image of Narcissus' doom. The spell is ended that Ishmael has persuaded us to participate in, merging ourselves in the moods that were not so much his as ours in common with all men in oceanic self-for-getfulness.

The moods have traced a curve from a somewhat re-served, deathlike emptiness of the soul to an enchanted "fullness" of communal subjectivism combining both dreaminess and intensity, and from this to a sudden con-frontation with the idea of self-destruction. This curve represents the centripetal movement of Ishmael's rhetoric, dissolving his sophisticated reserve and pulling us toward identification with him and a "pantheistic" consciousness. Now there is a rapid shift in direction as Ishmael once more refers to himself *in propria persona*. The tone becomes whimsical and rambling, a humorous, pleasant blend of old salt and schoolmaster as it ranges easily from the subject of broiling fowl at sea to that of Egyptian writing on broiled ibis. The voice is jauntier and more companionable than the one that we first heard, but still similar in its occasional darkly ironic overtones and willingness to take breathless jumps from 'fore-the-mast to metaphysics. Thus begins the centrifugal movement of the rhetoric, the curving away from the moment when all distances between reader, nar-rator, and dominant mood threatened to disappear. Now we again are aware of the distinction between what one critic has called "the conjured objectivity" and Ishmael's "conjuring subjectivity"[8] as Ishmael's shift in pitch and

[8] Glauco Cambon, "Ishmael and the Problem of Formal Discontinui-ties in *Moby-Dick*," *Modern Language Notes*, 76 (1961), 523. Cf. also Paul Brodtkorb, Jr., *Ishmael's White World: A Phenomenological Read-ing of Moby-Dick* (New Haven: Yale University Press, 1965), p. 148: "*Moby-Dick* tries to persuade us to become [Ishmael's] moods in order to discover their meanings within ourselves; it does so by submerging the initially amusing character Ishmael into the ambiguous voice of the narrator, whose feelings in relation to his strange world provide

focus reestablishes the distances and tactfully reaffirms his separate reality as narrator, and we recoil from our absorbed identification and return to a sharpened sense of ourselves.

In short, the opening of the book is an epitome of the way Ishmael's rhetoric engenders selftaste by manipulating the reader's distance from him and the world of his fiction. In the process of moving into and out of the vortex of the moods and subjects that obsess the narrator we are made to define him and our proper selves as intricately involved but finally distinct entities. We are made to value the absorbed passion that not only admits us but draws us into his obsessions and to relish also the ironic, elusive reserve that releases us from them. And the rhetorical cycle thus described is the formal counterpart of the younger Ishmael's cycle of self-generation.

Within the cycle of generated being, simple "either-or" tends to collapse into simple "both-and." But the significance of the cycle as a whole is that reality is a "neither-both." It is a dimensionless boundary between "subject" and "object" that exists by virtue of being crossed: it is a dynamic hyphenation of these "contrasted" terms that is activated by transactions of identification and distancing, seduction and alienation. Thus, although a simple "Cartesian" subject/object dichotomy is rejected as a general principle, the "Cartesian" view is useful as a corrective part of the whole design of lived experience. When the view is "lived" at the right point in the "plot" of the cycle, it therefore has its genuine functional truth, jarring one away from a "both-and" extreme of "pantheistic" merging. We may call the whole conjoint rhetorical and thematic design one of *identi-fiction*.

Everywhere in the novel the combination of allurement and distancing, attraction and disengagement, is in opera-

---

analogues for ours." I am indebted to the general argument of Brodt-korb's book, although Brodtkorb sees Ishmael's general tone as more consistently dread-ridden and bleakly ironic than I do.

tion. This affective sequence can be seen operating, for example, over the several chapters initiated by the first appearance of Ahab's boat crew. The creatures that modern men "only see in their dreams" (p. 199) are allowed to captivate the narrator's imagination, which indulges its fascination with them, gives them credence and credibility. The impulse is alternated, however, with what might be called Stubb's view, which in itself combines a certain imaginative insight with a commonsensical, comic skepticism. Ishmael's incantatory musings in "The Mat-Maker" introduce the apparitionlike appearance of Fedallah and his crew, but the apparition is followed quickly by a description of Stubb's ambiguous fashion of commanding his crew "in a tone so strangely compounded of fun and fury" that "pulling for dear life" they still pulled "for the joke of the thing" (p. 188). This in turn is succeeded by a centripetal intensification of mood as the whalemen pull toward the "charmed, churned circle of the hunted whale" (p. 193) and are overwhelmed by a sudden storm that obliterates distinctions ("Squall, whale, and harpoon . . . all blended together"). Ishmael's boat is left abandoned, as if "immortal in the jaws of death," alone in "the heart of that almighty forlornness" (pp. 194-95). The centrifugal movement is carried out in the grim laughter of "The Hyena" and its reflections on the universe as a vast practical joke. The pattern begins again immediately in Ishmael's renewed fascination with Ahab's unearthly crew. This is followed in the plot by the enchantmentlike appearance of the Spirit Spout and the spell cast over the entire ship going around the Cape of Good Hope in which the vessel is silent, "as if manned by painted sailors in wax" (p. 202); then by the foreboding interchange with "The Albatross" and another image of solitary, deathly abandonment while "in pursuit of those far mysteries we dream of, or in the tormented chase of that demon phantom that, some time or other, swims before all human hearts . . ." (p. 204). But we move away from this vision too in "The Gam," with its urbane tone and "gamesome stuff" (p. 206), and are off on another swing of the curve.

Other major attributes of Ishmael's style accentuate the alternating centripetal and centrifugal pressures of the book. Some of the most powerful of the former may be subsumed under the heading of the cognitive impulse, the desire to obtain final answers from an alluring world that stimulates interpretation. We see this in Ishmael's discursiveness, in his fact-mongering, and especially in his generalizing senten-tiousness, which tempts the reader to commit himself exclu-sively to a highly quotable passage as a way out of the end-less succession of qualifications and changing perspectives that Ishmael also gives us. This centripetal pull is reinforced by the immediate impression of formlessness given by the book, which, coupled with Ishmael's several teasing hints at his awareness of both formal difficulties and a kind of order —"careful disorderliness" he names it (p. 304)—stimulates the reader's projection and his attempt at closure of the all-but-completed form.[9] The centrifugal force is supplied by Ishmael's tentativeness—"Still, we can hypothesize," he characteristically says, "even if we cannot prove and estab-lish" (p. 313)—by his rambling chattiness; and by his ten-dency to subvert fact by blending it with legend, fancy, and frontiersman's tall talk. By turns intimate, urgent, frank, rhapsodic, but also superior, dry, and crafty, Ishmael's voice establishes our distinctiveness from the inspired poet even as he sweeps us along with him.

Ishmael's creativity is made a function of his relationship with his autonomous but intimately connected opposite, the reader, just as in nature distinctive qualities are created "by contrast." There is a revealing train of associations when Ishmael speaks of Ahab's use of "arts and entrench-ments," the usages of the sea behind which "he sometimes masked himself" in order to gain supremacy over his crew,

[9] Cf. Gombrich, *Art and Illusion*, especially part III, "The Beholder's Share."

and then implicitly links this use of stage tricks to the writer's own practice:

Nor, will the tragic dramatist who would depict mortal indomitableness in its fullest sweep and direst sway, ever forget a hint, incidentally so important in his art, as the one alluded to.

But Ahab, my Captain, still moves before me in all his Nantucket grimness and shagginess; and in this episode touching Emperors and Kings, I must not conceal that I have only to do with a poor old whale-hunter like him; and, therefore, all outward majestical trappings and housings are denied me. Oh, Ahab! what shall be grand in thee, it must needs be plucked at from the skies, and dived for in the deep, and featured in the unbodied air! (pp. 129–30)

Ishmael's problem of aesthetic form, imaged in the words "unbodied air," finds its partial solution in the habitual open speculation that reveals his art as he works out his problems of composition before his readers. This habit, like the language ("I must not conceal"), elicits our confidence as well as our sympathetic participation in helping the apparent fledgling to create. The "unbodied air" is precisely where the creation comes to life, in the joint instrumentality between artist and audience that is summoned up by Ishmael's apparent artlessness. But as should be expected from his interest in Ahab's masking devices, the relationship of creator and perceiver is more than a little disingenuous; despite Ishmael's protestations, we see within a few pages that he takes considerable pains to provide his hero with "majestical trappings and housings" when Ahab appears in the quarter-deck scene.

As recent critics have emphasized, Ishmael repeatedly calls attention to the illusionistic, "staged" nature of his book. In the first chapter, he completes our liberation from the spell of Narcissus by using a Barnum-like playbill to

MELVILLE: IN TRUST NEVERTHELESS

make the entire voyage a matter of literary genre: he imagines that on the "grand programme of providence" there must have appeared a brief interlude ("WHALING VOYAGE BY ONE ISHMAEL"), and wonders why "those stage managers, the Fates, put me down for this shabby part of a whaling voyage, when others were set down for magnificent parts in high tragedies, and short and easy parts in genteel comedies, and jolly parts in farces . . ." (p. 16). Stage directions ("*Enter Ahab: Then, all*"); essayistic character outlines ("Nor will it at all detract from him, dramatically regarded, if . . ."); bibliographical categorization of whales —these devices and many others throughout the book designedly remind us that Ishmael is staging an illusion. Nevertheless the power of the illusion compels us to participate in it, so that after Ishmael has called our attention to the leader's external arts, "in themselves, more or less paltry and base," we are still caught up in Ahab's mastery of the crew and in his grandeur as an artistic creation. Like his hero, Ishmael has an instinct for both spellbinding and spell-breaking—for unmasking as well as for its opposite.

Ishmael must "make" his reader able to see the book's "whiteness" and also to wear "colored and coloring glasses" (p. 170). We must be supple enough to participate in the book's reality by both putting our confidence in it and being able to see it as an illusion. We, too, must be gamesome, and godly as well in that we participate in our creation as readers by going through a cyclic succession of "contradictory" relationships with the book: the unconscious spell, thoughtless faith, doubt, skepticism, disbelief, and pondering repose of If.

As Ishmael periodically "disappears" and the enacting narrative consciousness seems to plunge self-forgetfully into the life of its story and become a nameless omniscience, we are submerged in the spell cast by the conflict of Ahab, the crew, and nature. But inevitably the narrator's voice intrudes to remind us of the artist-audience relationship and the roles we must play in the aesthetic game. The narrator not only addresses us, he often characterizes us in relation to his own roles in a way that contrasts sharply with the mesmeric communal subjectivism of a dramatically shared experience.

He sets himself up as the advocate of whalemen, and we become like the bumpkins the younger Ishmael mocks— mere landsmen who are duped by the world not because of excessive credulity but because of an insufficient imaginative appreciation of its wonders: "I am all anxiety to convince ye, ye landsmen, of the injustice done to us hunters of whales" (p. 98). As elsewhere, Ishmael the old salt is both condescending and anxious to initiate us so that we may begin to lose what he calls our "ignorant incredulity" and cease to be such "provincial[s]" (p. 285) concerning the truth. Ishmael is the artist above all: "I shall ere long paint to you as well as one can without canvas, something like the true form of the whale . . ." (p. 224). But before we can appreciate correct artistry we must first be disembarrassed of false notions and, most importantly, of an apparently formidable provinciality that Ishmael takes exception to in quasi-comic truculence: "Who ain't a slave? Tell me that" (p. 15); "Cannibals? Who is not a cannibal? I tell you . . ." (p. 255); "*The whale no famous author, and whaling no famous chronicler?*" (p. 100). Ishmael must have an audience that will give a particular kind of credence to his marvelous illusions, an audience retrained in the difficult balance of wonder and skepticism.

We must be reeducated because in the book's balancing of heroic and narrative wills, Ahab's view, which has lost what he terms "the low, enjoying power" (p. 147), is tremendously compelling in declamation and ritual act. To counter it we must see the aesthetic value of all the natural and social categories that are empty of meaning to Ahab. "There is an aesthetics in all things," Ishmael says of the whale-line representing the hazardous bonds between all men, and soon to be the death of the hero who spurned

97

mortal ties (p. 238). This aesthetics is the recognition that the gamesome reality is nonetheless undeniably substantial, its concreteness being a result greater than the sum of the parts. For the parts are not arithmetic atoms but are linked in corresponding contrasts, in interindebtedness. Like Ishmael admiring the forms of the deadly, concretely efficient whale-line, one comes to find satisfying the contours of the intricate connections binding all living and nonliving things in life and death, since without these mobile curves of connected opposites there would only be whiteness and the cosmic void. But Ahab, although theoretically aware of "linked analogies," spurns the knowledge. He refuses, precisely, to suffer knowledge anymore at any level at which the concrete impinges on his mind. He shakes it off like an irritable mastiff even as his receptive mind perceives the "wall shoved close." He wishes above all to do, not to suffer; above all to obtain knowledge by incredibly inflicting his will physically on the substantial "mask," instead of having some other agency or purpose afflict him with knowing. Thus sensitive men must suffer knowing from him, as Starbuck suffers "with soul beat down and held to knowledge" (p. 148).

Indebtedness to the carpenter's utterly impersonal artistry, with its symbolic "deaf and dumb, spontaneous literal process," plunges Ahab into solipsistic despair: " 'Oh, how immaterial are all materials! What real things are there, but imponderable thoughts?' " (pp. 432–33). The world is counterfeit for him because in his frame of reference there is nothing of ideational value "on deposit" to support its substance, so that he is maddened when the "pure manipulator" tells him, " '. . . I do not mean anything, sir. I do as I do' " (p. 432). If Ahab's role is to demand that the whale's Sphynx-head "speak . . . and tell us the secret thing that is in thee," Ishmael's is to question the weaver-god to illustrate that no answer is forthcoming except the loom's flow of will and energy: "The weaver-god, he weaves . . ." (p. 374). Ishmael's careful curiosity about the diverse concrete world weighs in the rhetorical scale against Ahab's heroic outrage, which looks past it.

In instructing us the former schoolmaster adopts a great number of pedagogically useful roles: in one chapter alone, "Cetology," he becomes in succession naturalist, herald, biographer, bibliographer, and architect. All his roles are obviously made playfully dependent upon whimsical élan, reflected in remarks like this: "Unconsciously my chirography expands into placard capitals. Give me a condor's quill! . . . Ere entering upon the subject of Fossil Whales, I present my credentials as a geologist, by stating that in my miscellaneous time I have been a stonemason, and also a great digger of ditches, canals and wells, wine-vaults, cellars, and cisterns of all sorts" (p. 379). Such statements express the abiding aesthetic will that picks up and drops whatever is needful for its continued free play, with the combined enthusiastic engagement and oblique smile of the true gamesman.

The result of all these unstable, "contradictory," combinations—tones, visions, illusions, roles, all embedded in a medley of genres each bearing its own traditional performer-audience relationship—is that we are prompted to a very special intuition. It is not simply of this or that implicit relationship. It is not even simply our re-cognizance of the social-relationship dimension of language that J. L. Austin has called its illocutionary component. The rhetorical focus and the ontological theme intimately redouble each other, so that we are offered an intuition of relation itself, in its essence, as *the* phenomenon-among-phenomena of our life-world. And the perfection of this selftaste, this *identi-fiction* of selfhood, is derived from Ishmael's gamesome equivocation. The narrator's playfulness and irony do not merely celebrate his authorial freedom; they coach the reader to secure his own liberty. Attacking our provinciality, they ask us to engage our imaginations in awe; then subverting our trust and willingness to grant belief uncritically, they ask us to "contradict" ourselves by entering into another phase of partial truth. So Ishmael assigns roles that encourage us to abandon our landsmen status and to share more completely in the teacher's pursuit of knowledge: "I would have you, as a sensible physiologist . . . investigate . . . now with the sole view of forming to yourself some unexaggerated, intelligent estimate . . ." (p. 284). We are invited, implicitly and explicitly, to assume a cosmopolitan frankness in response to the narrator's own tonality: "I freely assert, that the cosmopolite philosopher cannot, for his life, point out one single [more] peaceful influence . . . than . . . whaling" (p. 99). Similarly we are urged to be among the finer souls—"take your way, ye nobler, sadder souls" (p. 161)—and to be everywhere on our best individual mettle even as we are reminded of a communal sharing of vision: "But in a matter like this, subtlety appeals to subtlety, and without imagination no man can follow another into these halls. And though, doubtless, some at least of the imaginative impressions about to be presented may have been shared by most men . . ." (p. 167). We cannot simply forget ourselves, nor our responsibility in the aesthetic play: "But look at this matter in other lights: weigh it in all sorts of scales . . ." (p. 99); "But as you come nearer to this . . . it begins to assume different aspects, according to your point of view" (p. 282). The ultimate aim of Ishmael's rhetoric is to return us to ourselves. "I but put that [whale's] brow before you," says Ishmael. "Read it if you can" (p. 293).

Thus it is clearly much more than convention or carelessness that causes Ishmael to put the masthead reverie scene not in terms of his experience directly, but that of a mediating "absent-minded youth" who imperceptibly changes into the reader himself, in his own proper identity:

lulled into such an opium-like listlessness of vacant, unconscious reverie is this absent-minded youth by the blending cadence of waves with thoughts, that at last he loses his identity; takes the mystic ocean at his feet

for the visible image of that deep, blue bottomless
soul, pervading mankind and nature. . . . In this enchanted mood, thy spirit ebbs away to whence it came;
becomes diffused through time and space. . . .

There is no life in thee, now. . . . But while this
sleep, this dream is on ye . . . slip your hold at all; and
your identity comes back in horror. Over Descartian
vortices you hover. . . . Heed it well, ye Pantheists!
(p. 140)

If we heed Ishmael's warnings well, we are prepared to
read the long last enthralling section of the book, in which
we must do without his guiding presence, as our final exercise in self-definition; and to emerge from its illusion as
Ishmael does in the end, in the momentary repose of If.

III

To prepossess entirely and yet leave free and literally self-
possessed—might this not be one adequate definition of
love? And of Melville's art? Shortly after he completed
Moby-Dick, Melville expressed his skepticism of his public's
appreciation in a telling conjunction of ideas: "Appreciation! Recognition! Is love appreciated? Why, ever since
Adam, who has got the meaning of this great allegory—
the world? Then we pygmies must be content to have our
paper allegories but ill comprehended."[10] It is as if Melville,
through the medium of Ishmael, were giving his audience
one last chance to create itself, to discover its role in reading
the book. It is understandable that at times Ishmael's voice
has an edge on it. After *Moby-Dick*, there is no figure comparable to Ishmael in Melville's works to encourage and
cajole the reader directly and to set the example by responding to the world and to the problem of artistic creation as he
would have the reader respond to the act of reading—as
forms of self-definition. *Moby-Dick*'s metaphysics and its

10 *Letters*, pp. 141–42.

meditations on the phantoms that turn out to "be" oneself are inseparable from its rhetorical goal of helping an audience to create itself in a careful love.

That Melville did succeed in part with some members of his contemporary audience is indicated in a review of *Moby-Dick* that responds to something like the double, or cyclic, effect that I have described:

> The author's radiant imagination enthralls us in a delicious bondage, and the tide of his animal spirits sweeps all doubts and misgivings triumphantly before it. . . . He has a clever knack of identifying his own cause with ours. . . . His manner is so winning, and his language so persuasive, that there is no resisting him. . . . We share with him the perils he so graphically pictures, and merge our own identity in his. . . . As the gull (no inapt emblem, the matter-of-fact philosopher will say, of him who allows another man's imagination so to influence his own)—folds up her wings . . . and is wildly rocked through the hills and hollows of the waves—so does the mind of the sympathetic reader yield an unconscious allegiance to the resistless sway of this powerful writer.

The reviewer's gull metaphor piquantly sums up the opposite impulses felt in the book's rhetoric, which the reviewer elsewhere expresses in the language of the "Hyena" chapter: "There are occasions when the reader is disposed to believe that the whole book is one vast practical joke. We are half inclined to believe that the author is humbugging us, and with that suspicion comes its invariable accompaniment, a sense of offended dignity; but the spell of genius is upon us, and we are powerless to resist."[11]

The successor of that radiant, humbugging narrator is Melville's Confidence-Man, who represents a further work-

[11] London *Morning Post*, 14 November 1851, in *Moby-Dick As Doubloon: Essays and Extracts (1851–1970)*, ed. Hershel Parker and Harrison Hayford (New York: W. W. Norton, 1970), pp. 28–31.

ing out of the implications of Ishmael's art in a thoroughgoing game, at once of confidence and of Charity. The
Confidence-Man is the self-maker extraordinary, the player-
deity who masters roles and illusions. He not only recasts
himself in a series of forms, but defines and shapes the
identities of his audience, as the colorless "ray of living
light" does the experiential world; we can now comprehend
more extensively the attribution with which the present
study began: he is a "revolving Drummond light, raying
away from itself all round it—everything is lit by it, everything starts up to it." For the Confidence-Man is also the
poet, the Ishmael of negative capability who, like Melville,
finds himself an outcast. So Melville in the opening pages
of *The Confidence-Man* seems to echo the famous banish-
ment passage of *The Republic*:

> Suppose then there were a man so clever that he
> could take all kinds of shapes and imitate anything
> and everything, and suppose he should come to our city
> with his poems to give a display, what then? We should
> prostrate ourselves before him as one sacred and won-
> derful and delightful, but we should say that we cannot
> admit such a man into our city; the law forbids, and
> there is no place for him. We should anoint his head
> and wreathe about it a chaplet of wool, and let him
> go in peace to another city. . . .[12]

[12] W.H.D. Rouse, trans., *Great Dialogues of Plato* (New York: New
American Library, 1956), pp. 195–96.

4

Passion in Its Profoundest:
Mardi Once More; *Pierre* and "Bartleby";
"Benito Cereno"

*Passion, and passion in its profoundest, is not a thing de-
manding a palatial stage whereon to play its part. Down
among the groundlings, among the beggars and rakers of
garbage, profound passion is enacted. And the circumstances
that provoke it, however trivial or mean, are no measure of
its power.*

Billy Budd

I

BUT what does "will" signify in the phrases used earlier—
"one's will to distinctive form"; and "Individuality is a
willful fiction"? For Melville's view of existence comprehends not only hazardous protean process but, in each individual, a certain constancy of driving force that moves his
cycle of identity and delimits the kinds of change that can
occur. The caterpillar may change into a butterfly; it cannot
turn into an eagle. If all men, as Ishmael would say, share
"in their degree" in the general *Spieltrieb* or godly gamesomeness of individuation, what does this amount to specifically in a given individual case? Why does each cycle
move at all? What is it that abides in the very constancy of
ebb and flow? So far the question of motivation within any
individual's diachronic cycle of identity has only been
touched on by implication, and therefore the full meaning
of the conclusions just reached about *Moby-Dick*'s rhetoric
remains to be elucidated. Further, the question of what
propels the endless round of a man's self-creation requires
direct attention, and a firmer grip on themes previously
discerned, as we come to the remainder of Melville's ca-

reer and to the revolving illumination that *The Confidence-Man* casts on "the mystery of subjectivity"—where the local and general contexts make clear that subjectivity refers to both the experiencing subject and the condition of being subject to something else.

The repeated theme of the debates in *The Confidence-Man* is the inconsistency that the protagonist discerns in the transcendental disciple Egbert and his master Mark Winsome: the simultaneous assertions, first, that a man has an identity upon which he and others can rely; and, second, that he is completely malleable and thus untrustworthy— indeed, irresponsible. Related to this inconsistency is the book's questioning of fundamental human motives, which has so puzzled us that critics have tended either to treat the hero solely as a god (at this level of discourse, any imputation of motive is possible or seems redundant once the supernatural being is named), or to imply what one commentator forthrightly declares: "[the novel] does nothing to make the driving force of the 'original' trickster comprehensible."[1] There is no mistaking that the title character symbolizes the ambiguous supernatural; but the book explicitly identifies the human mystery with the divine, so that however one "understands" one mystery, the appreciation must work for the other. Like Kafka, Melville makes no final distinction between psychology and metaphysics, since, as he notes in *Pierre*, the stream bespeaks its source. To appreciate the paradox that underlies *The Confidence-Man*, we must be the "psychologic theologians" Melville mentions in *Billy Budd*. In all his works, Melville's accent falls on the adjective, not the substantive. Only the human enigma in some measure may be scanned: "There is no mystery out of ourselves" (*White-Jacket*, p. 398) because "Things nearest are furthest off. . . . It is because we ourselves are in ourselves, that we know ourselves not. And it is only of our easy faith, that we are not infidels throughout;

[1] Leon F. Seltzer, "Camus's Absurd and the World of Melville's Confidence-Man," *PMLA*, 82 (1967), 16.

and only of our lack of faith, that we believe what we do"
(*Mardi*, pp. 296–97).

Melville's views are paradoxical, not because he begins
with an exceptionally startling premise, but because in his
habitual manner he pursues and crowds his perceptions
through their every implication until he turns them "inside out"—as *Mardi*'s philosopher Babbalanja is accused of
doing to himself in seeking the elusive "old mystery" of his
deepest motivation. The relevant passages not only have an
intrinsic interest but provide a clarifying connection that
spans Melville's public career. The philosopher had begun
earlier with a dualism that is traditional except for the
telltale "pantheistic" hint: " 'soul and body glued together
. . . seamless as the vestment without joint, . . . twain—
yet indivisible; all things—yet a poor unit at best' " (p.
433). His next steps, moving to the perspective provided by
selftaste, are much more radical: " 'to myself I seem not
myself. All I am sure of, is a sort of prickly sensation all
over me, which they call life. . . . For aught I know, I may
be somebody else. At any rate, I keep an eye on myself, as
I would a stranger. There is something going on in me, that
is independent of me. Many a time, have I willed to do one
thing, and another has been done. . . . I was not consulted
about it; it was done instinctively. . . . I am a blind man
pushed from behind; in vain I turn about to see what propels me. . . . Thus, . . . it is not so much outer temptations
that prevail over us mortals; but inward instincts.' " Prod-
ded by his interlocutor to speak further of " 'him [who
has] . . . palmed himself off on you for you yourself,' "
and to say " 'something direct of the stranger. Who, what,
is he?' " the philosopher replies that he cannot: " 'the
incomprehensible stranger . . . is locked up in me. In a
mask, he dodges me. . . . So present is he always, that I
seem not so much to live of myself, as to be a mere apprehension of the unaccountable being that is in me. Yet all the
time, this being is I, myself' " (pp. 456–57).

The philosopher suggestively sums up a vision coming

more and more to the forefront of artistic consciousness: *Typee's* intercultural highlighting of subintentional reflexes; *Omoo's* picaresque aesthetic and rhetoric; Ahab's tortured sense that he is possessed by an alien presence; and the masked figure of the Confidence-Man, described as "in the extremest sense, a stranger" and as compulsively devoted to certain recurrent topics and images. If, as *Moby-Dick* postulates, individuality is a willful fiction in constant process of creation, the motivating "inward instincts" are so far below but sovereign to conscious will that when we are somehow made aware of them, they seem to constitute an alien being of whom the will itself is an expression. This stranger is not only motivating but generative: through its imperatives, Babbalanja explains, "in one lifetime we live a hundred lives." Melville writes similarly in a later book with an obsessed hero: "So, through long previous generations, whether of births or thoughts, Fate strikes the present man" (*Pierre*, p. 182). Looked at from the universalized perspective of Being, a man's acts of identity are terrifyingly contingent, confronted by the "corresponding contrasts" of indeterminacy and nonbeing. Looked at from the standpoint of individual being, ethos, but having a provenience antecedent to what is normally construed as ethics, the chain of hereditary and personal psychic generation binds the individual irresistibly in each successive act. In *Mardi*, the philosopher replies to the charge that disseminating his view is dangerous since it seems to relieve men from moral accountability, by asserting that the conscious moral sense is only a secondary, bridling influence, and that in any case the innate constitution of the individual's instincts—his "bonds" and "immunities"—cannot be altered by another person for good or ill. All men " 'are governed by their very natures.' " *Pierre's* study of "maternal contagion" will refine this view by stressing the permeability of morals and feeling in the protean world, but will also reassert the presiding instinctual constancy.

The distinction that Melville is making is an important

one, and it has been, in my view, frequently misrepresented or overlooked because Melville loves to advance it para-doxically and in all the forms in which it can be stated. The distinction is between a profound ontological indetermi-nacy linking all living things in "whiteness" (Being), and a characteristic temper within each individual (beings) generating out of the undifferentiated self (by the opposi-tional process previously described in *Moby-Dick*) all the diverse stages of the life cycle. In the present context in *Mardi*, the philosopher answers an accusation of incon-sistency: " 'And for that very reason . . . not inconsistent; for the sum of my inconsistencies makes up my consistency' " (p. 459). As the context makes clear, he is referring to the several voices, the polyphony, compounding his unitary identity. Though contradictory, they are all permutations of the coherent drive that Melville typically designates with the metaphor of the heart. This is the "very nature" of organic instinctive temper that governs, or "Fates," each individual in all his generations and impels him through their cycle. The distinction between, roughly speaking, "soul" and "heart," is of course an improvisation worked out by Melville in the course of imaginatively dealing with human behavior. It perhaps lacks complete philosophical rigor; but it has sufficient coherence for Melville's creative appropriation and for the dialectical shifting of emphasis from one term or perspective to the other that provides the reader imaginative purchase on elusive human identity. Indeed, it may be clarifying to anticipate for a moment by saying that in *The Confidence-Man* Melville demonstrates that the "purest," most inclusive motive drives toward full convertibility of the ontological and ethical perspectives: an interpersonal union corresponding to that which exists at the profoundest universal level.

Mardi's key discussion is unabashedly ethical in describ-ing the individual's complex of instinct: " 'Tell a good man that he is free to commit murder; will he murder? Tell a murderer that at the peril of his soul he indulges in murderous thoughts; will that make him a saint?' " (p. 458). However, Melville should not be made to mean more than the context permits. He is principally interested not in such neat divisions in deed or thoughts but in the way they express or conceal the exact texture and capacity of the motivating temper. In *Pierre*, the protagonist becomes, among other things, a murderer although he is "a good man." Similarly, in a famous passage in *White-Jacket*, the duplicitous master-at-arms Bland is described as an "organic and irreclaimable scoundrel" (p. 188); he is so regardless of what part he acts, just as Claggart later is intrinsically motivated by a "depravity according to nature." Pierre's fascination for Melville is "a dark, mad mystery in some human hearts" that "irresistibly impel[s] him" (pp. 180, 182), although, in seeming contradiction, from the first he has a "sympathetic, spontaneous friendliness," and "possessed a sterling charity" (p. 276).

In *Mardi*, the affective imperative is paramount beginning with Taji's incredible desertion from ship. Indeed, this intensely driven novel shows the opposite of the usual stimulus-response scheme: the quest-object is determined subsequent to the prior emotion; the quest for "Truth" is already cathected, waiting for an object that will give the chartless voyage a shape. In the largest allegorical conception, the imposter-god Taji is the embodiment of Babbalanja's masked incomprehensible stranger, the imperative silently accompanying the more intellectual voyagers on their rounds, his stubborn obsession moving their collective effort, but rejecting all proffered life-styles and intellectual formulations as inadequate to encompass his passion for intimate union. Of the intermediate destinations, Serena provides the nearest defining analogue to this truth of feeling in the recognition of the psychic hierarchy of cause and effect: " 'We love [Christ] from an instinct in us—a fond, filial, reverential feeling. . . . We love him because we do' " (p. 628). But even this vital mode of being, representing authentic union for some men, is compounded of a specific temper—a "heart of mild content"—crucially different from the narrator's reigning motive. His drive is deep but narrow; it lacks the commodiousness to include "mild content," which is for Melville always a suspicious as well as an intriguing virtue. Taji's rejection of Serena climactically emphasizes the importance of the particular instinctual configuration.

In another place in *Mardi*, the philosopher identifies the writer Lombardo's motivation as " 'Primus and forever, a full heart—brimful, bubbling, sparkling, and running over . . .' "; his " 'autocrat within' " is " 'his crowned and sceptered instinct' " (pp. 592, 597). The recurrent conflict in Melville's work is that between the gamesomely full heart and the heartless voids and immensities, both internal and external. Whatever the admonitions of philosophy or individual reason, the necessary connection between overflowing unsatiated desire and the richness of the cosmos can only be made by nonrational intuitive commitment to the data and accessibility of the human and nonhuman world. This, I believe, is what Melville means by the "grand belief" (p. 578) he declares to be widely shared, whatever one's rational skepticism. As a motto for tenacious human interdependency, it finds expression in Bardianna's sardonically generous will. The will in one item implies that *although* Bardianna has a high opinion of a good friend's probity (not *because*), he bequeaths him a benefit to administer for the sole use of a spinster: he bequeaths it "IN TRUST NEVERTHELESS" (p. 583).

Epistemic trust is the crux of *Mardi*'s intellectual discourse, and the gist of the rambling arguments validates the heart's inmost knowledge: " 'if all things are deceptive . . . what is truth?' "; " 'that question is more final than any answer' " (p. 284). Insofar as there is an "answer," it has to do only peripherally with abstract statement; it is only to be found for each man in the commitments and relinquishments to which his deepest motive impels him.

Understanding Melville's related but distinct ethical and

ontological perspectives on identity, we should be able to understand why in successive pages in *Pierre* he can speak of the protagonist's inherent "sterling charity" as one of "those peculiar principles" illustrating the "necessitarian dependence of our lives"; then of a boyhood friend's innate "generous heart"; and still go on to affirm that beneath all the strata of lives within, "appallingly vacant as vast is the soul of a man!" (pp. 276, 285). All the ambiguities pointed to by the book's subtitle are functions of the contradictory manifold of "soul" and "heart," the principles of permeable transformation and stubborn inclination, which in terms of identity is more significant than the usual division Melville criticism makes between "head" and "heart." (Perhaps in this one case commentators are too attentive to the letters to Hawthorne, whose habitual duality this was; I do not mean to say that the head-heart distinction is not prevalent in Melville and useful—I am assuming it myself at present—but only that in regard to identity it is a second-order phenomenon.)

It follows from the preceding paragraphs that Plinlimmon's ethic, based on the chronometrical-horological dichotomy, fails to carry authorial approval because with its icy temper of "non-Benevolence," (p. 290) utterly unaffiliated with the contingent, suffering human action it is distantly conscious of, it can be no more than the "re-statement of a problem" rather than "the solution of the problem itself" (p. 210). It is another question more final than an answer, though it pretends to be an answer. Melville makes clear that after a certain point the protagonist deeply comprehends the abstract truth of Plinlimmon's "re-statement," but what avails in actual life is Pierre's warmly responsive nature in contrast to the philosopher's essential unresponsive separateness: "Now, any thing which is thus a thing by itself never responds to any other thing. If to affirm, be to expand one's isolated self; and if to deny, be to contract one's isolated self; then to respond is a suspension of all isolation" (p. 293). In his instinctive intense response to

Isabel, Pierre comes to see his idyllic relationship with his mother and Lucy as a form of self-isolation not only to be suspended but completely terminated, despite their repeated pleas, as Lucy puts it, for "unbounded confidence and interchangings of all subtlest secrets" (p. 37; for other pleas for confidence, see also pp. 96, 185). Pierre's concluding extreme hatred is shown to be but the obverse of his youthful fervent love. His "sterling charity," as it is acted out in time, is thus defined as the generative capacity for both extremes of generous responsive identification, as in his shuddering, self-repulsive yielding to "incest" with Isabel and his murderous exclamation near the end: "'Oh Glen! oh, Fred! most fraternally do I leap to your rib-crushing hugs! Oh, how I love ye two, that yet can make me lively hate, in a world which elsewise only merits stagnant scorn!'" (p. 357). The initial instinctual motive has remained constant through the transformations that ironically return Pierre to isolation—isolation, finally, in the forms of prison and suicide. Yet the capacity for ardently responsive identification, once we discern its constancy, obviously exists in a different mode in Pierre's loving curses than it does in his youthful bucolic carolings. Pierre's murdering and suicide look like any other such deeds to the outside world, which would not relate them at all to an innocent sterling charity.

Pierre's earlier and later stages of development are analogous to the flight of the Catskill eagle in *Moby-Dick*, which whether in joy or woe dives or soars above the common level. Neither *woe* nor *joy* alone are adequate to name affective experience in its instinctually defining reach and quality, any more than the terms *murder* or *suicide* are adequate descriptions of the full human act, with its sovereign motive that propels a cycle of diverse identifying acts.

This discrepancy between deed and motive, funded act and external motion, implicit in discourse as early as *Mardi* and implicit in action as early as *Typee*, takes a fresh, central urgency in Melville's fiction beginning with *Pierre* and "Bartleby" and continuing through *Billy Budd*. Perhaps this suddenly renewed sense helps to account for Melville's blatant lack of interest in extended narrative events in *Pierre* and concomitantly acute essays on the varieties of motive. *Pierre* is a diagnostic inventory of what the later Melville fiction of the fifties will consolidate into narrative and narrative rhetoric. What increasingly matters for Melville is that the external event is altogether different depending on the motivation that informs it, the capacity and texture of "instinct," the energy and commitment of characteristic generosity or miserliness of spirit. The precise richness of invested being makes mere motion an individual *act*. Melville's despite for men in the mass is largely a reaction against their acquiescence in a life that is near the dead-level of undifferentiation and unconscious mechanical movement; Ishmael said that all men share his feelings "in their degree," but the cycles of most men's lives are flat, ignobly unaspiring. However, the most nobly aspiring are most likely to be tragically self-destructive, breaking out of the round of human life into isolation or suicidal deeds. They lack the wisdom to distrust productively the specific intellectual formulations to which their motives impel them. They are made tormentedly self-destructive instead of germinatively skeptical by the suspicion that their hearts' drive overgoes the human and conceptual environment in which they must act. If private men, they are liable to self-deception or equivocal action, as is Pierre. If leaders, they must deceive other men into a sort of desperate aspiration, as does Ahab, "who knew that to mankind he did long dissemble."

Even rarer than the noble activist, and in *Moby-Dick* directly distinguished from this type, are the men represented by the hero of "Bartleby the Scrivener: A Story of Wall Street." These are the Divine Inert, whose inertia makes them easily mistakable for the simply unaspiring. They are in motive as different from this prevalent sort as the emotions of the Catskill eagle spirit are different from shallower sensations also termed *woe* and *joy*, or the remote coolness of a Plinlimmon. The Divine Inert are noble in their awareness of the duplicitous arts by which "practical, available supremacy over other men" is achieved and in their committed refusal to conceal, rationalize, or palliate the instinctive, mysterious preferences that others fortify with ringed "entrenchments" (*Moby-Dick,* p. 129).[2] The result of their awareness and accompanying refusal of the "walls" Bartleby stares at is that they "prefer not" to will or, indeed, to act except inertially.

Bartleby's formula expresses a negative capacity analogous to, but crucially distinct from, the negative capability Ishmael tries to maintain in the universe of endless motion. In some moods, Ishmael declares himself infinitely weary of endless movement. The inert man refuses to consent to the repetitious motion itself, which the short story comically parodies in the solar determinism of Turkey's and Nipper's cyclic moods. He does so, not by a tangent of exclusive commitment in the manner of the active hero, but by remaining in every way as nearly like an inertial point as possible: " 'at present I would prefer not to make any change at all.' "[3] The irony of the charge of *vagrancy* brought against the stationary, monotonic scrivener clinches the story's point with chilling and poignant neatness: the language of men has no name for Bartleby's challenge to the life of automatic, misunderstood motion and artful relationship that copies the "original" universal process. They can only reflexively name their own vagrant lives in radically misnaming Bartleby's action. For his is an action: a "pure action" of unalloyed preference, finally eschewing deed and motion altogether, and carefully distinguished in the story from a conscious will and even physical appetite,

---

2 The root of "inert" is *in ars,* without art. In the original context in *Moby-Dick,* the idea is implicitly contrasted to the (previously noted) "art" of the "tragic dramatist" as well as the social "arts" of the leader; and, more subtly, to Ishmael's rather equivocal phrase, "I must not conceal. . . ."

3 *Piazza Tales,* ed. Egbert S. Oliver (New York: Hendricks House, Farrar Straus, 1948), p. 50. Hereafter cited in the text.

which are also abandoned: " 'You *will* not?' " presses the narrator; " 'I *prefer* not' " is Bartleby's self-consistent reply (p. 30).

Bartleby, as every reader has said, is mysterious; but the nature of his mystery is amply defined in Melville's work, and it is of the first importance. His story figures Melville's understanding of motive in the most succinctly direct and controlled fictional statement up to this point. Yet the very nakedness of Bartleby's simple declaration, "I prefer not," has set readers to positing intellectual reasons roughly equivalent to the lawyer's attempt at rationalizing his own discovery of human suffering by accounting for Bartleby's action with the Dead Letter Office rumor. The attempt is to comprehend Bartleby's unusual preference as the result of some cause (intellectual, experiential, etc.). Rather, it is the root "cause" in itself, unfolding in action, in time, to its logical conclusion: to conjointly refuse artfulness and motion in an artful, mobile world means death. As to the level at which his refusal is made, it must be noted that the *present* form of the instinctive inertial preference is stressed in the story; "at present" is the scrivener's repeated introductory qualification. At first, Bartleby "seemed to gorge himself on documents" yet "he wrote on silently, palely, mechanically." Then in a "singularly mild, firm voice" he begins to make his series of overt refusals (p. 24). From the outset, the quality of motionlessness is attributed to him; it is a quality inhering in his person, as the "motionless young man" (p. 23), not in his physical behavior. His exceptional initial industriousness yet openly mild detachment are as much indicative of deep, artless need as is the sudden, composed negation that indicates unbroken continuity of motive without, in his words, "any change."

Both the initial and final manifestations indicate a fundamental instinctual withdrawal of consent from the contrivances of will, whatever the visible motions of the mechanical body may be. This is the "negative" instance of the powerful act of Queequeg, which delivers him from death by reconnecting deep instinct and conscious will to determine his bodily condition in a fashion miraculous to occidental men. (The culmination of this self-mastering integration will occur in *Billy Budd*.) For "Bartleby was one of those beings of whom nothing is ascertainable, except from the original sources . . ." (p. 16). He has the same indifferent promptitude that Melville noted in primitive men in close touch with their inmost natures: he declares several times that he is "not particular" about forms of overt activity even as the logic of his innate preference rapidly acts itself out in increasingly artless behavior. The unfolding momentum of the story partakes of the mildly imperative inevitability of one of Bartleby's replies: "as if to settle that little item at once" (p. 49).

The narrator's incomprehension that one instinctual motive can give rise to overt deeds that seem as altogether different as hyperindustrious copying and refusal to copy is indicated in an ironic echo of *Pierre*: "no man, that ever I heard of, ever committed a diabolical murder for sweet charity's sake" (p. 43). As long as Bartleby's mode of inertia, his exceptional industry, outwardly mimics the motions of others, he is safe from physical harm. When his manner of being inert becomes the cessation of overt activity, Bartleby becomes a threatening reproach to a society of walls, barriers that facilitate a limited ("monetary") human interchange and massively frustrate any unmediated, artless expression of motive. In a phrase: in this fictional world, the best of men, the lawyer, confuses Charity with prudence. As a simple, pure act in itself, Charity is as incomprehensible as Bartleby's artless "I prefer not."

Melville in *Pierre* tried to be directly (and scornfully) profound; "Bartleby" is more profound as achieved fiction by employing a limited consciousness as narrator. The attempt to be totally unguarded and frank showed Melville conclusively that all statements, no matter how explicit and conscientiously complete, are but statements so-to-speak in falling short of the truth about any realm of experience.

They are all, intentionally or not, statements within quotation marks—within walls. Melville had always known as much theoretically and had practiced, in his earliest works, rhetorical techniques for inviting attention to narrative consciousness and the spirited skepticism it enacted, as well as for limiting investigation with picturesque *sprezzatura*. *Moby-Dick* is an eccentric masterpiece created with this knowledge interlaced in theme and rhetoric. But Melville did not fully appreciate his knowledge until, flush from the whale hunt, he had gone after kraken, in the words of his well-known letter to Hawthorne. *Pierre*, with its writer-hero's imprecations, bears in it the disdainful foreknowledge that the public will reject it. Just as thoroughly, in its bizarre "philosophical" jargonizing of language, the book shows a revulsion at its own philosophizing bent while attacking philosophical systems.

With *Pierre*, Melville clearly discloses and fiercely attempts to consume the chain of disillusionments: first, loss of naive confidence in human trustworthiness, and, following hard upon this, loss of confidence in God and loss of confidence in the *public-ation* of the writer. For Melville, the three reference points of trust are finally inseparable, bound up together in his sense of his own identity as a professional author.

The writing of the sprawling *Pierre* and the concise "Bartleby" in rapid succession, and the entire conviction of his successful first venture in short fiction, suggests how thoroughly Melville digested the lesson of writing the long book. *Pierre*'s open contempt for the kind of fiction the public seemed to want, and for the public itself, simply could not be sustained by a writer of Melville's nature. Confidence must be renegotiated, and Melville with scarcely a pause, in poor physical health and distracted mind, proceeded at once to the task in short works that mark a new departure in their maturely paced verve and command of pointed brevity. The task is accomplished largely by Melville's taking on a narrative persona nearer to that of his ordinary reader, *l'homme moyen sensuel,* than any thus far except for that of *Typee.* The persona's whole representation is automatically in quotation marks, and thus Melville can turn his complete attention to a fable that holds both overt statement and implied truth in illuminating contradistinction.

In "Bartleby," then, the motive of artlessness is objectified in a problematic figure; and Bartleby is viewed through narrative eyes whose myopia would only be apparent to discerning readers, while the narrator's pragmatic but sympathetic sensibility might be wholly identified with by the "mass of men." The myopia is discernible partly in the narrator's habit of imputing to himself motives—the "new commandment" of Charity most especially—that he clearly does not have. But a major rhetorical effect resides exactly here. The lawyer's confessed, frankly prudential practice of avoidance provides a lower-case, quasi-comic version of Bartleby's refusals, and the lawyer's repeated offers to help Bartleby and the latter's apparent ingratitude invite an identification on abstract moral grounds (with the lawyer and against the recalcitrant Bartleby) that is directly contradicted by the imaginative pull of sympathy. The result is a rhetorical chiasmus that permits one kind of reader to respond to the story much as one would to *Typee*—as an example of ethically tempered picturesque "charm," quickened by comic caricature and by the sensibility evident in the narrator's closing exclamation: "Ah, Bartleby! Ah humanity!" In this view, the story seems one of those the narrator describes: "divers histories, at which good-natured gentlemen might smile, and sentimental souls might weep" (p. 16). Certainly the narrator's tone often seems to fit the description, as when he depicts the wallscape seen from his chambers:

> This view might have been considered rather tame than otherwise, deficient in what landscape painters call "life." But, if so, the view from the other end of my

118

chambers offered, at least, a contrast, if nothing more. In that direction, my windows commanded an unobstructed view of a lofty brick wall, black by age and everlasting shade; which wall required no spy-glass to bring out its lurking beauties, but, for the benefit of all near-sighted spectators, was pushed up to within ten feet of my window-panes. (p. 17)

But we may wish to examine what underlies this kind of perception when we see that these wallscapes are also the focus for Bartleby's silent observation. Again, *Pierre* writes as essay what "Bartleby" more subtly embodies in fiction.

The essay is a key one for not only *Pierre* and "Bartleby" but the entire course of Melville's later writing, which is intent upon the pollution of being. It concerns the difficulty of Pierre's exercising with genuine spontaneity and precision of feeling the "sterling charity" that identifies him, without "maternal contagion" by the overall environment of optimistic sentimentality symbolized by his mother. Melville likens this atmosphere to the *"povertiresque* in the social landscape," which is the ethically debased counterpart of "the picturesque in the natural landscape." It is the false aestheticism of seeing the world (however unwittingly) as solely an object for morally disengaged gentlemanly appreciation, duly garnished with attenuated, wistful apperceptions of suffering to heighten our complacency: "the time-tangled and want-thinned locks of a beggar, *povertiresquely* diversifying those snug little cabinet-pictures of the world, which, exquisitely varnished and framed, are hung up in the drawing-room minds of humane men of taste, and amiable philosophers of either the 'Compensation,' or 'Optimist' school." And before we think we fully comprehend the lawyer's final exclamation ("Ah, Bartleby! Ah, humanity"), recall that Melville goes on to say of Pierre's mother that, overhearing the seemingly gallant words of her dying tenant farmer, she looked on him "with a kindly and benignantly interested eye to the *povertiresque*;

and murmured, 'Ah! the old English knight is not yet out of his blood. Bravo, old man!' " Following this, in another anticipation of the lawyer's words, Melville parodies the Compensation and Optimist philosophers: "There, beneath the sublime tester of the infinite sky, like emperors and kings, sleep, in grand state, the beggars and paupers of earth!'" (pp. 276–78). This essayistic treatment is far more cogent for the novel's central concerns than is the related melodramatic device of the mysterious picture, the likeness of Pierre's father. Along with "Bartleby," *Pierre* thus winds still more deeply into the bipolar concept of picturesque that Melville began with, as theme and rhetorical technique, in *Typee*.

Melville penetrates the unconscious ingenuity with which we furtively baffle and divert our deepest response, as by the hero-making sensibility determined either to admire suffering or to be oblivious to it. Probing beyond Pierre's mother to Pierre himself, Melville questions the mythopoeic faculty and discloses this form of heroic seeing as at once a form and deflection of love. *Moby-Dick*, we can now see even more clearly, manifested this understanding in a rhetorical shaping of the reader as an ideal partner—a process coordinate with its making of heroic myth.

What *Moby-Dick* embodies and turns to rhetorical advantage, *Pierre* pessimistically analyzes: the hero's would-be Charitable response to Isabel becomes the ennobled version of *povertiresque* in an environment where all the literary and nonliterary forms of feeling have been corrupted for use. "Bartleby" in turn subtilizes the same perception on a more realistic scale of contagion, this time regarding not an enthusiastic aspiring author but—and here the compassionate ironic wit is nothing short of breathtaking—a pragmatic Wall Street lawyer who begins his tale by lamenting "that no materials exist, for a full and satisfactory biography of this man. It is an irreparable loss to literature" (p. 16). The lawyer's Isabel is Bartleby, and the lament is of a piece with the epitaphic comment on Bartleby's death, that he is asleep

"With kings and counselors" (p. 53). The moving quality of the epitaph makes the ironic clarity the sharper: this softening deflection into heroic peacefulness is the topmost reach of what the pragmatic seeker after easy complacency can do for Bartleby. In a sense it acknowledges the scrivener's totally unassuming stature, but above all it climaxes the narrator's willingness to see, to "explain," to palliate Bartleby's suffering as anything but that of (an) unaccommodated man. However well meaning, it is art in response to artlessness. Faced with the unguarded motive of the scrivener, to which only an uncalculating Charity might have responded, the lawyer is either too practical or too sentimental. But perhaps these come to the same thing as ingenious contagions of the exact feeling that Melville imaginatively situates by the narrator's emotional oscillations to either extreme of it. Such ethical and affective precision makes the story a quiet, unqualified triumph of the very fiction making that it and its companion novel tacitly put into question.

Thus the rhetorical chiasmus of competing identifications also fosters a meticulous attention to the distinctions of motive that identify Bartleby as exactly the man, and the representative man, that he is. In terms of narrative technique, perhaps the story's most remarkable feature is that, though out of context the hero Bartleby would strain credulity, the narrative presence itself does not hazard the reader's confidence. As the average man's surrogate, the narrator reposes, as he reiterates, "singular confidence in Bartleby's honesty" (pp. 31, 39), and we repose ours in what he reports (though not necessarily in his assessments). This is so whether or not his limitations are apparent to us even at the beginning of the tale—for he is quite clear about them, they are never in doubt, and it requires no great shrewdness to see them. The narrative consciousness is not paradoxical, not unsettlingly confiding, but remains always at the same distance from us, as a lucid shallow stream. The narrator is troubled about Bartleby, and we are also; but in the important relationship on which the story's communicated form depends, we are confidently composed. Given Melville's previous volatile narrators and controversial stances, this confidence is worth final comment.

The considerable problem Melville faces in "Bartleby" is to present the rarest of natures, motionless and absolutely self-composed amid a frenzy of uncomprehending attempts to cope with it. The raw material of the story—the tersely enigmatic copiest who calmly refuses to participate in the humdrum life of the workaday world—offers a writer a large temptation for a rendering that is hollowly portentous, sophomorically captious, or meagerly allegorical. "The Bell-Tower" is a reminder that in this period of his career Melville can yield to such temptations. But Bartleby with his preternatural confident composure, however rationally baffling, strikes the reader with entire truthfulness of feeling in large part because the story's rhetoric creates a corresponding composed feeling in the reader-narrator relationship. Bartleby's profoundly assured preference has an immediate intuitive accessibility for us because it is delivered through a narrative channel of whose burgher-solid preferences and largely unchanging voice we are assured. This confidence is the pervading tonal base line from which the story's disturbing impact can be measured as we read; and the ultimate disturbance, the ethical frustration, retrospectively does not allow us to feel very superior, if superior at all, to our narrator.

Simply, what would we have done about Bartleby? The story with understated relentlessness isolates the small, unconscious screening contrivances of bad faith by means of which we can fail to deal with each other while seeming to; and by means of which we can seem to feel pathos and yet shield ourselves from its simple agony. We have art, Nietzsche was to say after Melville had demonstrated it, so that we do not die of life. Because Melville suspends judgment concerning which implicit Nietzschean choice a particular man should make, he permits us to see the implacable grounds for any choice. Thus his intricate but almost homely, resolutely unheroic narrative puts us in touch again with the wisdom generating such formulations as Nietzsche's. Here Melville's writing withdraws from the grandeur of such aphorisms and of his own heroic fictions to remind us of the wisdom's daily application. "Bartleby" does not allow us any answers concerning a protagonist who refuses heroism, whose fortitude asks to be incisively recognized without the all-too-human mystification its very simplicity invites. The story does not traffic in consolation. It demands of all but the most self-shielded and complacent an honesty about the adequacy of *our* unmediated responses even as it uncompromisingly shows where utterly unguarded artlessness leads. Perhaps, in view of the criticism (doubtless including my own) that has attached itself to Melville's honest tale, we may add this postscript to Nietzsche: we have criticism so that we do not die of such art as this.

II

Beginning with *Pierre* and "Bartleby," Melville's works become concerted examinations of human love, returning again and again to the purest, most ideally inclusive form Melville calls Charity and to the fates attending its corruption. His authorial voice, paradoxically now that it is no longer seeking bold frankness, seems often no longer under constraint. Its ironies and quiet condemnations are the more impressive, and on occasion more devastating, because they are delivered with the control of that disinterested passion foreshadowed in Ishmael's godly gamesomeness. If there is such a thing in practice as, to use Melville's term, *Charitable* criticism, without personal rancor but with the whole weight of character passionately behind it, Melville's fiction beginning with "Bartleby" often affords splendid evidence of it. It is like what Kenneth Burke has called redemption or transformation of complaint. This communicated temper is what the more abstractive ideational approaches to Melville seem to miss, and sometimes miss badly. One wants to say that it is everything. The process of transformations is carried out across the whole front of experience, from immediate poverty-burdened lives to exotic Encantadas; in repeated dyptich contrasts, and ascents to "Pisgah" heights, movements up close and back far that give a sense of the overall tracery of actions as well as the proximate look of suffering. The works of Melville's second phase form a series extending itself with great patience as if according to some agenda of training in suffering and the ways it is actually borne and seen by ordinary men. The voice is that of a man despising complacency even while attracted to fellowship (as in "The Paradise of Bachelors"), and sympathetically examining agitation by a controlled participation in it (as in "Cock-a-doodle-do"). Far from being mild and mellow, it is skeptical of these states if they are uninformed by disillusioned knowledge. All these concerted attitudes serve as evidence for the honesty of a training in patience that does not sell out to consolation. Thus, in "The Two Temples": "Maternal charity nursed you as a babe. Paternal charity fed you as a child; friendly charity got you your profession. . . . You, and all mortals, live but by sufferance of your charitable kind; charitable by omission, not performance."

The stories experiment with angles of vision on those who are self-reconciled, whatever their attitude toward the external world, and on those who have somehow failed in this assurance of being—who, like Marianna in "The Piazza," have placed their focus of vestigial confidence outside themselves in picturesque wistfulness. "Cock-a-doodle-do" provides a good contrast with "Bartleby" because in this less successful but still very interesting story the equivocal narrative consciousness, intently fixed upon a phenomenal impractical self-assurance, produces an effect of grotesquely painful compassion, a verbal grimace of painful sympathy. This tale notwithstanding, the stories of the fifties substitute patience for abundance, both in theme and narrative art. The patience Melville frequently depicts is matched by

that with which he submits himself to the limited perceptions of his narrators, especially in his two greatest stories
of the period.

In this respect, the storytelling of "Benito Cereno" is remarkable for maintaining a pace that tests the bounds of
delayed narrative closure. The narrative patience of "Benito
Cereno" is a schooling in patience for the reader whereby he
is instructed to see, in the appearances of things, warped,
one-sided versions of whole potentials that with thought-
fully sympathetic application can be intuited in their
fullness. In both "Bartleby" and "Benito Cereno," the
narrators' trivial goodheartedness provides an imaginative
first approximation for a breadth of harmonized insight of
which the narrators themselves are incapable. If they are,
as Pierre said of his boyhood friend, plus heart and minus
head, we must also see that the two are not to be discon-
nected in operation, that the heart is constricted in its
scope of response by the paucity of imaginative intellect,
and this in turn is contaminated by cultural restrictions of
sensitive imagination.

"Benito Cereno" is about "soul beat down and held to
knowledge," in Starbuck's fine phrase. As with Ahab and
Starbuck in the quarter-deck confrontation, the subjection
that enlightens is a direct charismatic infusion of powerful
force, just as it will be in *The Confidence-Man* when the
protagonist momentarily casts aside his ploys and over-
whelms the barber's resistance. In every case, that of Ahab,
the Confidence-Man, and Babo, both the love of ritual and
the charismatic dominance are manifestations of overflowing psychic energy. Indeed, radiating through the modest
viewpoint of Delano and the impersonal legal language of
the trial deposition is Babo's elicitation of confidence for
its own sake, to manifest and covertly to feed his power.
Even after his death, his "unabashed" perspective, his implacable leadership, still dominate. They dominate the culminating paragraphs not only in imagery but in the rhythms
of the prose, which has been transformed from the non-

committal, shifting suppositions of the story's beginning into strong, rhythmically inevitable connectives of grammar and idea that trace the lasting web of his ego's assured power.

The reader must not feel that Babo is simply a cruel and treacherous man or, at the other extreme, a romanticized Slave in Revolt. Domination, or enslavement, as fact, not as obscuring melodrama, is the central event and idea of the story. Slavery, made as visible as an overturned rock in the inverted form of black dominating over white, is manifested as a drama of embodied forces in which none of the characters is a villain. Thus we see how awesomely perverted is the nature of the phenomenon in its dissolving force on personality, as master and slave change places covertly and present a mysterious spectacle of motivation. The image of Benito Cereno leaning helplessly on his slave is a snare for the unwary, but it also becomes a provocation for discovery when Cereno pronounces his last words in the story: "The negro."

Like Babo's concluding gaze, the two words and the ineradicable suffering they indicate throw us back upon the tale to account for an emotional wound in Cereno seemingly in excess of the events we have witnessed, illumined in the deposition's facts. The declaration turns us back, then, specifically to the deposition, which has been offered to us as a "key" by Melville. First, and as a precondition for everything else, the important rhetorical function of the deposition is to present the story's pervasive enslavement as ineluctable fact, existing in Melville's own time and place as a cardinal instance of the "maternal contagion" of human bonds. But this does not mean that the explanation provided by the deposition is ultimately explanatory; it is there aesthetically, to serve aesthetic ends. In the form of a general critical proposition, such a statement is commonplace. In practice, it seems to be overlooked more often than not. Since Newton Arvin long ago objected to the device in stipulating why he thought the story inept, to my mind critics have offered little to counter the objection plausibly or have maintained a silence on the subject that does not do justice to its importance.[4] It is well to recall also Melville's general habit of incorporating more or less modified factual or historical materials. Partly, as here, this is Melville's way of assuring his overly optimistic public that his periodic bulletins concerning the world's evils were not the products of a morbid mind, but were solidly grounded in documented experience.

But if "Benito Cereno" is, as criticism has generally asserted, an important achievement, the deposition material must not be simply an artistically neutral, discursively efficient method of giving background; it must make a signal contribution at this important penultimate point in the story's structure. To restate the matter: coming after the elusive devices of prose style and point of view in the story's opening section, and followed by the calm, firm tonalities of the brief concluding section, the foursquare, formally punctilious language of the deposition is in every important respect Melville's prose and is to be analyzed as such. Like the slowly developing first movement, the deposition risks the reader's patience even as it promises explanation of "what happened." As this form of explanation it is excessive, as "superfluously punctilious" (p. 114) as Cereno's manner seems to be at times, since a brief summary would have done better; as a *discursive* explanation of Cereno's curt "the negro," it is clearly inadequate. The effect of our recurrence to the deposition is not only one of oppression in that the story has seemingly imposed on us falsely; it is as if the reader is impatiently pulling against a language chary of real explanation. The effect, in other words, is that of Delano's puzzled view compounded with Cereno's soul-burdened knowledge. The story thus becomes, even more than Melville's other short fictions that employ the dyptich

[4] *Herman Melville* (New York: William Sloane, 1950), p. 239.

or double-perspective form, a twice-told tale. What Ishmael had done for us in *Moby-Dick*, by asking us to look again at the facts, we now must have wit enough to do for ourselves.

As we re-read the "key," the flat, postulatory language of the deposition in its impersonal efficiency and neatness in detailing phenomena simultaneously fumbles at painful emotional reality and—systematically refusing to impute motives—gives an enormous sense of motivational implaca-bility. The resultant defamiliarization is rather like the reading of an old tragedy in a half-understood ancient tongue, or like the surprised picture-frame view that Hunilla gets of the death of her husband and brother in "The En-cantadas." The delimiting screening, and simultaneous pin-pointing, of view results in a feeling something like this: "this distanced event clearly is objectively *so*, but it is so unexpectedly intimate in its bearing that it seems odd, like one's own features seen fleetingly in the face of a stranger." The use of juxtaposition in long sequences and the mathe-matical causational "precision" of the verb forms and over-determined identifying epithet (always "the negro Babo" and "the generous Captain Delano") produce a fine-tuned tensile irony that seems compassionately clairvoyant. At this point, only quotation, although much too brief to do justice to the accumulating mass, can begin to give an adequate idea of how all this is articulated. Here, at a climactic point, we watch the developing verbal lines of ordinance that sen-tence-by-sentence rigorously create an iconoclastic image of pleas, prayers, commands, and we see their final grim issue in symbol and taunting question:

> [a number of sailors] the negro Babo *ordered to be thrown* alive into the sea, although they made no resistance, *nor begged for anything else but mercy*; that the boatswain, Juan Robles, who knew how to swim, kept the longest above water, *making acts of contrition*, and, in the last words he uttered, *charged this deponent to cause mass to be said* for his soul to our Lady of

Succor; . . . [*sic*] that, during the three days which followed, the deponent, uncertain what fate had befallen
the remains of Don Alexandro, *frequently asked the
negro Babo* where they were, and, if still on board,
whether they were to be preserved for interment ashore,
entreating him to so order it; that the negro Babo an-
swered nothing till the fourth day, when at sunrise, the
deponent coming on deck, the negro Babo showed him
a *skeleton which had been substituted for the ship's
figure-head—the image of Cristobal Colon*, the dis-
coverer of the New World; that the negro Babo *asked
him whose skeleton that was, and whether, from its
whiteness, he should not think it was a white's*. . . . (pp.
128–29; my italics)

Then follows the overbearing irony of Babo's further
orders, which has been prepared for and extended in
comprehensiveness by the preceding, but more surreptitious,
ironies. Everything stresses Babo's imposition of self: the
double-edged wording of the key phrase "follow your
leader" (Babo is, at the very moment he points at the
skeleton, the leader "in spirit," and he warns the sailors
repeatedly lest they "soul and body" go the way of Aranda);
the mock-riddling game of fidelity implicit in the reiterated
questions and the phrase "keep faith," combined with the
game-formula "follow your leader"; the ritual obliteration
of personal distinctiveness in identical gesture ("that each
Spaniard covered his face; that then to each the negro Babo
repeated . . ."), imaged in the uncovered skeleton and recurrent allusions to whiteness; and, more generally and
subtly, the syntactical necessity for reidentifying personal
pronouns ("he, Gandix"), as if all identities had been put
into question by the dominance of "the negro Babo."

Thus it is that Cereno's cryptic "The negro" carries an
extraordinary stylistic as well as thematic weight converging
on this summational pinpoint. The proper name need not
be spoken, and would be in part misleading. Ultimately,

everything in this story is reducible to, or expandable from, these two words, this intaglio of black identity on white. In the intertwining guilt and innocence of white men and black, this psychically inscribed image is the one irreducible fact, for "innocence and guilt, when, through casual association with mental pain, stamping any visible impress, use one seal—a hacked one" (p. 85).

White man leaning with exaggerated dependency on black, and each evoking the other as the centrally obsessive fact of his own life—these are, we can see now, delayed-effect revelations. They point to far more than reductive social stereotypes. Combined, image and vivid pronouncements show us that such universally preemptive possession, such obsessed fidelity to one internalized image—the *negro*, or conversely the *white* Babo bitterly celebrates in his taunting questions upon coming to power—is a perversion of love's freely chosen interdependent fidelity. Slavery, in brief, is unsentimentally identified as an institutional perversion of love—the very love Delano thinks he sees. This corrupted motive acts behind the concealing masks, which also, once they are seen *as* masks, iconically present the force alone for our imaginative inspection. Babo's elaborate costume-drama inversion of the usual roles of master and slave, which acts as a screen for Delano's perception as well as ours, has also shown forth the institutional contagion of human image-making to which Blacks have been subjected, whether benevolently or nonbenevolently. For Melville, this means that slavery contaminates existence itself, at its very base. It methodically corrupts literally self-creative human inter-indebtedness into a parasitic dissolution of individual fiber, or the equally destructive total absorption that is hatred. Tainted love and false or ironic creations go together, beginning with the fundamental shaping of individuality. This ingeniously parasitic corruption of fidelity is not merely notional in the story but is experienced as a covert charisma passing from one side of human interchange to another, as in Babo's final electric gaze that connects with Cereno's grave.

The perspective of Babo's gaze, once we have truly earned it in reexperiencing the deposition, tells us why the unconsciously patronizing benevolence of Delano and Aranda is enraging to Babo. This limited but nevertheless real variety of charitable impulse identifies the self and others with a tincture of benign superiority in the compassion, as is clear from Delano's cultural stereotyping of Spaniards as well as Blacks. To be thus identified with, especially for Babo's ego-expansive personality, constitutes a corrosive intrusion on psychic privacy, a particularly offensive enslavement to the image-making of another. For Delano's and Aranda's "povertiresque" benevolence images Blacks as creatures incapable of violence and guile, too faithful for evil—and thus not fully human.

The enslavement the story is concerned with, then, is the soul's subjection to the shaping projections of others. Babo's revenge concentrates on the iconoclasm of parody; he establishes himself as the stereotypical image of the Black in order to gain control, and strips Aranda's body into a mockery of iconic leadership. In another tenor of emotion, perhaps, but just as deeply, Babo must feel about men like Delano and Aranda as Ahab felt about Moby-Dick: he is a wall shoved close, "he tasks me, he heaps me." Melville's heavily iconographic presentation greatly amplifies the culturally dominant and counteractive processes of imaging: the narrator's stark, ambiguous imagery of greys, blacks, and whites in the opening pages; Delano's culturally determined perceptions of Blacks as benign jungle animals, easily domesticated into "Newfoundland dogs" (p. 100), as well as the whole wayward succession of "images [that] flitted through his mind" (p. 88); and Babo's intricate showmanship, its iconic aim summed up in the incisive barbering metaphor: "the negro seemed a Nubian sculptor finishing off a white statue-head" (p. 104).

All the charades of motion (symbolically elaborated in the movements of the wind, in drifting, hatchet polishing, etc.), all the mere deeds of others, are acts of "the negro" because governed by his motive. Even Cereno's desperate escape is his last semiautonomous act, since after this the Black rules him "in spirit" more effectively than before. The one exception stresses the importance of innate susceptibilities and immunities: Captain Delano, for whom the deposition is sufficient to clear up every obscurity that would concern his native curiosity. The very nature that makes him vulnerable to Babo's confidence game, and particularly to the mimicry of goodhearted fidelity, also establishes the limits of Babo's influence over him. Like the "safe" lawyer in "Bartleby," his prime rhetorical function is to serve as a directive surrogate for one kind of curiosity. (Let me add that it is no mean curiosity either, since the story's impact is in part a function of accomplished suspenseful storytelling, of the elementary arousal and satisfaction concerning what will happen and why it did.)

The one remaining darkness, it can be said without exaggeration, gives the effect of being noumenal: the negro. Everything in style and fictional event points toward this abrupt declaration, everything identifies what elements of behavior constitute it, and everything—the explanatory deposition most obviously—is inadequate to *explain* it, so that it strikes the reader as the psychic thing-in-itself, like Bartleby's "I prefer not." This accumulated result is largely why, apart from the obvious dramatic mummery of Cereno's artificially stiffened scabbard, the religious imagery, and other rhetorically galvanic symbols, the adventure story in itself has strong parabolic overtones. With this vision in mind, and in anticipation of *The Confidence-Man*, it will be useful to take a brief corresponding view of the point the discussion has reached. The question is one of defining versus explaining, and the distinction seems to me so fundamental concerning Melville that I am going to risk diagrammatic prosing.

In Melville's habitual frame of reference of first and last causes, only a complete originative or teleological rationale of the supernatural can explain any individual being's behavior, for it takes place in the universal motivational context. But Melville can define in fictional action the mystery of one individual's motivation, just as classical science can define a body's motion by describing the complex of internal and external forces acting, but without providing a metaphysically adequate explanation why these forces exist at all. For the classical scientist qua scientist, the question of why in this sense is not pertinent; but for Melville as public artist and private man it clearly is. He designates it by the word "mystery." As a writer he is concerned both to define the mystery in the sense discussed above and, in his most ambitious works, above all to communicate its felt reality—in Wallace Stevens' famous words, to give not ideas about the thing but the thing itself. In order to perform this aesthetic substitution for an impossible explanation, Melville deploys the creative phenomena at his disposal—words in all their arrangements of tone, point of view, event, discourse, character, and image—in such a way that they heuristically direct our attention toward the noumenon yet suggest their own intrinsic "inadequacy" and so fall back; the result is that, having done their indicative but self-subordinating rhetorical work, the phenomena transmit a strong sense of the motive-in-itself.

Thoreau's inspired urging has a bearing here: "The volatile truth of our words should continually betray the inadequacy of the residual statement. Their truth is instantly *translated*; its literal monument alone remains." Plainly, my account may be capable of generalization beyond Melville's works; but each writer has his own method of "volatility." Melville's intense, evident desire for adequate explanation, his making the frustration of explanation a primary dramatic issue, and his exhaustive employment of discursive explication give his heuristic artistry an exceptional honest conviction and tensional power, as if the solid element of facticity resisted its own necessary translation. This clear sense of mystery, in Melville's signification of the term, is the very opposite of mystification, or obscurantism. The noumenal effect is heightened in "Benito Cereno," as in *Moby-Dick* and "Bartleby," by being punctuated by silence ("the only Voice of our God," according to *Pierre*): the tongueless whale, the refusal of Bartleby to state in "positive" terms what he desires, the soundless end of Babo. The noumenal is only present in the quickest perils of phenomena; motive is only present in action, to be defined there and nowhere else: "[Babo's] aspect seemed to say, since I cannot do deeds, I will not speak words" (p. 140).

To return now in conclusion to the noumenal motive in "Benito Cereno": in an important sense, it is an act of fidelity. My purpose is not simply to pun but to summarize by recaptiulating how for the confidence-trickster Babo "act" and *act*, iconoclasm and image making, are the same. The psychosocial motive is ego-expansion through a dominating performance of fidelity, whether in masquerades of confidentiality that seduce Delano's belief, or in the tirades ("the negro Babo harangued them") in which the crew is told they must "keep faith with the blacks." If "to affirm is to expand the isolated self," the expansion is the more satisfying for the confidence-man because the tendered currency of affirmation—confidence in all its presented images—is counterfeit, in the one case being an extravagant mimicry and in the other being a direct imposition supported by an icon-centered game of follow your leader that mocks itself and those constrained to play it. Like Bartleby's act of denial, Babo's act, though opposite in valence and method, is "pure." The confidence it purportedly affirms is a null category that, thus, cannot dilute or qualify the self-expansive mummery of ritual motion. Babo's binding ritual becomes a real absurd fiction, directly equivalent to the institution of slavery that it inverts, and so achieves the superpersonal force imaged in the final dominating gaze of one dead man over another. A charismatic "follow your leader" both defines and displaces the institutional form of leadership. The longer one meditates on the story, with its stark revelations of ascendancy beyond personal death, the more the phrase, "the dead hand of institutions," takes on fresh meaning. The effective reality of the essential act is the impress it accomplishes on the Spanish captain, who does indeed keep faith with the negro; and so, finally, do we, with the noumenal imprint of the black's motive on our imaginations, as the hacked imprint of the white obsesses his. Babo and Bartleby, each in his own separate but related wisdom of manipulation and refusal, know that life follows art, as Cereno comes to know and Pierre had discovered earlier:

> ... he had habituated his voice and manner to a certain fictitiousness in one of the closest domestic relations of life; and since man's moral texture is very porous, and things assumed upon the surface, at last strike in— hence this outward habituation to the ... fictitiousness had insensibly disposed his mind to it as it were. ... [T]o Pierre the times of sportfulness were as [if] pregnant with the hours of earnestness; and in sport he learned the terms of woe. (*Pierre*, p. 177)

In a general view, "Benito Cereno" confronts the recurrent Melvillean problem of mysteriously ambivalent behavior—Cereno's seemingly temperamental changes from exaggerated cordiality to haugthy reserve in "day-long enigmas and contradictions" (p. 115)—at the heart of which is a single, implacable agent of motive dominating from first to last. Babo is only one of a number of figures in Melville who exhibit some or all of the characteristics of a confidence trickster. Their diversity of character is such that by itself the descriptive term is only generally indicative. Yet they do tend to fall into roughly cognate types within which there is greater or lesser malignity; for example, Bland, the hermit Oberlus ("The Encantadas"), and Clag-

gart; Dr. Long Ghost and Stubb; Benjamin Franklin
(*Israel Potter*), the Lightning-Rod Man, and Plotinus Plinlimmon; and even Ahab, who is sui generis as a dissembler
and manipulator of confidence. The study of a character
under the rubric of confidence-man, therefore, should take
into account tonal and psychological differences as much
as, or more than, similarities. This is true above all concerning the protagonist of the novel that culminates Melville's public literary life. For *the* Confidence-Man is the
hero as rhetor. He is the fitting hero of an author whose
career is a long persuasive act of increasing hazards that
lost him his contemporary readers and won him the post-
humous audience that the opaque last novel seems almost at
times to address in anticipation.

In the novel's more immediate public reference, another
review of *Moby-Dick* can represent the question that the
last novel pursues, to summarize a career: "In the earlier
portion of his yet brief career, there was much questioning
whether Herman Melville was a man of genius or not.
There was something so new in the author's style, and in
the sentiments it clothed, that sundry decision-loving critics
hesitated not to pronounce him a charlatan, whilst the more
cautious or sager veterans shook their heads with a world of
meaning in the motion, or demurely suspended their opinion. It is ever thus when a man of original genius appears
before the public."[5]

[5] *Bentley's Miscellany*, Jan. 1852, in *Moby-Dick as Doubloon*, p. 80.

5

Hidden Suns and Phenomenal Men:
The Confidence-Man, Billy Budd

"With what heart have you told me this story?"

The Confidence-Man

. . . its own betrayer, its own deliverer, the mirror turn lamp.

Yeats

WE can situate *The Confidence-Man* in Melville's body of work, and particularly with reference to *Moby-Dick*, by recognizing it as a parody of the regeneration of life. Its ironic comedy at once points to and dryly despairs of the radical transfiguration and rebirth of the world by the apocalyptic power of faith. For transfiguration and rebirth the novel substitutes an April Fools' Day masquerade. For the reality of faith it substitutes the word *Fidèle*. For fructifying human interchange it offers a "game of charity" and of confidence (p. 11). The book's hero and its narrative voice ring the changes on the solar and vernal symbols of generative renewal, and clustered motifs like *original, genial, genuine, generous, genius,* and *charity* encapsulate an entire theme in the implied difference between their root senses and their "debased" acquired meanings. Indeed, this verbal mutability is a significant adjunct of the transformational process that mimics the original generative power painfully missing from the world.

Although in this fictive world the complete metamorphosis of spiritual renewal seems to be wholly frustrated, human changefulness is boldly underscored. The primary experience aboard the riverboat seems to be uncertainty of identification. Yet Melville through his hero probes for some indelible identifying stamp, some "maker's mark" that, in however grotesque or perverse a form, can be discerned through the metamorphoses of time and fortune. Amid selves seemingly scribbled like mottoes on the *tabula rasa* of each individual, Melville concentrates on the relationship of apocrypha and apocalypse (in the root, respectively "concealment" and "revelation"), as in the punning interplay of the book's last chapter. In common with the hero, Melville seeks a revelation by means of the more ambiguous kinds of concealed, "uncertifiable" truth. This truth, like that of *Moby-Dick*, is firmly grounded in human experience, human reality; but it has proved more difficult to keep this reality steadily in view in *The Confidence-Man* because of the novel's literary, historical, and especially religious allusiveness.

If the danger for Melville's contemporaries was that they would naively or impatiently disregard the supernatural undercurrent of significance, like the barber near the novel's conclusion who needs to be reminded that " 'You can conclude nothing absolute from the human form . . . ,' " the danger for modern readers is that they will be too quickly impressed by it, as Warner Berthoff has remarked in another connection.[1] As Melville shows (in common with Mark Twain and Nathanael West), the whole psychic life is traditionally trained to flow along religious channels, or more exactly along the affective channels long shaped by religious concerns handed down over generations and inculcated strongly from the outset in the imaginatively impressionable person. It is thus not surprising that, first, strictly secular emotional situations will be figured according to an implicit religious model and, second, these situations, taken at large, will never be finally distinguishable from "religious" concerns for ultimate, universal significance. In this case it is hurtful for the modern reader to drink shallowly from the spring of religious tradition. We are in danger, in other words, of falling into the same habit of convenient customary labeling that the Confidence-Man

[1] The reference is to *Billy Budd*; in Berthoff, pp. 183–88.

plays upon in announcing what he is and what his solicitations are for, which comforts the barber as soon as he can categorize his customer as philanthropist. As was proposed earlier, to take the allegorical means as ends is to resist the book's exhaustive examination of motive. What does motive count for, after all, if we immediately comfort ourselves intellectually that the Confidence-Man "is" Satan masquerading as Christ? To impute a motive then is redundant, unless we are subsequently willing, as few if any readers of Melville are, to ask what we really mean by a satanic motive. The same reasoning holds if we at once decide that the protagonist is Christ being rejected on his Second Coming as on his first, or that he is a grim, tricky God/ Satan; or if we follow H. Bruce Franklin's interesting suggestion that the oriental Vishnu-Siva combination provides the most adequate traditional model to explain the contradictory hero.[2]

After the complex human reality of the book has been absorbed, such readings undeniably have much to recom-

[2] See the discussion of *The Confidence-Man* in Franklin's *The Wake of the Gods: Melville's Mythology* (Stanford: Stanford University Press, 1963) and his introduction to his edition of the novel (Indianapolis: Bobbs-Merrill, 1967). Proposals that the protagonist is either God, Satan, or Christ, in benign or sinister form, have been numerous. For example: Elizabeth S. Foster, in her landmark edition of the book (New York: Hendricks House, 1954), argues for a Satanic interpretation; Lawrance Thompson, *Melville's Quarrel with God* (Princeton: Princeton University Press, 1952), sees a manifestation of God as Practical Joker; and Carolyn Lury Karcher identifies the Christ parallel as most important, in "The Story of Charlement: A Dramatization of Melville's Concepts of Fiction in *The Confidence-Man: His Masquerade,*" *Nineteenth Century Fiction,* 21 (1966), 73–84.

In somewhat closer analogies to my approach, R.W.B. Lewis, "Days of Wrath and Laughter," in *Trials of the Word* (New Haven: Yale University Press, 1965), calls the hero a trickster god, a malign Hermes; and thinks the novel is the ancestor of "comic apocalypse" in American fiction, foreshadowing Twain's *Mysterious Stranger,* West's *The Day of the Locust,* and several important contemporary fictions. Joseph Baim, in a superficial treatment, applies a notion of Trickster, in "The Confidence-Man as 'Trickster,'" *American Transcendental Quarterly,* 1 (1969), 81–83.

mend them, as critical metaphors for Melville's fictional metaphor writ large, since it is apparent that the author defines the human and divine enigmas "circularly" in terms of each other. The metaphysical resonances are partly designed to trouble Melville's contemporaries into sharp cognizance of their ambiguous lives and the full circumference of that ambiguity, but for the casually skeptical modern audience they not only retain little such capacity but can readily offer a reductive critical bolus against the novel's power to disturb its readers into fresh vision. To leap over the human mystery that Melville time and time again brings before us and read the book's abounding plenty of compact life histories as simply recurrent instances of evil tricking good, Devil versus God, seems to me a procedure that is exactly backward—and reminiscent of early *Moby-Dick* criticism. I am of course committed to the Trickster paradigm, but this, too, leads to a sterile shell-game of taxonomy unless we first make human sense out of the hero's behavior in terms of *this* novel's particular fictional vocabulary. Then, since it is a signally religious lexicon, the discussion can profitably return to consider what may be said of the "metaphysical scamps" (p. 118) that constitute the one hero. In sum, I wish to examine the book by using its traditionally religious terms while suspending for a time their extra-human applications beyond what they can illuminate concerning human experience.

I

But considering that goodness is no such rare thing among men—the world familiarly know the noun; a common one in every language. . . .

The Confidence-Man

The Missourian Pitch accuses the protagonist of being wordy. The novel, too, falls under the same accusation. Itself giving the impression of being stuffed with words, the book returns repeatedly to the three-way pull between words, ethics, and self, and convinces us of how much human experience is purely verbal. But, in doing so, the work takes its greatest risks as a responsible act of communication. Human nature, as the catchall term is usually understood, is the supreme fiction and verbal thing involving all the categories of philanthropy and misanthropy; the proper verbal sorting of men is prerequisite for acts of the one kind or the other. Although the "grand points of human nature are the same to-day they were a thousand years ago" (p. 60), it is doubtful whether the human form "may not be a kind of unpledged and indifferent tabernacle" (p. 50). Human natures—these do exist, though in essence, as the Confidence-Man's tactics reveal, they are strange to their possessors as well as to others, so cloaked are they by accustomed deception attempting to reify the fluid, "inconsistent" psyche. Or better, they seem to be the real possessors, the incomprehensible strangers that *Mardi*'s philosopher apprehended as the permanent residents of changing human forms. In the public life of "human nature" that words are formed to acknowledge, the private intersubjective enigma of individual men seems incredible, a "mystery of human subjectivity" (p. 112). Therefore judge and jury cannot place confidence in the unfortunate husband's story of Goneril's contaminating power and the incalculable pressures, sympathies, and revulsions that comprise it. For example, in the discussions of the press, in the Confidence-Man's popularized nostrums, and in the verbal misunderstandings between the hero and his confidants, the book dramatizes a linguistic degeneration to the grossest common denominators of agreed experiences that protectively conceal mutual human strangeness. This verbal cheapening is felt the more keenly as we measure it against the increasingly fine discriminations manifested in the protagonist's ironies and stratagems. The contrast of language, highlighting the difference between public life and private, is one encouragement to our awareness of his identity.

Moby-Dick rhetorically situated us vis-à-vis a natural

world whose unceasing web of relations we see spinning
out before us, which calls us to it in dangerous love. *The
Confidence-Man* rhetorically situates us in regard to a
verbal world, also in systemic motion. But this world,
after the first chapter dramatically presents a pure and
strange principle of complete intimacy, seemingly repels us.
It situates us by putting us out. In the one book, a symbolically alienating mediator, an Ishmael, teaches us to
connect with the world but not dissolve into it. In the
other, the narrative presence steps from the wings on a few
well-spaced occasions to perform the equivalent (so measured and quizzical seem his overtures) of ironically asking
us if we are enjoying, in his words, the "man show." He
says that he offers us both a comedy of words in his few
interjected appearances, and a comedy of action in the body
of the narrative; but in so uneventful a work one might
want to reverse the descriptions, or say that words have
swallowed up everything, like another Ishmaelean white
world. In an important way, this latter supposition is correct, although not in the manner it first seems to be. The
words seem to glide into one another, yet time apparently
has stopped in this otherwise static world. It appears to be
a structuralist's heaven. But in a work that multiplies surfaces and is preoccupied with "seeming," the first step of
wisdom is to distrust these appearances too.

It seems clear that the author, like his hero, seeks to
escape the universal tyranny of words by indulging them in
a certain fashion. After completing *Moby-Dick*, Melville
wrote Hawthorne of the peculiar contentment the book
produced, a sensation of "irresponsibility; but without
licentious inclination. I speak now of my profoundest sense
of being, not of an incidental feeling."[3] Irresponsibility is
the cardinal concept in the Cosmopolitan's discussion of
Shakespeare's "hidden sun": " 'At times seeming irresponsible, he does not always seem reliable' " (p. 149). The
enlightening-mystifying irony of a character such as Auto-

[3] *Letters*, p. 142.

lycus shows Shakespeare to be a Cosmopolitan also, "tied to no narrow tailor or teacher" (p. 115), as irresponsibly freed as the vernacular character Black Guinea, who avowed himself " 'widout massa' " (p. 7), or as nature "unfettered, . . . transformed" by fiction (p. 158). In the second important instance of its use, "irresponsible" is one of the words with which the Cosmopolitan and Mark Winsome puzzle each other as the Confidence-Man presses Winsome to acknowledge a man's responsibility to fellow mortals in need, in contrast to nature's amorality, typified in the irresponsible rattlesnake. Not the least significant instance of Melville's "irresponsibility" is his ironic employment of this pivotal term to stand for these two related, but crucially different, ideas in aesthetics and ethics.

The feeling of being freed of the ethical weight is indeed akin to Melville's aesthetic notion of "nature unfettered, exhilarated, in effect transformed" in fiction. More specifically, the irresponsibility in question in *The Confidence-Man* is that associated with irony. In the mode of irony, so Kierkegaard wrote, one is responsible neither to object nor ego—neither, that is, to the matter to be defined nor to any formulable definition of oneself, much less one's views, the public projection of what one is.[4] In the freedom from responsibility for knowing or being known finally, the writer achieves an exhilarating liberation and the "profoundest sense of being" concurrent with his liberation of nature. He escapes, both as private entity and civil creature, from the

---

[4] *The Concept of Irony, with Constant Reference to Socrates.* My statements reflect primarily Kierkegaard's notorious criticism of Romantic irony. The more positive traits of Socratic irony in Kierkegaard's view—especially the liberation of subjectivity from externally imposed rules, a liberation with ethical potential—are descriptive also of Melville's irony, which is both Romantic and *maieutic* in the Socratic tradition.

For Melville's deeply influential readings in Plato and the Platonist tradition, see Merton M. Sealts, Jr., "Melville's 'Neoplatonical Originals,' " *Modern Language Notes*, 67 (1952), 80–96; and Merrell R. Davis, *Melville's Mardi: A Chartless Voyage* (New Haven: Yale University Press, 1952).

inadequacies of the verbal world, which "familiarly know" goodness and human nature as nouns.

The rhetorical dilemma is clear. The discussion of the biblical Apocrypha in the novel's last chapter is one of a number of promptings Melville gives the reader to face the issue common to works of systematic irony. If the author is free, what of the reader who must put confidence in the author's words? Is he not left with apocrypha, uncertifiable statements, the imposed, undesirable freedom of Kierkegaardian *angst*? To put the matter another way, what Melville hazards in his accurately named "comedy of words" is the value of verbal communication itself. This is because the eccentrically excessive qualifications, the sometimes maddeningly broken prose rhythms, and the serpentine syntax gradually conspire against the reader's confidence in authorial guidance. The impression given is that of caricature: an author with finger placed alongside his nose who might say a great deal if he wished. Instead of the confiding or too-confiding presence of the early books, we have an opposite extreme of reserve that elaborately calls attention to itself, and especially its verbose reticence in ascribing motives to fictional characters. Even if we at length make sense of what is said, the exaggerated impersonation is not calculated to leave the reader at ease.

A traditional function of rhetoric is to divide one's audience into the shrewd and the credulous; at the extreme, into potential "knaves" and potential "fools." In *The Confidence-Man*, in large part through the agency of the hero as rhetor, there is a refinement of this rough division, which corresponds to the procrustean labeling endemic aboard the *Fidèle*. This refinement, determining our view of the implied author and our relationship to him, can be seen in terms of two stages in the reader's perception.

If we are not content with eschatological allegorizing, the first stage of response is likely to be that Melville's irresponsibility seems total. This view is coupled with a similar opinion of the hero. The statement, quoted earlier, that the book "does nothing to make the driving force of the 'original' trickster comprehensible" is one rather hedged expression of the idea. Everything seems to be the subject of satiric attack, it is impossible to tell where the author's allegiances lie, and therefore the book is "nihilistic"; or it is only a verbal construct cleverly mirroring a purely verbal, fictional human world of deception. This is the stage of shrewdness: determined not to be taken in by the novel's suspicious prose and the apparently baseless identity of its role-playing hero, we see through Melville's con game. It's all a sham; modern readers may admire its artistry as artifice, and sympathize with or deplore the nihilism to which Melville has come, leading to the celebrated "long silence." The first stage, of course, may be the last.

A second stage is possible, however, one that is likely to proceed along with an investigation of the paradoxical motive of the persuasive hero. This is because the narrative presence for the most part disappears behind and into the long dialogues of persuasion that form the bulk of the novel. Aside from three short essays addressed to the question not simply of how to react to this book but how to read in general, and the character descriptions that give impersonations of noncommital statement, one is left to decipher the hero's words and actions through the confusing series of encounters and roles. This device of rhetorical withdrawal on the part of the author is called to our attention by a tortuous show of reticence going beyond any requirements of mere irony, and leaves one fully dramatized rhetoric before us: that of the attitude-purveying title character. Rhetoric is the action of the book because it is the hero's action; once we are attentive to this fact, the speculations of the hero's fictive audience can rouse our curiosity about the motives and grounds of persuasion. Why, in short, does a man persuade?

As the hero's persuasive excesses begin to mount, and particularly as his constant hammering on "confidence" is joined to the contradictory social demeanors that the essay chapters prod us to notice, the narrator's impersonations and the hero's begin to disclose a pattern of consistency within the contradiction—and, in fact, a common concern with inconsistency. One may begin in the first stage with the observation that, in contrast to simple inverse irony that clearly means exactly the opposite of what is stated, the book's characterizing irony cuts two ways. The hero's vantage point of perfect confidence allows a caustic view of everything he comes in contact with, and yet it is apparent that it is not itself the real norm but is also undercut. This two-way effect does not result because everything is censured irresponsibly, but rather because the irony is oblique. It smiles at both the presented value and its explicit or implicit opposite because it views a *tertium quid*, a position that resolves or completely does away with the black-white opposition by reconceiving its terms.

As an illustration, it is useful to recall the scene in *A Portrait of the Artist* (chapter 1) in which an older schoolboy asks young Stephen Dedalus if he kisses his mother before retiring to bed. Stephen answers, " 'I do.' " " 'O, I say,' " the boy calls to his schoolmates, " 'here's a fellow says he kisses his mother every night before he goes to bed.' " Stephen, blushing hotly at the boys' laughter, retorts, " 'I do not.' " Gleefully, the older boy calls out, " 'O, I say, here's a fellow says he doesn't kiss his mother before he goes to bed.' " The sensitive Stephen puzzles in agony for some time about which answer should be the right one. He cannot escape conceiving the problem on the terms in which it has been given him. Reconceiving the situation as one of social dominance would allow Stephen a way out of his dilemma of choices, both the objects of satiric attack. It would be idle to see Stephen's tormentor as a "nihilist" about filial love (though he is sufficiently sensitive to it and detached from it that he can wield it as a rhetorical tool): he is interested in discerning something about Stephen's naiveté and using the information for personal advantage with his fellows. We can say something comparable of the Confidence-

Man and his creator. The Confidence-Man habitually catches people in contradictions in which—if the idiom is allowable non-literally at this point in my discussion—they are damned if they do and damned if they don't.

In the tradition of Erasmus, Montaigne, and Swift, oblique irony delights in playing with doctrinal disputes. In *The Confidence-Man*, broadly speaking, the normative *tertium quid* is the generative motive that Melville metaphorically designates the heart. In pervasive image and motif the novel establishes an entire thesaurus of this term, and locates in it a principle transcendent of doctrinal disagreements, both sides of which may be ironically slighted if not openly satirized. The paramount issue is not what is believed but the personal temper that informs and motivates the belief.[5] Here is a radical—foolish—simplicity indeed, but the easy, even obvious, insight seems one most easily forgotten in practice. It is the implicit truth of Melville's accentuated narrative consciousness from the first, and the theme that comes sharply to the fore beginning with *Moby-Dick*. "Ironically," the function of personal temper in *Moby-Dick* has been obscured by an exaggerated critical concern with abstract verities, which has spilled over into the interpretation of all Melville's works. As Melville writes later in the "Jack Gentian" sketches, "in the crooked mouth of the invidious . . . in effect even veracity lies." It would be wrong, of course, to claim that the substance and object of confidence is of little or no importance. Although the paramount issue is the quality, the how and why, of belief, as it is implicitly in good literature gen-

---

[5] Cf. Robert Penn Warren's statement concerning *Clarel*, in "Melville's Poems," *The Southern Review*, 3 (1967), 831: "Ideas are not to be judged abstractly as true or false: in one sense, the personal tone, the quality of commitment a person has to an idea and the depth and richness of his experience of an idea, are related to the 'truth' of an idea. . . . Melville is trying to show ideas not as abstractions but as a function of the life process." I have been arguing, of course, that this view of Melville's far antedates the period of his poetry.

erally and Melville's writings in particular, the singular individual behavior of the novel's characters results from the diverse combinations—some ludicrous, some pathetic, some tragic—of the focus as well as the manner of confidence.

Melville's controlling insight animates the rhetorical device of presenting stories (chiefly those of Goneril, Colonel Moredock, and China Aster) in a style and tone that do not reflect the native outlook of the character who is the ostensible narrator, so that the latter's "moral" is qualified significantly or is negated by the imposed narrative temper. We are invited to dissociate the categories of manner and matter, form and content, that we normally take for granted as being united. This reading experience is elicited not once but three times, carefully pointed out by the narrative "we" or by the characters who are turned into ventriloquists' dummies for the usurping narrative voice—Egbert (already a puppet for Winsome) complains forcefully of the tyranny (p. 177). The oblique norm is also indicated, for example, in the revelation that the Missourian's heartfelt impulses go directly counter to his verbosely announced doctrine of misanthropy; in Colonel Moredock's story, in which the practice of Indian hating is inseparable from Moredock's Charitable nature (I will return to this shortly); in the long confrontation of the "poor, old, broken-down, heart-shrunken dandy" (p. 192) Charlie Noble, with his cosmetic youth, and the Cosmopolitan, both of whom plump for the doctrine of convivial confidence; and in the Confidence-Man's summation of the Winsome-Egbert philosophy, which has been presented at length: " 'Why wrinkle the brow, and waste the oil both of life and the lamp, only to turn out a head kept cool by the under ice of the heart?' " (p. 192). But again it is primarily the rhetor protagonist who enacts the novel's meaning, and his enactment demands our attention.

In his effort to persuade everyone to a uniform temper of confidence, the protagonist is the agent of the transforming power of imaginative fiction. Through his masquerade, as through the power of fiction as Melville describes it, the Confidence-Man transforms the world from what it appears to be into what it is, and so presents "more reality, than real life can show" (p. 158). This momentary artistic act is the highest transfiguration possible in a permanently fallen world, where the New Jerusalem is one of the hero's exploratory swindles.

The Confidence-Man's contradictory behavior with different characters, or in different guises with the same character, provides hints of his more fundamental metamorphoses of identity. In these changes the hero demonstrates the process of human self-creation in a fantastically magnified form. As he makes others become what they are most fundamentally, the Confidence-Man and his "victim" co-agents create each other by a process that might be termed a dialectical revision of Locke's thought. Transforming himself to illuminate the most basic needs and expectations of those he meets, the hero becomes the man-of-confidence when, in his first avatar as the unformed, "white," deaf-mute, he is victimized by a crowd's lack of trust. Initially mute, and in his second identity able to speak only a rough-hewn dialect, he finally becomes the "wordy" man of confidence Black Guinea predicts (p. 10). Initially deaf, he becomes capable of the "mute eloquence of thoroughly digesting attention" (p. 124) as he seeks the motives of those he encounters. At first dressed in shabby white, and "in the extremest sense of the word, a stranger" to the world, he becomes a multihued man of the world as he dialectically absorbs the variety of the "multiform pilgrim species" (p. 6). He "federates, in heart as in costume, something of the various gallantries of men under the various suns" (p. 115). But the absorption *is* dialectical: for all his protean mimetic skill, the Confidence-Man has a tablet not altogether blank. It contains a confederating first principle as constant as the one unchanging word on the deaf-mute's slate.

The arguments in chapter 18, "Inquest into the True

Character of the Herb-Doctor," provide an important clue to the protagonist and the novel. Observing the Confidence-Man in action, two men debate whether he is a credulous fool or a cunning knave. An earlier chapter title had ironically presented the reader a similar ostensible choice: "The Man with the Weed Makes It an Even Question Whether He Be a Great Sage or a Great Simpleton." In the later chapter's inquest, one of the men maintains that " 'He is not wholly at heart a knave, I fancy, among whose dupes is himself. Did you not see our quack friend apply to himself his own quackery? A fanatic quack; essentially a fool, though effectively a knave.' " Subsequently, having seen the herb-doctor donate half of his recent earnings to an apparently needy man (and a rather dubious case for charity), the other disputant asks if the Confidence-Man might not be " 'an original genius' " or in fact " 'knave, fool, and genius altogether?' " (pp. 76, 78).

It is crucial to remember that the whole book argues against either-or intellectual simplifications of fugitive truths, especially concerning "that spirit which is affirmed by its Creator to be fearfully and wonderfully made" (p. 59). The fool-or-knave debate about the Confidence-Man yields the solution: a third term, genius, that includes the first two terms, does not negate them, but transcends their simple oppositional antithesis. The mistake lies in seeing the first two terms, in other words, as mutually exclusive rather than complementary.

For the Confidence-Man, just as he appears to be in his first avatar, is the fool of Charity, willing for its sake to undergo endless trouble with no visible recompense.[6] He

[6] For readings of the novel that come at the centrality of Charity from different suggestive angles, see William Ellery Sedgwick, *Herman Melville: The Tragedy of Mind* (Cambridge: Harvard University Press, 1944), pp. 187–93; and Warner Berthoff, "Herman Melville: *The Confidence-Man*," in *Landmarks of American Writing*, ed. Hennig Cohen (New York: Basic Books, 1969), pp. 121–33. Nathalia Wright briefly discusses the importance of St. Paul to the novel, in *Melville's Use of the Bible* (Durham: Duke University Press, 1949). A good treatment of the idea of verbal degeneration is Cecelia

and the hero of his major parable, Charlemont, are analogous to the man the Cosmopolitan describes: "a man of a disposition ungovernably good-natured . . . [who] still familiarly associate[s] with men, though, at the same time, he believed the greater part of men false-hearted—accounting society so sweet a thing that even the spurious sort was better than none at all" (p. 141). Suddenly, in these words, Melville's entire body of writings presents itself to us, unveiling its core of commitment appropriately through the analysis made by a trickster hero. The Missourian reflects much more wisely than he can know between two of his three encounters with the hero: "Was the man a trickster, it must be more for the love than the lucre. Two or three dirty dollars the motive to so many nice wiles? And yet how full of mean needs his seeming" (p. 113). In oblique reply, the hero puts the moral of his hero Charlemont's tale as an ironic question to the ludicrous small-time con man, Charlie Noble: "lovingly leaning towards [Noble], 'I rest it with your own heart now, whether such a forereaching motive as Charlemont hinted at he acted on in his change—whether such a motive, I say, were a sort of one at all justified by the nature of human society?' " (p. 160).

Charity per se, as an urging of the heart, is to be understood in pre-moral terms, though without its vivification all virtues are but sounding brass. In the New Testament, whose vocabulary Melville stitches through nearly every page of *The Confidence-Man*, Charity is the archprincipal of union and the keystone motive in "the new testament of the spirit" that the Christian apologists advocated over the Old Testament "of the letter." Chiefly in the writings of Paul and John, it is the gift, the charisma, whereby men identify themselves with one another as one body that is in turn identified with

---

Tichi's "Melville's Craft and Theme of Language Debased in *The Confidence-Man*," *ELH*, 39 (1972), 639–58. Appearing after I had written this chapter, Tichi's article can be read as a complement to it because of her emphasis on Melville's "Artistotelian" sense of linguistic and ethical relationships.

the mediator Christ and with the Deity in "the fellowship of the mystery" (Ephesians, 3:9). Charity thus means that one's sympathetic capacity is large and that the need to exist with others, for others, overrides all other considerations, so that the motivating power seeks recompense only in fulfilling itself. Like all genuine ideal virtue, it is its own reward. By himself, the Confidence-Man is only an unused potential; and the plaint of Melville's early heroes, filled with nostalgia by the thousand leagues of blank sea about them, sounds startlingly aboard the Mississippi steamer: "Society his stimulus, loneliness was his lethargy. Loneliness, like the sea-breeze, blowing off from a thousand leagues of blankness, he did not find, as veteran solitaires do, if anything, too bracing. In short, left to himself, with none to charm forth his latent lymphatic, he insensibly resumes his original air, a quiescent one . . ." (p. 37).

Charity is the Confidence-Man's original genius, and he is an original genius in the sense that he embodies the principle purely. As his identification with both heart and sun imagery indicates, his governing drive corresponds to the basic quickening force of life. Thus the narrator's firm insistence on the instinctual nature and on the originating, engendering power of the "original character": "while characters, merely singular, imply but singular forms, so to speak, original ones, truly so, imply original instincts. . . . [S]o that, in certain minds, there follows upon the adequate conception of such a character, an effect, in its way, akin to that which in Genesis attends upon the beginning of things" (p. 205). As with the Deity, this shaping, unifying motive-spring of the profoundest instinctual life, essentially unchanging as the deaf-mute's word "originally traced," provides the all-sufficient axiological foundation. The hero enters the book with the air of one "evenly pursuing his duty" over obstacles; thereafter, in a series of verbal interlacings, words such as *agent, call, part* ("for my part"), and *office* denote the obligatory nature of his pursuits. Even to apply the word *charity* in the usual ethical sense to a deaf-

and-dumb individual imperative that is the prior condition for all choice is in a sense to begin to falsify, because to limit, the originating drive. This is part of the reason that, at the same time the Confidence-Man is described as an original genius in the opening pages, he is also called a mysterious imposter. A genuine Charity endures all things, believes all things like a fool because it cannot help but do so. Whether appearing as the lamblike man or the Cosmopolitan who says that one must "stand ready in a sensible way to play the fool" (p. 116), the Confidence-Man evinces the "fraternal and fusing feeling" that denies his own condition of alienation by asserting that " 'No man is a stranger' " (p. 115). His is therefore the classic motive for rhetoric, the call for re-identification in union. And the appeal is according to the classic Christian shibboleth, the engrained largeness or meanness of spirit in each individual. For, in terms of the plot, the overarching irony is that of *Pierre* once more, but now given in a fiercely comic yet unagitated and comprehensive statement of the absurdly contradictory forms that sterling Charity must take to act in this world.

The three primary figures for the Confidence-Man's creative persuasions, as well as for the traditionally appetitive and confiding nature of the profoundest social union, are light, eating, and music—the imagery of the symposium, the dialogue of love. The Confidence-Man seeks to betray into the light the innermost spring of action, so that each person in response to this "original character . . . [which is] like the Drummond light, . . . starts up" with his own original life. Throughout the novel the hero offers himself in images of consumption (e.g., bread, medicine, tobacco), speaks of tasting men as fine food and vintage wine, and finds one kind of heart "an inviting oyster" (p. 136) to inspect and to sample. From still another view of the secret union that he seeks with apparent openness, the musical-voiced protagonist is the " 'profane fiddler on heart-strings' " that the invalid Titan names him (p. 75).

The Confidence-Man says that he must have mankind

"thick" about him (p. 119), and the two meanings of the pun apply with equal validity to his nature as both fool and knave. In this contradictoriness he is not unique, but magnifies a fundamental property of humanity that Melville is at pains to indicate, as most obviously in this well-known passage: "he, who, in view of its inconsistencies, says of human nature the same that, in view of its contrasts, is said of the divine nature, that it is past finding out, thereby evinces a better appreciation of it than he who, by always representing it in a clear light, leaves it to be inferred that he clearly knows all about it" (p. 59). That the same fundamental motion of the spirit can give rise to behavior commonly seen as morally self-contradictory is precisely the theme of the important chapters on Indian hating that have attracted a great deal of critical attention.

Generosity of spirit is a necessary, but not sufficient, condition for practical moral life; however, under the conditions of the frontier, the powerfully driven, Janus-faced behavior that made Pierre a social pariah makes Colonel Moredock a local hero. The frontier experience, like the Typeean, provides accepted roles enabling the ardent spirit to live out both social love and unsparing cruelty. The frontiersman, as Melville says suggestively, is poised on a moving margin—at once social, natural, and intercultural—like a Polynesian surfing on a wave-crest (p. 126). The Indian-hater is a typically Melvillean tragic figure in that he is at once morally deluded and repugnant, having narrowed his vision of evil to one exclusive manifestation; and humanly sympathetic, since it is the very capacity of his warmhearted sensibility that produces his undying outrage, his implacable, self-sacrificing revenge, as well as his unusually cordial sociability: " ' "It were to err to suppose," the judge would say, "that this gentleman was naturally ferocious, or peculiarly possessed of those qualities, which, unhelped by provocation of events, tend to withdraw man from social life. On the contrary, Moredock was an example of something apparently self-contradicting, certainly curious, but, at the same time, undeniable: namely, that nearly all Indian-haters have at bottom loving hearts; at any rate, hearts, if anything, more generous than the average" ' " (p. 134). Colonel Moredock's life history is a central elucidating parable of motive for the novel. Set over against the labyrinthine concealments of the *Fidèle*'s civilized life, and yet sufficiently related to it to be recognizably pertinent, the tale allows Melville an imaginative return to the approximate state of nature in which the prereflective inner life rules more openly than covertly: "instincts prevail with the backwoodsman over precepts" (p. 125). The integral motivational ground for the Indian-hater's extremes of generous behavior is most dramatically evident when the object of hate suddenly becomes the object of love: " '[in some] instances . . . after some months' lonely scoutings, the Indian-hater is suddenly seized with a sort of calenture; hurries openly toward the first smoke, though he knows it is an Indian's, announces himself as a lost hunter, gives the savage his rifle, throws himself upon his charity, embraces him with much affection, imploring the privilege of living a while in his sweet companionship' " (p. 131).

When the story of Colonel Moredock ends with a repetition of the parallel between this frontiersman and the surly Missourian, the Confidence-Man quickly strikes to the heart of the matter: " 'If the man of hate, how could John Moredock be also the man of love? . . . In short, if ever there was such a man as Moredock, he, in my way of thinking, was either misanthrope or nothing . . . ' " (p. 136). As elsewhere, the Confidence-Man here plays the ingenuous audience of a storyteller, affirming the either-or simplifications that the narrative voice chides for denying the human contradictions presented in profound creations. The truth is shown again in short order when the Cosmopolitan slyly speculates about the man who must associate with others although he considers most men falsehearted, and then predicts the advent into the world of the "genial misanthrope" (p. 200). The protagonist in one sense is describing himself and his own advent. He is most capable of hating men because, even more than the rifle-clicking Pitch and the Indian-hater, he is most capable of loving them. In the carefully misunderstood parable of the Indian-hater and the semi-caricature of Pitch, Melville seems to be playing with, as if having already considered and (perhaps somewhat reluctantly) rejected, the notion that hatred is the only form of emotional contact that can be trusted in this world.[7]

The Confidence-Man is a knave because, differing in degree but not in kind from all men, he undergoes whatever changes, tells whatever story, plays whatever role necessary to achieve the goal dictated by his foolish genius. He is bizarrely successful at assuming other identities by means of his extraordinary Charitable capacity for identification with others. He is effectively made a charlatan because he discovers in his first appearance that the outright, vulnerable fool's profession of love produces the diametrically opposite reaction in others. The obstacle to the frank exchange of heart that Charity entails is schematically presented by the barber's sign set in opposition to the deaf-mute's slate: "NO TRUST" (p. 3). Later, having learned the lesson of furtiveness and the ambiguous forms that the

---

[7] The phrase "genial misanthrope" does triple service typical of the novel's layered prose: besides its applicability to the protagonist, it implies a criticism of his interlocutor, the pinch-hearted, hollowly companionable Charlie Noble, as well as a criticism of the contemporary age whose developing genius seems to forecast the "new kind of monster" who, "in the process of eras," will express spiritual meanness perfectly.

For Melville's own "inconsistent" genial dislike, see his suggestive statement to Hawthorne: "It seems an inconsistency to assert unconditional democracy in all things, and yet confess a dislike to all mankind—in the mass. But not so.—But it's an endless sermon,—no more of it." *Letters*, p. 127. For a useful reminder of how important is the idea of geniality not only in *The Confidence-Man* but Melville's works in general, see Merton M. Sealts, Jr., "Melville's 'Geniality,'" in *Essays in American and English Literature Presented to Bruce R. McElderry, Jr.*, ed. Max Schultz et al. (Columbus: Ohio State University Press, 1967), pp. 3–26.

subterranean vitality can take, the Confidence-Man warns the good-natured merchant against "the emotional unreserve of his natural heart; for that the natural heart, in certain points, was not what it might be, men had been authoritatively admonished" (p. 56). It is worth noting that the hero's frustrated ideal of openness is balked by the same social strictures that the narrator points out in the persistent Melvillean equation of fiction with unreserve: "And as, in real life, the proprieties will not allow people to act out themselves with that unreserve permitted to the stage; so, in books of fiction, [the best readers] look not only for more entertainment, but, at the bottom, even for more reality than real life can show . . ." (p. 158).

Here, then, is the ethical crux that the book's traditional vocabulary, and especially the implicit references to Paul, can help us to see: love is logically prior for an authentic virtuous act since it is the vivifying, all-certifying motive.

Without it, there can be only empty motions, the "game of charity" that the crowd plays with the second avatar, Guinea (as Paul had written, though a man give all he owns to the poor, if he *has* not Charity, the deed counts for nothing). In a complete "horological" reversal of priority, the passengers aboard the *Fidèle* perform on the implicit belief that trust in other men is the necessary prerequisite for love, and even for the lesser social virtues. The original fool becomes the original confidence man because a scarce confidence is the prime negotiable instrument in this world —"this ship of fools" indeed (p. 12), but not Pauline fools in Charity. The cataclysmic change as well as the dialectical continuity between the first identities should, therefore, be clear; the Confidence-Man turns from the embodiment of potentially unmediated spiritual interchange into the embodiment of debased transaction and grotesque social coherence—a Guinea, and a tarnished, false one at that. After the first avatar undergoes a metaphorical death, becoming "like some enchanted man in his grave" (p. 5), there is sufficient liberal vitality to be found aboard the ship that, from the man punningly identified by his weed, to the P.I.O. man who espouses trust in young, growing things, there is a steady progression (of a verbal sort) away from dourness and death and toward the robust vitality of the Cosmopolitan. Yet there is not enough confidence that the protagonist can cease being a con man.

The Confidence-Man's knavery is consequently not so much that he disbelieves what he preaches about confidence as that the strictly objective, descriptive truth of his hortatory statements is a matter of ultimate indifference to him. The quality of his belief in the efficacy of confidence and the benign nature of life might be called the belief of indifference—which is not the same thing as indifferent belief. Melville's psychological truthfulness is brilliant: the Confidence-Man believes in his confidence/no-confidence litmus test in roughly the same way that a scientist ordinarily invests the belief of indifference in a calculus of approximations whose operation will yield a truth that he ultimately is interested in, one that is not a matter of essential indifference. The Confidence-Man is able to invest the calculus of his faith-gospel with sincere conviction because it is a tool, a negotiable currency, for discovering the hearts of those he encounters. (We might even suspect in the Confidence-Man's strategy a *reductio ad absurdum* of the Pauline emphasis: the subsidiary virtues such as belief must have no value solely in and of themselves if, as Paul passionately reasons, they are nothing without Charity.)

The Confidence-Man's is, nevertheless, a real variety of belief, and more common perhaps than is readily admitted. Here, too, the hero is symbolic of both the artist and the artist's audience, in the investment of an instrumental belief for the purpose of truth. Analogously, a competent actor or writer capitalizes on the wide range of affective-intellectual manifolds that lies between extreme, exclusive belief and disbelief. Most of the Confidence-Man's statements, the most outrageous optimist lies, can be seen as a species of heuristic truth once we recognize the hero's motivations and the strategies of his confidence game, which with equal justice can be called utterly naive and utterly cunning. When at one point the Confidence-Man speaks of " '[gambling] games in which every player plays fair, and not a player but shall win' " (p. 46), the only possible corresponding situation is one in which the very act of hazarding something with another person would itself be sufficient reward. The irony describes a game of Charity in a nonironic sense.

II

The Trickster archetype underlying Melville's creation is the master metaphor for the ready convertibility of a coherent, constant psychic energy into forms usually conceived as mutually exclusive. The Trickster tricks because everything—whether law, proposition, or role—is immaterial to him as an end and completely credible to him as a means, in the light of his powerful instinctual life. The point may be further made pertinent to Melville's novel, in view of an exceedingly verbal quality that makes verbality questionable, by adapting as a parable Kenneth Burke's idea of the paradox of substance.

Stated briefly: ordinary, discursive language is designed to deal with differences and to discriminate among them. Since it is by nature abstractive, when it attempts to cope completely with irreducible unitary phenomena it falters, for it must either define a thing in terms of its opposite—by what it is not, as freedom is defined by reference to restraint —or it must shift to the paradoxical metaphors that characterize fictions. Thus phenomenologists, attempting to give an account of the basic self-in-time consciousness of the "now," must use such a phrase as "the primitive othering of the same." The more one attempts to *under-stand* the intrinsic *sub-stance*, the more one is forced contradictorily to refer to the extrinsic phenomenon that *stands under*;

the more thoroughly one formulates the personal, the more it must be seen in terms of the impersonal or the interpersonal (or, Charity).

I believe that Melville, characteristically tenacious concerning the nature of identity as seen in essential manifestations, imaginatively came upon a comparably paradoxical result. That is, the human motive of self-identifying union corresponds to the vital, all-fusing principle, so that the more one is moved by this internal necessity, the more one is aligned with the protean energy of nature. The greater the capacity to identify oneself with other lives (to be consubstantial with them, in Burke's terms) and consequently the more authentically vital one's selfhood, the more it is an "identity-less identity" or a "selfless selfhood" approaching the indeterminacy of the underlying life-principle. This is not the same as saying that the hero is without an identifying constant, although instinctual generosity is entirely immanent, having no existence outside its diachronic, and thus often morally and verbally perverse and countervalent, manifestations. The Confidence-Man stands out clearly defined in his very capacity for becoming, in his own language, *congenial* with others by means of paralogical, "paraverbal" lies and disguises. His original genius is unique in its exceptional power of manipulating the counters of unification. And his knavery, defensively adopted, is effectively the ludic means of resistant nay-saying that acts against the powerful pull of entire identification and dissolution of separateness.[8]

One corollary in this novel is that the narrower a character's dialectical bounds revealed in his emotional contradictions (as distinguished from Winsome's emotionally abstracted, purely intellectual inconsistencies), the more his selfhood is identified with the inorganic and life-frustrating.

[8] Cf. the words of Isabel, another of Melville's extreme strangers, but one who makes little shift to forgo her exile: "I feel that there can be no perfect peace in individualness. Therefore, I hope one day to feel myself drank up into the pervading spirit animating all things. I feel I am an exile here." *Pierre*, p. 119.

This is the really monstrous, because more humanly ordinary, transubstantiation of life represented chiefly by the clay-eating, icicle-hearted Goneril, the hero's alleged wife, whose blighting, alienating secret touch attests to the concealed social motive even in this grotesque of intimacy.

One of the best illustrations of Melville's own knavishly contradictory irony in detailed operation is furnished by the encounter between the gentleman with gold sleeve-buttons and the Confidence-Man in his guise as the grey-coated mendicant for Seminole Widows and Orphans. By means of equivocal imagery and descriptions such as "good man" and "winsome aspect," the chapter foreshadows some of the most important debates to follow; and the ironic imitation of ethical hairsplitting anticipates the Confidence-Man's credo, significantly expounded to Mark Winsome: " 'Let casuists decide the casuistry; . . . compassion the heart decides for itself' " (p. 163). A long mock-casuistical paragraph (including a citation from St. Paul that "irresponsibly" distorts its meaning out of context) effectively obliterates any distinctive significance in the two identifying terms, "the good man" and "the righteous man," that are nevertheless applied with a straight face to the two persons at hand. They are applied as readily, in fact, as are the basic non-distinctions of apparel, gold buttons for "identifying" one man and grey coat for another. Then as the protagonist begins his solicitation, the gentleman with gold sleeve-buttons unintentionally parodies the Confidence-Man's imperative and so pays homage to the implicit norm: for himself, the gentleman coolly declares, "charity was in one sense not an effort, but a luxury; against too great indulgence in which his steward, a humorist, had sometimes admonished him" (p. 42). The hero's subsequent enthusiastic mimicry reduces to absurdity the gentleman's notion of "the charity business," as he calls it (p. 32). The Confidence-Man's slick, facile tone amplifies the gentleman's ruling disposition: " 'You see, this doing good to the world by driblets amounts to just nothing. I am for doing good to the world with a will. I am for doing good to the world once for all and having done with it' " (p. 35). This is one of the times in reading Melville (as with parts of *Omoo* and the story "The Happy Failure") that one seems to be reading Twain, in this case under the guise of Colonel Sellers. The chapter's final contrast of the gentleman's "pleasant incredulity" and the life-transforming potential inherent in the Confidence-Man's ideal—pleaded with a Pentecostal "persuasiveness before which granite hearts might crumble into gravel"—gives the encounter its sardonic Q.E.D.

Thus, seen as a whole, Melville's ironic verbalism effects a liberation from procrustean verbal choice by suggesting a train of thought, or rather of temper, lying obliquely to the argument's apparent grain. Frequently the quiet undertone is unsparingly critical, but just as frequently it has a carefully weighted sympathy that acknowledges the shapes of diverse individual lives. Consider the following sentence: "Like the benign elm . . . the good man seemed to wave the canopy of his goodness over that suitor [i.e., the protagonist], not in conceited condescension, but with that even amenity of true majesty, which can be kind without stooping to it" (p. 41). One would have to be tone-deaf not to hear qualifying reverberations here, but in an important respect the sentence means exactly what it overtly says; in giving the gentleman with gold sleeve-buttons his due, it is representative of a number of such statements in the book. The point is worth emphasis because Melville's irony is often made to seem too monotonic, whereas it is almost always polyphonic—to use Melville's own term, a "concert," like the voices of Taji, the poet, and the philosopher in *Mardi* (pp. 367, 560, 581). The complacent gentleman festively dressed in white, and detached from vice as he is from virtue by merely material generosity, is a tempting target for an uninflected tone of ridicule. But Melville in *The Confidence-Man* is not interested in the easier forms of satire, which in fact would obscure the profound disjunction with which the novel is concerned. There is a lucid, unmitigated disenchantment in the authorial eyes that view this "good man," this modern version of Pontius Pilate; they are like the "indifferent eyes" (p. 217) of the Confidence-Man as he leads away a similar, though rather more likable, soul at the novel's conclusion. It is only when brought into the electric glare of radical Charity that the social virtue looks shoddy, and the gesture that is "kind . . . without stooping," although a real complement to egalitarian social easiness, begins to look like a pale mockery. The passage is ironic because the gentleman, in being a veritable triumph of conventional social grace and goodness, is *thereby* a spiritual cipher. Only a voice that is itself a polyphony of mutually poising voices, a Socratic *convivium*, can do justice to the diversions and self-protective confusions of Charity.

In summary, the Confidence-Man is an original genius in fashioning fictive situations to reveal the truth originally.[9] The term *genius* comprehends both the fool and knave roles: motivated by his desire to touch the hearts of others, the fool uses the knave's tactics to make everyone fools. This means, not necessarily to win a certain sum of money by outright deception, but to try to make another person act contradictorily, "foolishly." The self-contradiction delimits the range of feeling and so discloses the original potential of a man's sympathetic genius. The good merchant Henry Roberts is led into such a contradiction, "stimulated into making mad disclosures—to himself and to another—of the queer, unaccountable caprices of his natural heart" (p. 58). And the warmhearted misanthropic Missourian, who goes off "like a rocket" (p. 100) in response to the Confidence-

[9] Further meanings of the term *genius* correspond to the roles of the protagonist: especially as the Cosmopolitan, he is obviously the genius loci of the "all-fusing spirit of the West, whose type is the Mississippi itself, . . . one cosmopolitan and confident tide" (p. 6); in light of his culinary metaphors and frequently festive air, he is truly a tutelary spirit, "viewed as propitiated by festivities; hence, one's appetite"; and his final role as psychopomp is a traditional function of a person's private genius, "finally to conduct him out of the world" (*O. E. D.*), as well as that of the trickster god Hermes.

Man's bait, contradicts himself emotionally at every turn, whether he accepts or rejects what the hero ostensibly offers. The common ground of socializing motive that the Confidence-Man shares with these co-agents, and the largely unconscious but unquestioned ancillary values that make his challenge constantly relevant to them whatever their response, exists as a competitive tension between sociability and sensitive self-protection. This is another version of the rhythm of merging and recoil in *Moby-Dick*. As *speculum mundi*, the Confidence-Man puts others through the cycle of commitment and disengagement that Ishmael experienced, a cycle whose amplitude depends on the degree to which each individual shares the common motive.

The hidden sun of genius discovers by an act of fictional creating; but the genius, whether he is the Confidence-Man or Shakespeare, can only create what in some way already covertly exists, by collaborating with the concealed genius of others through equivocal measures that are outlandish according to quotidian standards, which judge by externals. Thus the eccentric Cosmopolitan repeatedly insists on being *convivial*—a word one of his victims helpfully defines for him as meaning "living together" (p. 152). For there is also a sense in which no creativity is original, as the narrator argues, since "all life is from the egg" (p. 205).

This is an egg that, appearances to the contrary, cannot be cracked. The potential *arche* can only be known as it acts, in its acts. So Melville's book of originations fittingly ceases in darkness, and without an ending: "Something further may follow of this masquerade." A more unteleological fiction could not be imagined. In contrast to the passage from *Omoo* earlier examined, or to the end of *Moby-Dick*, we are left without even an "event" to tell us what "finally" happened. We are left with the tentative narrative consciousness and its final trick of pointedly refusing to tell. But the ambiguity, the subject of much critical conjecture, in its blatancy makes the seeming curtness function really as an invitation to understanding. Like the conclusion of "Benito Cereno," the words, "this masquerade," beckon us to read the book again, or at least to consult again with its original, its unmasked first reality.

The lack of *telos* is the point. The original Charity is equally the point at which understanding begins. There is no "event" because nothing *finally* happens. Quite to the contrary. Something originally is undone in a quiet de-creation. For the most remarkable truth about the novel is that it goes backward, not in history but in human process defined in traditional terms. It shows ethical process reversing itself from the New Testament of the spirit, in Charity, to the Old Testament of the letter, the words that swarm like flies to honey to cover the embarrassingly naked and artless, deaf and dumb, love. So the book is directly the reverse of what criticism has tended to call it: apocalyptic. It is anti-apocalyptic and counter-teleological. More exactly, in the root senses, it is apocryphal and archaeological; it disappears into the *arche*, concealing itself there, in the primal darkness of a reverse creation. The design has been to take us back from one origin to another: from dumb spiritual generation into ultimate origin in the concealing letter. Pope's famous lines are the literary parallel:

> Lo! thy dread Empire, CHAOS! is restored;
> Light dies before thy uncreating word:
> Thy hand, great Anarch! lets the curtain fall;
> And universal Darkness buries All.

In the closing scene, with the satanic boy and the childless old man, who is capable only of helpless, immobilizing doubt, we see that the uncreating word is the negative *"auto-da-fe"* (p. 210) that replaces the existential act of faith. The image of the reading light whose horned altar and haloed figure represent the Old and New Testaments points in turn to the conquering old letter whose conquest by word we have been watching throughout the book. The

Trickster blows this lamp out in a reversal of the Deity's inspiriting primal breath and light. We are back before Creation, in the darkness of a truly hidden sun.

Where does one go after darkness? Beyond darkness? Whatever the answer might be to such ideational speculations, the reader is left without words, and is turned back to the book's origin, its original speechless Charity. When there is no *telos*, no Revelation, there is no other place to go: "the profounder emanations of the human mind, intended to illustrate all that can be humanly known of human life; these never unravel their own intricacies, and have no proper endings . . ." (*Pierre*, p. 141).

And as for the reader's conviviality with this fictional symposium of Melville's, we have been tutored by the surrogate rhetor to see that, according to the dictates of innate temper, one may hold belief—as for example, a belief that the majority of men are falsehearted masqueraders—in a wide variety of modes, and may derive from this conclusion directly contradictory behavior toward others. We are in a position to understand fully why the narrator is skeptical of those who, using "fixed principles," "cherish expectations with regard to some mode of infallibly discovering the heart of man" (p. 60). Here, as with the whale in *Moby-Dick*, one only discovers the "living truth" in the heart of quickest perils, by the risk of cordial commitment.

On these grounds we can begin to appreciate more completely Melville's impersonation of extravagant authorial reserve concerning the characters he has himself created; as if, like the Deity that Melville describes, he too is a little puzzled at the result. In the hero's comedy of action, the "proper," because *personally* inescapable, behavior is hazard and testing—but with a complete clarity about what is risked. In the narrator's comedy of words, it is a parodic withholding of judgment because of the narrator's, and our, verbally self-conscious distance from the story. We read "as if" we withhold judgment because of our awareness of verbal limitations and the masquerades of appearance; yet this suspension is repeatedly undermined by the more heavily insinuated comedy of action. We yield, and cannot for long withhold judgment after all. Thus, combined, the hero's and the narrator's examples rhetorically elicit from us the stance of sensible foolishness. But the crowning comedy is that this persuasion will only be successful if the requisite instinctual imperative already exists in us in some unfrustrated germinal form. The two examples, of action and of words, inculcate the probative commitment of confidence directed toward moments of release when a character is persuaded to contradict himself. In these rhetorical moments in the novel's white-toned comedy, as in the more steadily maintained epic cycles of *Moby-Dick*, the bedeviled self is made real to itself.

The question the Cosmopolitan asks one of the book's subordinate storytellers is, and must be, also that of Melville's reader: " 'with what heart have you told me this story?' " (p. 190). The distinction on which the book's creative argument rests is between Winsome-Egbert's sort of irresponsibility—the failure of an icy heart—and the aesthetic irresponsibility—"without licentious inclination"— of privileged utterance by which the artist can voice the deepest sensations of life repressed by his age's moral proprieties and our shared habits of civility, and most notably verbal tropisms. Melville's ascetic irony in *The Confidence-Man* is remarkable because it is motivated by his innately compassionate feeling for human community combined with his embattled awareness of his readers, the external but also internalized reality in consciousness that would receive his words. As a writer, Melville is authenticated for himself and for us precisely in our experience of his elusive, choral-voiced narrative consciousness and in our placing in him "trust nevertheless." But whereas in *Moby-Dick* Melville coached us to create ourselves as his faithful readers, in *The Confidence-Man* we are challenged, in as many ways as the trickster hero challenges mankind, sensibly to play the fool by acknowledging the irresponsible heart, our own hidden sun, in the very act of reading.

And now, as an appendix to the discussion, if we turn briefly to the delayed question of the book's religious allegory, we are challenged to play the fool in another fashion. When we canvass the possibilities concerning what figure among the immortals is masquerading as what, we are involved in Melville's game of "which is the original?" His several statements in his works to the effect that in all the universe there is "but one original," are to the point. But so are the Confidence-Man's unmistakable traditional associations with Satan. An excellent case can also be made for considering the Confidence-Man as Christ, even on the basis of a modern familiarity with the New Testament not likely to be as deep as Melville's was. For example, not to mention the traditional associations others have pointed out, Christ was accused repeatedly by the orthodox of being a deceiver and a blasphemer, and of being in league with the devil and thus deriving his powers. He was throughout his career involved in entrapping debates in which he outwitted his opponents even when he did not persuade them. Further, it could be argued that after first properly appearing aboard the *Fidèle* as one whose kingdom is not of this world, Melville's Christ metamorphoses into the princely Cosmopolitan, the very "prince of the world" who is Satan.

Approximately as good a case can be made for the apostles, in fact, for they came under the same accusations as their "original." In this respect, Paul, of course, is by far the best candidate for paralleling the Confidence-Man, who paraphrases the apostle's many statements directly regarding confidence and charity as if he had written them. Paul was originally a man of hate savagely persecuting the Christians; after his abrupt transformation he was as fervent an advocate of love as he had been of hate, joining the Christian community of despised pariahs much as the Indian-hater embraces those he had previously been slaughtering. Paul was constantly traveling and in hardship, in even pursuit of his duty across the known world, and had again and again to defend himself against the suspicions of other Christians, his fellow "strangers and pilgrims on the earth" (Hebrews, 11:13). To vindicate his typically paradoxical language and his flexible tactics of persuasion with different sects, he made a list of the various parts he had played and concluded it: "I am made all things to all men, that I might by all means save some" (I Corinthians, 9:22). And to defend his continual requests for money, the purpose of many of his endless journeys, he protested by ironically repeating the accusation: "for I seek not yours but you. . . . But be it so, I did not burden you: nevertheless, being crafty, I caught you with guile" (II Corinthians, 12:14, 16).

Or again, we may conclude that the book means to show that God and Satan are the same.

In any of these ways, and others like them, we may decide to solve what Melville firmly declared a mystery of ultimate metaphysical origin. Melville's declaration surely does not arise from his inability to conceive ironically of such solutions, for he holds out evidence for all of them and more. As with metaphysical identification of the White Whale, the problem is one of overdetermination: we are given too many possible "explanations," not too few. It is, as Melville wrote Hawthorne, "this *Being* of the matter"[10] by which we hang ourselves in giving ontological names. If *The Confidence-Man* is indeed an April Fool's book, there is a pertinent problem of choice in the New Testament that may help to uncover the jest. When the Pharisees attempted to determine which of two sources was responsible

---

10 *Letters*, p. 125. The whole quotation is as follows: "But it is this *Being* of the matter; there lies the knot with which we choke ourselves. As soon as you say *Me*, a *God*, a *Nature*, so soon you jump off from your stool and hang from the beam. Yes, that word is the hangman."

for Christ's extraordinary actions, they were warned severely against confusing the spirit of Satan and the spirit of God. Melville's study of the impact of a phenomenal being tempts us to the same literal confusion, no matter what we finally decide about the hero's metaphysical source. The book's grimmest jest may be that, according to authoritative explanation (Matthew 12:22–23), such a confusion is the sole unforgivable sin, which shall "not be forgiven . . . neither in this world nor the world to come." If we are tempted to commit the unforgivable sin, perhaps our only solace is that Melville was also.

III

For in tremendous extremities human souls are like drowning men; well enough they know they are in peril; well enough they know the causes of that peril; nevertheless, the sea is the sea, and these drowning men do drown.

Pierre

What I have to say in conclusion about *Billy Budd* may be said in a few pages. The initial itinerary the story follows is one in which gentleness transforms into, or becomes a tool or expression of, violence: Claggart's meek demeanor subserving the aim of destroying Billy, Billy's killing of Claggart, Vere's love of the hero being subordinated to the military duty of executing him, and, at the most general social level, the "religion of the meek" subserving the "atheistic" "brute Force" of war.[11]

This developing pattern reveals that in every case fundamental motive clashes with practical result or appearance. What is more, we are asked in the case of every major character to consider motives that are far from apparent in the overt deeds of each. The one that has proved most troublesome to readers is Vere's confiding love for Billy,

[11] *Billy Budd, Sailor,* ed. Harrison Hayford and Merton M. Sealts, Jr. (Chicago: University of Chicago Press, 1962), p. 122. Hereafter cited in the text.

given extension by the statement that the captain is one of "Nature's nobler order" (p. 115). The paradox is that Vere feels compelled to argue before the court that motive is beside the question in judging Billy's deed. The resulting irony is therefore that we are being asked to respond to Vere by using a frame of reference that he officially and fatally denies Billy Budd. Or to paraphrase: a just assessment of Vere must include primary considerations that *he* declares inappropriate in legally judging Billy, although privately he acts to console the protagonist. What then can be said of Vere's motive and the instinctive trust between the two men who are executioner and victim? I believe that we are meant to see the same generous spirit in Vere's sworn allegiance to military life, with its prospects of glory, that is manifested in his quick, warm private response to Billy. The first manifestation effectively supplants and frustrates the second, for military *superbia* has an institutional power and practical necessity that the private expression lacks: in a word, duty. When Vere in a quasi-Kantian manner sets duty rigorously against natural inclination, he unmasks yet another humanly institutional diversion of the need for human solidarity, as slavery was unmasked in "Benito Cereno." The parallel reversal of private feeling occurs when Billy's confidence in Vere, combined with the necessity to defend himself publicly against Claggart, precipitates what is in effect murder of a superior in wartime. Although perhaps most readers would think that they would have decided differently from Vere—and Melville's tone carries a full awareness of how far Vere's decision is from absolute justice—to be too much exercised over this question is to obscure Melville's tragic point, which is the same for Vere and Billy Budd as it is for Claggart, who might have "loved Billy but for fate and ban" (p. 88). Each individual's form and frustration of love is his fate in "the jugglery of circumstances" (p. 103); and, given this man, this time, and this circumstance, thus it will happen: each man's act will be effectively reduced to a motion, as if he had no private motive whatsoever. The sea is the sea.

To anneal us to this steely appreciative temper, which is neither "acceptance" nor "rejection" but tragic love in full possession of its consequences, Melville rhetorically insists that he is primarily writing fact, not fable. This is also why he openly refuses, as he refused implicitly in "Bartleby," to invent a subsidiary "romantic incident . . . to account for" Claggart's hatred of Billy (p. 73). The reason for Claggart's feeling is to be found, insofar as it can be, by the emotionally engaged but musing analysis one employs when confounded by fact. More exactly, Melville treats his putative historical facts with a combination of two rhetorical stances: one judicial or judicially commemorative, the other epideictically analytical (like, say, *Middlemarch* in this latter respect). The two perspectives are subtly intermixed in the following passage, which in its concerns and measured lucidity condenses an entire literary career:

> Now envy and antipathy, passions irreconcilable in reason, nevertheless in fact may spring conjoined like Chang and Eng in one birth. . . . To [Claggart], the spirit lodged within Billy, and looking out from his welkin eyes as from windows, that ineffability it was which made the dimple in his dyed cheek, suppled his joints, and dancing in his yellow curls made him preeminently the Handsome Sailor. One person excepted, the master-at-arms was perhaps the only man in the ship intellectually capable of adequately appreciating the moral phenomenon presented in Billy Budd. And the insight but intensified his passion, which assuming various secret forms within him, at times assumed that of cynic disdain, disdain of innocence—to be nothing more than innocent! Yet in an aesthetic way he saw the charm of it, the courageous free-and-easy temper of it, and fain would have shared it, but he despaired of it.

With no power to annul the elemental evil in him, though readily enough he could hide it; apprehending the good, but powerless to be it; a nature like Claggart's, surcharged with energy as such natures almost invariably are, what recourse is left to it but to recoil upon itself and, like the scorpion for which the Creator alone is responsible, act out to the end the part allotted it. (pp. 77–78)

Melville gives both the judicial and epideictic stances symbolic extension to point out what has bearing on analysis and feeling; that is, an understanding of the broadest archetypicality of character and event, which represent not only human history but the nonhuman universe as well (as, for example, Claggart's is a "depravity according to nature"). Exceptional characters, what Melville calls "certain phenomenal men," are the most typical in this sense because they most clearly reflect the pure motivational entities that are mixed and weakly diffuse in other men. The recurrent word "phenomenal" can be applied in its full meaning to them: the noumenal *shines* in them: in "Starry" Vere, in the "phenomenal change" in Claggart's luridly gleaming eyes (p. 98), and particularly in the "phenomenal effect" (p. 123) of Billy Budd's execution in which he shines with the dawn light. To underscore this point, Melville guides the reader to distinguish between the accustomed seeming strangeness of human deeds and the genuinely phenomenal. He does this by rhetorical directives—most bluntly, "Marvel not," he tells us, in regard to the chaplain's behavior— and by using the oracular Manxman's gnomic wisdom as a rough indicator for the intellectual level at which the story is to be received (although the Manxman's rather too cool elevation is outweighed by the warmer tones of the folk ballad at the story's conclusion).

Partly, the truth of the story, as with any tragedy, is that the hero is dead, no matter what the motives, whether we might say Claggart loved him and Vere hated him. Claggart's willful misinterpretation of Billy's trivial accident in spilling soup is the key instance in which motive becomes merely what the observer wishes to conceive it:

> An uncommon prudence is habitual with the subtler depravity, for it has everything to hide. And in case of an injury but suspected, its secretiveness voluntarily cuts it off from enlightenment or disillusion; and, not unreluctantly, action is taken upon surmise as upon certainty. And the retaliation is apt to be in monstrous disproportion to the supposed offense; for when in anybody was revenge in its exactions aught else but an inordinate usurer? But how with Claggart's conscience? . . . Claggart's conscience being but the lawyer to his will, made ogres of trifles, probably arguing that the motive imputed to Billy in spilling the soup just when he did . . . made a strong case against him; nay, justified animosity into a sort of retributive righteousness. (p. 80)

War is the general epitome of this reduction, for it " 'looks but to the frontage, to appearance' " (p. 112), which is to say, to the mere motions of men. This reduction to motion is the primary function of the first phase of the plot. Not only war, but also Billy Budd in his innocence looks but to appearances, being unable to conceive evil of anyone who speaks to him kindly. Given the right time and circumstance, his speech impediment means the "effective abrogation of everything but brute Force," so that his fatal striking of Claggart is significantly defined as an act of war: like "the flame from a discharged cannon at night" (p. 99). Following this nadir, the second phase of the story is the tragic reinstitution of genuine action, a phenomenal reversal of ironic reversals.

The cardinal irony of *Billy Budd* can be put briefly, then, as the triumph of mere motion over act—and most tragically, over act fully recognized by the principals. The tragic triumph of *Billy Budd* is in the luminous act, one of an implied sequence in history, that in receptive human hearts does full justice to the individual's total mode of being. For his hanging is an act on Billy's part, a heroic choosing of what he is constrained to; and consequently in a significant human sense it is a conquest of that reductive mechanical motion whose most fearful individual expression is death, and especially the dramatic involuntary convulsions of the hanged man. Billy's overcoming of involuntary mechanism is a metaphorical attestation to the activity not only of Billy's conscious will but more importantly of his entire subintentional vitality. His rare self-integral gesture, fully articulate and unimpeded through his blessing, is presented as the only real act in the execution itself, bending all wills to his dominant unifying drive, immobilizing Vere and making the crew's voices "echo" to his "clear melody" (p. 123). It is, to use Melville's term, the "priestly motive" manifest in Admiral Nelson's preparation for death, one of those epic "exaltations of sentiment that a nature like Nelson, the opportunity being given, vitalizes into acts" (p. 58).

As Charles A. Reich has observed of the hanging scene, "It is a . . . formal, solemn act of society which every onlooker regrets. It is as if society has become a will separate from the will of all its members."[12] To create the poignant sense of loss and, just as crucially, to isolate and make accessible to our intuition the deeper motive acting, the scene must display the social disjunction in which this inexorable abstraction of will kills Billy Budd. Yet, concretely, it is Billy Budd who chooses this abstraction, incarnates it, and transcends it in a blessing that is "conventional" as mere form, a traditional "felon's benediction"; but is "unanticipated," "a clear melody of a singing bird on the point of launching from the twig," as the hero's indi-

12 "The Tragedy of Justice in Billy Budd," *Twentieth Century Interpretations of Billy Budd,* ed. Howard Vincent (Englewood Cliffs, N.J.: Prentice-Hall, 1971), pp. 60–61; rpt. from Yale Review, 56 (1967), 376–89.

vidual act. His words are spoken without bravado, and as a conventional formula are in keeping with his nautical society's mores, so that the common social bond is maintained in Billy's individual stylistic transcendence. The melody suffusing the words is the purely gratuitous human excess that transforms this death into a vital mode of being. This gratuitousness has its counterpart in the apparently overflowing godly energy of spontaneous natural beings, as the singing bird metaphor reminds us; but it is uniquely human in its awareness not only of choice but the sordid death confronting it. Billy's first fully integrated human act is his last, but his verbal melody is more deeply authoritative over the crew than the martial music that follows it. And further surpassing the mechanical motion-stimulus of martial form, it is creative in inspiring the folk art that "for a term" (p. 131) venerates the hero. As Melville had affirmed in *Redburn* (p. 291), the manner of death provides the index to the real life and faith of each man. This deep acceptance of inevitable death is the converse of what *Mardi* called "the only true infidelity": "for a live man to vote himself dead."

The solemnity of the execution is surprisingly disrupted by a brief chapter breaking into the absorbing chronological treatment, which is then picked up again in the next chapter as if the discontinuity had not occurred. The pitiful, tragically heightened mood is shattered by the grotesque "scientific" discussion in which the doctor refuses to admit will power as the cause of the hanged man's lack of "mechanical spasm" (p. 124). The disrupting chapter must seem a perverse blunder or clumsy "comic relief," unless one recognizes it as a rhetorical shock designed for two ends. One purpose is precisely to reestablish at this crucial point the reader's distance from the story's events so that, without ceasing to be moved by them, the reader will not lose a disinterested appreciation. It provides in the learned medical fool a gradient, if not a scapegoat, whereby the reader's (and Melville's) residue of merely egocentric bitterness at the innocent man's death may be largely drained off. The second purpose, dovetailed into the first, is to underline with almost harsh detachment Melville's discrimination between Billy's heroic union of being in an act both willed and profoundly instinctual, and the usual mechanical human motions and concomitant limited understanding of conation. Like the deposition in "Benito Cereno," the doctor's net of factual language focuses our attention exactly on what it seeks to capture and fails to, if understood simply in the manner intended by the speaker. But whereas the deposition was to be re-read, the doctor's discussion is primarily a signal for re-reading, sending us back to the story's fulcrum of action, the preceding execution scene, with a vision specifically alerted. For cast in a different tone and given a further frame of understanding, the doctor's denial that mere conscious will alone could explain Billy's manner of death is exactly correct. The chapter thus works up to the highest pitch the story's pervasive tonal and structural irony: the awareness of the distance that separates an act from the rational understanding of it. This irony is the predicate of the story's presented emotion, its fine-hammered woe and love.

At the general level of the Mutiny Act and international war, organized society seems to structure the distance Melville ironically identifies. But in the most immediate terms, the network of social reality is at the center of the story's values; it is imagistically extended, in fact, across the boundary between the human and nonhuman that the "upright barbarian" (p. 52) hero symbolically occupies. The aim is to show the subterranean continuity of this network even when the lines of society and the natural law have been broken by revolution or by war's officially sanctioned violence. As in *The Confidence-Man*, images of harmony and eating delineate this connective web. One imagistic set subliminally enacts the indifferent process of physical absorption: Billy's spilled soup, the birds gathering for food over the hero's sea burial, and the dawn cloud-fleece being "licked up by the sun that late had so glorified it" (p. 128). Another set helps to valorize Billy's act of harmony and the crew's identifying response to it: the "musical chime" of the "innermost man" in the *Rights-of-Man* captain (p. 45); the martial piping, "Shrill as the shriek of the sea hawk" (p. 126), and the sacred airs that are used to move and placate the sailors; the swelling inarticulate murmur of the crew that blends with the crying of the gulls; the echo of "Billy Budd" on Vere's lips in death; and the final song that commemorates Billy surrounded by companionship, and harmoniously will-less in the deep currents of the sea.

Whether a man claim, as did Vere, that his allegiance lies with his king and not with nature, or whether men act in enmity or amity, the story reasserts the ground of identification—not only beyond good and evil, but beyond conscious will—that the rare, fully integrating individual human act can illuminate. Many of Melville's usual rhetorical directives occur in the story, but the structural and tonal weight fall on the phenomenal persuasive act itself, Billy's death. Earlier in his career Melville portrayed Ahab in the self-contesting ritual declamation by which he sought to bind to himself other men and even the universe. At the end of his life, with as sharp a sense of audience-awareness in his obscurity from the public as he had ever had in his eleven public years, Melville offers us a rhetoric of direct, overt act that for one instant could be intuitively unambiguous because it was final. Then, before ending his story, his fidelity to what he calls "Truth uncompromisingly told" made him testify to the ambiguity and infidelity that close in again like the sea over a body—nevertheless.

But this is still not the end. For with our tempering in unflinching rigor, we are now ready not to misconceive, in thought or feeling, the conclusiveness of music. We are ready for the ballad, moved and moving with the hero's germinal harmony, which like a chord sounds all the notes.

PART TWO

Mark Twain: The Authority of the Courtier

AGAMEMNON: *This Troyan scorns us, or the men*
of Troy
Are ceremonious courtiers.

. . . .

TROILUS: *What's aught but as 'tis valued?*
HECTOR: *But value dwells not in particular will;*
It holds his estimate and dignity
As well wherein 'tis precious of itself
As in the prizer. 'Tis mad idolatry
To make the service greater than the god. . . .

Troilus and Cressida

Man will do many things to get himself loved,
he will do all things to get himself envied.

Pudd'nhead Wilson's New Calendar,
Following the Equator

Introduction

On the evidence of the last half-century, the literary fiction known as Mark Twain seems to be amenable only to a body of criticism that is diagnostic and combative. This condign result is a token that he has exerted his authority posthumously as surely as he did during his life; it is less a matter of regret than a sign of Mark Twain's success. For, finally, Twain presents himself as the American literary problem-child, combining awesome gifts and equally awesome ineptness. Several other major American writers from Cooper through O'Neill readily permit a diagnostic approach; but Twain demands it now as he did when he played a courtship game of delinquent regressiveness with Olivia Clemens, William Dean Howells, and—more coyly and distantly—with a huge popular audience. He is, and has been, a perennially contemporary author precisely in this covert demand, proposing to us in his literary identity itself recurrently fresh problems of literary behavior to solve. And his authority is no less forcefully indicated in the popular reputation as lovable humorist he still maintains. It is the curious authority of a writer not only practicing a most fragile persuasive art, humor, but attempting to extend his dominion in every possible fashion, in the service of the extraordinary will to power that Van Wyck Brooks first formally noted and reacted to.

After a brief period of relative calm following the reverberations of the Brooks-DeVoto battle (in which Brooks quarreled with Twain and DeVoto with Brooks), a period also of consolidation capped by Henry Nash Smith's fine studies, more recent scholarship and the current reviews of volumes published thus far in the Mark Twain Papers evidence a renewed uneasiness or outright distaste regarding much that Twain wrought in his life and art. Even if one had not, as Leslie Fiedler once remarked, made the mistake of reading too much Mark Twain, two very Twainian hoaxes recently discovered seem to have reestablished the quasi-militant spirit apparently suited to the case, and hint that there is more to be said about Fiedler's "duplicitous Mark Twain." The first hoax was that perpetrated long ago by Albert Bigelow Paine, the writer's official literary vicar, in patching together a story from unfinished manuscripts to produce *The Mysterious Stranger*.[1] The second involves the large disparity between Twain's many hints about his valuable, explosive unpublished material and the abortive material made accessible to date in the Mark Twain Papers. But whether we berate or condone or eulogize Mark Twain, we are being brought under the power of his courtly humours; these are principal agents of an enterprising imaginative aggrandizement for which his copyrighted name and a still-powerful Mark Twain Estate are the legal metaphors.

As it happens, Melville was long used, rather like the model boy in one of Twain's stories, to criticize by contrast Twain's angling for public acclaim instead of defying it in favor of individual integrity and "purely literary" standards. Though the previous section should suggest that the evidence concerning Melville does not permit a simple contrast between the writers, recent studies have thoroughly confirmed that Twain to a great extent composed his works

---

[1] William M. Gibson is forthright in leading off his edition, *Mark Twain's Mysterious Stranger Manuscripts* (Berkeley: University of California Press, 1969), p. 1: "Mark Twain's *The Mysterious Stranger, A Romance*, as published in 1916 and reprinted since that date, is an editorial fraud perpetrated by Twain's official biographer and literary executor, Albert Bigelow Paine, and Frederick A. Duneka of Harper & Brothers publishing company. When I first read the three manuscript versions of the narrative in the Mark Twain Papers, like other scholars who had seen them, I found this dismaying conclusion to be inescapable." For the initial discovery of the fraud, see John S. Tuckey, *Mark Twain and Little Satan* (West Lafayette, Ind.: Purdue University Press, 1963).

Fiedler's cited remark is in *Love and Death in the American Novel* (New York: Criterion, 1960), p. 564.

with immediate, financially rewarding popularity in view. Hamlin Hill's investigations of the writer's publishing ventures disclose his knowing, enthusiastic participation during almost his entire career in a scheme of merchandising markedly resembling a confidence game, played upon the largely rural and small town public that did not frequent bookstores. Hill writes,

> Coming to "literature" from the commercial background of newspaper work and journalism, he tended much of the time to look upon his travel books as merchandise whose worth was its market value.
>
> The world of subscription book publishing into which Clemens moved in 1867 could only have strengthened his commercial approach to "literature." It was a world of cynical and dishonest practices aimed at amassing the largest possible profit from material all too often of dubious value. Publishers betrayed not only their customers but their authors, their general agents and their canvassers as well. Prospectuses— sample pages in a sample binding carried by the door-to-door canvassers—were contrived to distort and misrepresent the volumes they described. Instructions to agents contained advice that could only insult whatever integrity they possessed. . . . Although [Twain] condemned aggressive materialism in narratives written during a wide span of years . . . there was still more than a hint of public confession in his portrayal of schemers, inventors, and entrepreneurs. One of Mark Twain's aquiline eyes was on the cash box, while the other focused on the almost ascetically high-minded world of the New England literary Brahmins.[2]

Today it should be obvious that, though DeVoto's or Parrington's populist arguments will not satisfy our curios-

[2] *Mark Twain's Letters to His Publishers*, ed. Hamlin Hill (Berkeley: University of California Press, 1967), pp. 2–3. See also Hill's *Mark Twain and Elisha Bliss* (Columbia, Missouri: University of Missouri Press, 1964).

ity about Twain, neither can we merely, by a Brahmin a priori, automatically ascribe whatever is mediocre in Twain's work to his lust for tangible recognition, and whatever is excellent to something else. Neither can we any longer afford to think, with Lionel Trilling, in the following fashion:

> Call the passion [i.e., Twain's drive for money and prestige], like Balzac's, an aspect of the Faustian will and it at once has a different complexion. The Faustian will was strong in Mark Twain; he knew that it was passing brave to be a king and ride in triumph through Persepolis; a new idea, even for a "modest little drilling machine," is, as he says in one of [his] letters . . . "something imperial." But perhaps it will be objected that his imperial will should have gone into his writing. Maybe so. Yet the true charm of his best work is exactly its relaxation of will, perhaps the result of the will having been, for a while discharged in business enterprise.[3]

But if such a position seems no longer at all tenable to many students of Twain, we have not thought through the concrete literary consequences of the opposite case, which seems much nearer the whole truth: that Twain's writings are imaginative acts with the same basic motive as his practical, and certainly his publishing, endeavors. If we could justly describe Melville's typical narrative voice as *addressed*, how are we to characterize that of a writer whose creative eye seems to be largely on the main chance? The critical reckoning that still remains incomplete concerns the particular nature of the fictions shaped by this authorial awareness.

---

[3] "Mark Twain—The Genius in Business," in *A Casebook on Mark Twain's Wound*, ed. Lewis Leary (New York: Crowell, 1962), pp. 181–82; revised from "Mark Twain—A Dominant Genius," *The New York Times Book Review*, 3 Feb. 1946, pp. 1, 14.

6

Idolatry Mad and Gentle:
The Innocents Abroad, Roughing It

This crown of the man who knows laughter, this rose-chaplet crown: I have placed it on my head, I have consecrated laughter. But not a single soul have I found strong enough to join me.
              Nietzsche, *Thus Spake Zarathustra*

Every truth requires some pretence to make it live. Let this be your pretence, your pose. Speak magistrally no matter how you may feel.
              Joseph Conrad to Edward Garnett

UNTIL recently, Twain has been regarded as a trickster only in the limited generic sense (for instance, in a hoax like the "Empire City Massacre") or as a hazy, largely biographical commonplace that was a dead end more than it was a starting point for critical thinking. But now, even though the term "trickster" is itself used only incidentally, the precise bearing of trickery on Twain's works has become a prominent question. For example, the two scholars who have devoted book-length studies to Twain's humor are agreed in the broadest sense: Pascal Covici (*Mark Twain's Humor*) deals with Twain's works in general as forms of hoax; and James M. Cox, in a much more ambitious undertaking (*Mark Twain: The Fate of Humor*), stresses the idea that the reader is pleasurably "taken in" by Twain's impersonations of seriousness.

For the moment, my preliminary text will not be Twain but the last-named study, Cox's provocative and unpatronizing diagnosis. More than any other single book on Twain, this important investigation opens up the most vital rhetorical issues. The aim of the book is a coherent thesis regarding Twain's development as a humorist above all else. In general, Cox takes Brooks' thesis and turns it upside down: Twain's basic problem was not that he repressed his really artistic, non-humorous ability, as Brooks urges, but that he eventually suppressed his natural ability as a humorist after initially committing himself to a humorous literary identity and thus to "the fate of humor." (In proposing one-half of Twain's humorous-pathetic whole as *the* essential element, Cox at least borders on the genetic fallacy—that something necessarily is what it begins as—although in interestingly Twainian fashion he plays this as a trump by calling it "fate" and deriving helpful insights from it.)

In particular, Cox's treatment of Twain's first two major books, *The Innocents Abroad* and *Roughing It*, makes them at once available for a discussion of rhetoric. Cox makes several similar points about them. He convincingly dispels the claim that the works represent in action anything more than a mock initiation. However, apparently influenced by the preface of *Innocents Abroad*, he does find an educative process: "a training of the reader to see with his own eyes."[1] Indeed, Cox states that the truth of Twain's early writing is that it "moves the reader to ask what the truth is" by rousing him to a "skeptical state of mind . . . forcing him to maintain a questioning alertness in the face of experience." Further, this same truth is "the humorous narrator Mark Twain," who converts his experience into entertainment that we "indulgently suspect"—so that we may question whether any apparently serious passage is subverted by deadpan humor—and nevertheless "helplessly enjoy" (p. 104).

I am not altogether sure what skepticism means in such a context. In one frame of mind, one wants to indulge Cox's paradoxical combination of permissive helplessness concerning the entertaining Mark Twain and athletic vigilance regarding the very experience converted into this entertain-

---

[1] *Mark Twain: The Fate of Humor* (Princeton: Princeton University Press, 1966), p. 54. Hereafter cited in the text. As the following pages will show, I owe Cox a good deal, both in agreement and disagreement.

ment. But the matters raised by the combination are too important not to be disentangled if possible.

I

Instead of training in independent perception, as Cox argues, *The Innocents Abroad* offers imaginative acts of substitution. The first substitution, from which all else follows, is indicated in the preface when Twain says that the book's purpose is "to suggest to the reader how *he* would be likely to see Europe and the East if he looked at them with his own eyes instead of the eyes of those who traveled in those countries before him. I make small pretense of showing anyone how he *ought* to look at objects of interest beyond the sea. . . . I offer no apologies for any departures from the usual style of travel writing that may be charged against me—for I think I have seen with impartial eyes, and I am sure I have written at least honestly, whether wisely or not."[2] The preface is a request for concession of authority to Mark Twain, who, because he is an honest man, will reveal what the reader *would* see if he looked with his own eyes instead of those of men who wish to change his sensibilities. The underlying assumption is that author and reader share certain fixed evaluative premises of vision, and that the author's "departures from the usual style" are the impartial attestations of a particular vision already secured by the author.

This remission to man and style granted, the reader is quickly assured that he can proceed with easy confidence in his ambassador and guide. On the first page of the narrative proper, there is an invitation to comfortable thoughtlessness. The language makes no demands, indeed seems to bask complacently in the least thoughtful commonplaces of agreeable middlebrow gentility. Yet, following upon the sober introduction, the narrative's rather giddy beginning has the

2 *The Writings of Mark Twain*, Author's National Edition (25 vols.; Harper, 1907–18), I, xxxvii. Hereafter cited in the text by page number alone unless the volume identification is required for clarity.

effect not of foolishness but of a mature man's *being* light-headed, and properly so for the festive occasion of the "great pleasure excursion . . . chatted about . . . everywhere." The book will depict the pleasure trip as a fraud; but Twain, as Cox notes, will substitute his own pleasure trip, his book, for it. But, I would add, it is emphatically *his* book. Twain will perform this displacement by a "system of reduction" (II, 238–39) and of reinstating expansion that demolishes one banality or travel-book romantic illusion only to supplant it with Twain's own authoritative version.

One broadly comic method that he uses is playing with clichés just as "the boys" play with languages in jumbling together English and French. The play is quite conscious: "Perhaps the savage reader would like a specimen of [the Poet Lariat's] style. I do not mean this term to be offensive. I only use it because 'the gentle reader' has been used so often that any change from it cannot but be refreshing" (II, 133). The unobtrusive elegant phrasing ("cannot but be") is a perfect garnish to what Twain is accomplishing here: but it can be performed in other keys, as in his treatment of the Venetian gondolier. First comes the reduction of illusion: "This the famed gondola and this the gorgeous gondolier!—the one an inky, rusty old canoe with a sable hearse body clapped into the middle of it, and the other a mangy, barefooted guttersnipe with a portion of his raiment on exhibition which should have been sacred from public scrutiny" (II, 279–80). A few pages later, after he has admired the gondolier's "easy confidence" as a boatman, Twain gives a superior representation of the figure's romance: "The gondolier *is* a picturesque rascal for all he wears no satin harness, no plumed bonnet, no silken tights. His attitude is stately; he is lithe and supple; all his movements are full of grace. When his long canoe and his fine figure, towering from its high perch on the stern, are cut against the evening sky, they make a picture that is very novel and striking to a foreign eye" (p. 295). Twain's authority is secured throughout the book by his ability to displace whatever is jaded and meretricious—and the major part of the Old World is initially presented this way—by his own creation, a revised perspective that by contrast seems "refreshing" and "novel" and thus "striking to the foreign eye."

The intermediate aim of *Innocents Abroad* is to cultivate in the reader, not skepticism, but comfortable confidence. Confidence of what? Confidence of entertainment by a virtuoso whose bag of tricks, though they are recurrently humorous in tendency, really consists of a telescoping set of humours in the old sense.[3] As they flash before us, these humours impress upon us that we are in the hands of one who will not fumble the occasion of wit, or the opportunity to render a description with conventional ease or a criticism with pungency. We are required to accede authority to him as the stylist of his own fascinating authorial personality, and with this hypothesis of coherence-by-performance, we primarily respond to the immediate returns of satisfaction that each separate episode or anecdote furnishes.

Mark Twain does our seeing for us, and his vision is regulated by a temperament even more volatile than that of Melville's Ishmael; but it differs from Ishmael's in being more immediately aimed at sharply dramatic effects and so offering little encouragement of an independent view. The abrupt shifts in emotion are imposed on the reader by an altogether eccentric authorial temperament designed to be enjoyed for its displayed eccentricity, its inflationary psychic economy. One of the most dexterous manipulations of Twain's deadpan idiosyncrasies is the handling of Lake Como. After a dutiful treatment ("Last night the scenery was striking and picturesque") the Italian lake yields by comparison to Twain's private, and at the time of writing

---

[3] The idea of a virtuoso authorial personality is also stressed in a discussion of *Huckleberry Finn* by Louis D. Rubin, Jr., *The Teller in the Tale* (Seattle: University of Washington Press, 1967), pp. 52–82.

relatively arcane, memory of Lake Tahoe: "Como would only seem a bedizened little courtier in that august presence . . . [which is] a sea whose every aspect is impressive, whose belongings are all beautiful, whose lonely majesty types the Deity!" (p. 263). Having accomplished this substitution of his view for the standard, disappointing object of admiration, and having established a miniature hierarchy of "courtier" and "august" singular authority, Twain without warning plunges from this divine height into his well-known diatribe against the noble red man in the passage beginning "Tahoe means grasshoppers." The sentences grow out of one another, one phrase seemingly exciting the next descent in degree of worth, in a delighted release of animus that turns mock-philological possibility into personal conviction: "It means grasshopper soup. It is Indian and suggestive of Indians. They say it is Paiute—possibly it is Digger. I am satisfied it was named by the Diggers—those degraded savages who . . ."; and so on. Even Twain's own contrasted substitutions seem not to be proof against his temperamental waywardness. But while rhythm and syntax change here, the language is so simple that the swerve of emotion produces a double take. Double take is exactly what Twain has done: he has used Lake Tahoe as a means of mounting rhetorically to a pinnacle, then pivoting on this god-term has quickly descended his pyramid by reenvisioning it in the revised descending order Tahoe-grass-hoppers-Indians. (Considering the same habit imagistically, compare Twain's extended treatments of ascent and descent, as when he uses the "Ascent of Vesuvius" as the formal humorous pretext for digressions, which indeed ascend and descend rhetorically; and as when the repeated rapid ascent and descent of the Egyptian pyramids imagistically second Twain's reverent treatment of them as well as the irreverence of the game he stages on them with the guides.)

The communicated posture regarding such deadpan switches from polite picturesque adulation to fuming at "Cooper Indians" in the middle of Italy is partly a head-shaking acquiescence, as if the reader were being led to say, "Old Twain, he sure does despise them Indians." There is clearly little sharing on our part of literally invoked feeling; rather, the reader's vicariously experienced shameless animus is a direct function of the *stylistic* verve of the malediction. Twain is the performer making sharp discriminations of status, and we are the audience, put in *our* place by his turning the emotional tables on us. In *Moby-Dick*, Ishmael's turns and counterturns of mood were movements along a smooth continuum. Twain's are displacements too abrupt not to cause discontinuities in the reader's emotional progress; instead of having a curve to follow, the reader must repeatedly jump the track. The consequence is that, although the writing is usually simple, style and the pleasures of style are thrown into strong relief because stylization, and not an accustomed sequence of emotion, seems to offer the only affective bridge if we are again to follow the writer. In particular, Twain's outbursts in excess of the immediate putative stimulus are whipped up and carried to exhaustion by the stylistic emotional release in direct strokes of the pen.

One announcement in a correctly described "chapter of vituperation" (p. 332) overtly states the sovereignty of Twain's momentarily reigning humour: "And now that my temper is up, I may as well go on and abuse everybody I can think of" (p. 330). This is a humorously exaggerated statement, no doubt, as is more obviously his subsequent claim to have destroyed and eaten a "friendless orphan" in order to calm himself. But the very fact that Twain makes such a statement at all and then follows it by indeed being abusive is a left-handed claim in favor of whatever mood it pleases him to pursue at the moment. The humor at once downplays and reasserts Twain's authority. Twain can usually bring off this gambit successfully because the straightforward vigor of his attack carries all restraints before it, while the intermittent skirmishes with decorous circumlocution heighten the pleasure of aggressive unrestraint by making pretended inhibitions and moral concerns ancillary objects of comic play:

> This Civitavecchia is the finest nest of dirt, vermin, and ignorance we have found yet except that African perdition they call Tangier, which is just like it. The people here live in alleys two yards wide, which have a smell about them which is peculiar but not entertaining. It is well the alleys are not wider, because they hold as much smell now as a person can stand, and of course if they were wider they would hold more, and then the people would die. These alleys are paved with stone and carpeted with deceased cats and decayed rags and decomposed vegetable tops and remnants of old boots, all soaked with dishwater, and the people sit around on stools and enjoy it. They are indolent, as a general thing, and yet have few pastimes. They work two or three hours at a time, but not hard, and then they knock off and catch flies. This does not require any talent, because they only have to grab—if they do not get the one they are after, they get another. . . . Whichever one they get is the one they want. (pp. 334–35)

Typical of Twain's view, and a reinforcement of his rhetorical stance, the scene is presented in terms of entertainment. Once the notion of enjoyment is mentioned ironically, it seems to provide the cue for further development by a comic conceit. The depicted ambience is inherently "not entertaining," but the people are represented as not only enjoying it but elaborating its possibilities with a game that requires no talent. For Twain, here as elsewhere, people are largely defined by what entertains them.

In sum, Twain's displacement of substance into style is also a displacement into personal humours—both dominate the objective world of fact. Twain's improvisational, opportunistic effects put his readers in the position of a circus audience, for whom, ideally, the tonal contrasts and

Barnum-like combinations cannot be too sudden or grotesque. We are invited to pleasurable anticipation about what Mark Twain will do next, how he will take advantage of the disparate opportunities for "effect" to put everything in its place and us in ours. The specific instance of Twain's rancor at the sanctimonious Pilgrims and at the begging, cheating mobs besieging the travelers, or his fleetingly expressed hatred of those who suffer or unaccountably "let" themselves be degraded, may not be enjoyable in itself. But in context the sudden eruption serves to heighten the overall effect of comfortable pleasure by unsettling our emotional stability momentarily, so that we are the more appreciative of having our equilibrium reinstated by light humor or by competent journalistic information. Twain's responses preoccupy the reader so much that he is little concerned about an independent look at empirical reality.

Twain is using the same punctuation technique in this first book that he had recently begun developing successfully before a live lecture audience: a sudden change in direction reinforced by the slightly minatory air of a deadpan face with its aquiline look. The whole communicated demeanor helps to put listeners slightly off balance from time to time and makes them the more receptively attentive to a proffered emotional recovery. The result, while touched with mild anxiety, is just the opposite of *questioning* alertness. As an early lecture review put it, "The audience gets into a queer state after a while," in which "It knows not what to trust."[4] But if Twain's punctuation is judiciously applied, finding a stay against its queer state becomes a primary consideration for the audience. When in the passage cited earlier Twain concludes his fulmination against the Indians by "apologetically" underscoring his eccentricity with the abrupt "But I am growing unreliable," his return to a placid comparison of Lakes Como and Tahoe is received with something very like relief from a momentarily exciting,

[4] Cited in Henry Nash Smith, *Mark Twain: The Development of a Writer* (Cambridge: Harvard University Press, 1962), p. 19.

but nonetheless disquieting, discharge. The rhetoric, though it bears Twain's inimitable stamp, evinces an engrained dialectical attitude toward experience that parallels Melville's. As a favorite image indicates, Twain knows to his very bones that comfort is most enjoyable when a storm threatens outside one's refuge. Thus Huck and Jim watching the storm from their Jackson Island cave can point backward toward Ishmael and Queequeg snug in winter darkness, and forward to the Ishmaelean statement in *Captain Stormfield's Visit to Heaven*: ". . . happiness ain't a *thing in itself*—it's only a *contrast* with something that ain't pleasant. That's all it is. There ain't a thing you can mention that is happiness in its own self—it's only so by contrast with the other thing. And so, as soon as the novelty is over and the force of contrast is dulled, it ain't happiness any longer, and you have to get something fresh."[5]

As regards the character "Mark Twain," the narrative rhythm is that of emotional ruffling and placation: either an excitation of excess and the allaying of it, or balancing an eccentric private excess by a conventional (usually sentimental) overflow in the opposite direction. However, we remain always at approximately the same psychological distance from the protagonist and his world, and thus our emotional swings are only nuances compared to his hair-trigger changes. A large portion of the work's humorous delight proceeds from the disjunction between the two: in a situation in which the reader might merely wince, the humours actor "Mark Twain" is pyrotechnic. Above all, Twain's persona sports with the role of adulatory audience or viewer, either displaying maudlin asininity at Adam's showpiece tomb; or succumbing to an attractive swindling salesgirl or to his own "infant dream" of some nonexistent luxurious comfort; or playing "that game which vanquished so many guides for us—imbecility and idiotic questions. . . . Relief for overtasked eyes and brain from study and sight-

5 *Report from Paradise*, ed. Dixon Wecter (New York: Harper, 1952), pp. 42–43.

seeing is necessary or we shall become idiotic sure enough. Therefore this guide must continue to suffer" (pp. 366–67). Where the reader would be merely nettled by a guide's complacent confidence in his power to draw worshipful exclamations from tourists, the protagonist and "the boys" tyrannize over a succession of "Fergussons" by a virtuoso game of idiotic impassivity, and so effect an ironic homeopathic cure for frustrated excitability by transferring the condition to their tormentors.

What counts in *Innocents Abroad*, as well as in *Roughing It* and to a large degree all of Twain's works, is not a new vision of reality, at least as this is commonly understood. What matters is an eccentrically mixed and timed hierarchical arrangement of perspectives that are easily accessible in themselves, and whose value is in their rapid mobilization by the author. Taken separately, Twain's culturally instinctive admirations as well as disgusts were his public's, as for instance his contrast of the renovating, energetic confidence of Napoleon III with the torpid rule of the Turkish Sultan over a population sunken in ancient poverty. Twain is typically concerned with exposing a sacrosanct hoax. But this exposure is always performed in the context of "marketable sentiment" (p. 191), a phrase occurring in a context that epitomizes it: the sentimental outrage, sentimentally irreverent buffoonery, and pathetic worship that luridly comprise his rendition of the Heloise and Abelard story. His ready manipulation of the conventions of feeling, ostensibly for the sole sake of truthful exposure, licenses him to indulge unexpectedly in any of them or in any mimicry of them, and gradually tends to blur the normal boundaries between them and their impersonations. The really pertinent test of sincerity in the book's rhetorical system is whether or not a given Twain performance accomplishes the twofold end of relieving excitable feelings and achieving authority over the reader.

The all-inclusive affective import of Twain's first book is that it makes the great stiff mass of conventional modes plastic once more to individual feeling, subject to the torsions of his disbelieving humor as well as his rage, humiliation, frustration, elation, and nostalgic adulation. They become expressive once more, not by being satirically attacked wholesale, but by being surprisingly stretched to accommodate his extremes of sentiment and disbelief. The reader is not freed from them but bound to them the more securely and comfortably for Twain's having made them elastic for expression—*his* expression—once more. We are brought repeatedly, in other words, to the border condition of play where conventions are suited for the articulation of wide-ranging feeling and for mastery by the trickster ego— Twain's ego. Our portion, resulting from the virtuoso's eccentric efforts, is an increased comfort in affective stylistic usages, which seem not as imperiously constricting as they were before.

It may help to clarify my major points thus far if we return once more to James Cox's study. Cox's position is that we come to suspect that Twain's irreverent irony is ubiquitous; thus we are led to ask at any given moment the absurdly humorous question regarding Twain: "Is—is he humorous?" Even granting, for the sake of argument, that this is so, I think Cox clearly has not followed the consequences of his view far enough, since for him Twain's irony only works subversively within the text. To take the example Cox uses: that we should "suspect" Twain's apparently sincere adulatory posture in regard to the antique Pisan tear jug because of the discrepancy between the apparent tone and the object admired. I have also shown that we are systematically faced with such discrepancies because Twain's reactions—irony and satiric invective included—are recurrently in excess of what seems warranted. Surely, for example, Twain's ranking of Tahoe (certainly in excessive terms) over Lake Como is not subverted—by which Cox appears to mean "canceled out" since he speaks of Twain's transformation of everything into irreverence. Twain's pivoting on the name *Tahoe* in an opportunistic attack on the

Indians who named it does not destroy his previous excess but answers it with another. The effect is the establishment of a hierarchy reaching from the Divine down to degraded humans, and, transcending this order, Twain's will to praise and scorn and thus to create such hierarchies. And surely the same reasoning holds true for the tonal mixtures Twain applies to telling the Heloise and Abelard legend. The point in almost every case is that Twain's courtier's feelings of admiration and rebuke overwhelm their objects. In the sense that these feelings have this priority, the objects are a "ruse," the texts a pretext. At this level of argument we can call this situation ironic. We can also with equal justice call it eulogistic, with the focus of eulogy being Mark Twain precisely in his role as supreme courtier exercising his power of verbally discriminating among degrees no matter the inadequacy of the objective environment. Once this is understood, Twain's running battle with other travel writers is seen as more than an incidental drama. He wishes to make them collectively appear the "bedizened courtier" he terms Lake Como, the standard object of their admiration. In the contest over the proper allocation of adulation and blame, Twain is to be the real thing, the courtier whose verbal rankings establish his stylistic authority. The court-ship is a grand enlargement, a one-man performance, of the process of hierarchical identification and "self-interfering" distancing that Kenneth Burke describes, as we noted in the first chapter. Malediction and devotion are mutually facili-tating for Twain. He is always engaged, on a vertical scale of rhetorical ranking, in *reculer pour mieux sauter* as well as *sauter pour mieux reculer*.

Within the narrative, the thematic correlative for this vertical mobilization is that "Mark Twain" cannot con-fidently touch bottom (or top) on original reality and con-comitant original response. Indeed, as if foreknowing, he makes little concerted effort to do so but instead acts out a temperamental failure of discovery. The major reason, we are asked to agree, is that conformist, theatrical conventions of feeling face the protagonist like a physical encrustation at every point of his cultural and religious journey. The ready-made set of worshipful attitudinizing built in at each point frustrates any attempt at response that is not inherently dramatic and in some respect derivative. But the crucial difference between Twain's dramatics and these ready-made sets lies in their utter inertness. The complacently unchanging emotional platitudes in effect ask the attitudinizing pilgrim audience to be the supernal idiot that "Mark Twain" periodically mimics in order to outbid such demands and to move freely up and down the scale of praise and blame. For the coercive conventions cannot be attacked piecemeal, nor will they lend themselves to a revelation of any reality underlying their strata upon strata of commonplaces. They constitute a hierarchy and can only be countered as such. The hierarchy establishes degrees of response ranging from the most elevated praiseworthy objects to the most debased blameworthy, but it has no power to reach the objects it ostensibly gives access to. It is not so much that "Mark Twain" does not think that traditional objects of worship are not worthy as that he can find no unobstructed way to them to find out. In particular, whatever originally was of religious value has been so smeared over with incredible fabrications and centuries of gaudy secondhand emotions that confidence in it is continually baffled and distracted. This is the real vandalism that the book deals with. "Mark Twain's" madcap performances, reaching their appropriate peak in Jerusalem, increasingly become those of a son of Protestantism striving at least to re-juggle the order of interlocked impediments to living imagination that cannot be cleared away.

Both Melville and Twain obtain imaginative leverage on inert play and masquerade by employing the reciprocal metaphors of picnic and pilgrimage. *The Confidence-Man* conceived of life as a picnic *en costume* for "that pilgrim species, man." The Quaker City's voyage launches "a picnic on a gigantic scale" and also, in the words of the book's subtitle, The New Pilgrims' Progress. In Melville's work, the protagonist's advocacy expresses the author's, if not the speaker's, genuine skepticism. In *Innocents Abroad*, flat disbelief, not skepticism, is the primary point here: both metaphors are shown objectively to designate false dreams of anticipated entertainment and piety; yet they also signify true dreams in regard to Twain's own entertaining guidebook.

In his guidebook, Twain restlessly uncovers the necessity for fashioning "new dreams and better," as his last significant hero will counsel in *The Mysterious Stranger*. Yet they are better than the inert illusions only insofar as their manipulation does the authoritative work of beguilement well: they are equally powerless to reveal any deeper, permanent substantial reality. Their fluid hierarchy of feeling also is a reference without a referent outside of the relief it brings its inventor and his reader. Even the undeniably concrete Holy Land is experienced by the protagonist as a counterfeit reality since it trades on religious pieties while its wretchedness and tawdry religious displays frustrate all sense of a transcendent reality and a proper adulation. Twain has but one consideration to fall back on: the comfortable pleasure into which distance, time, and his art can transform the journey's dreary, disappointing frauds. A favorite transformational device is the anticipating memory. This instant nostalgia has a necessary undertone of irony since it implies that the arduous journey through the space and time of the historical Old World is only of value when one largely cancels it in time or space. There is "full comfort in one reflection," that in time "all that will be left will be pleasant memories of Jerusalem, memories we shall call up with always-increasing interest as the years go by, memories which someday will become all beautiful when the last annoyance that encumbers them shall have faded out of our minds never again to return. . . . We are satisfied. We can wait. Our reward will come. To us Jerusalem and today's experiences will be an enchanted memory a year hence—a memory which money could not buy from us" (II, 362–63). Analogously, Twain says of the scene of the Annunciation, "I could sit off several thousand miles and imagine the angel appearing, with shadowy wings and lustrous countenance, and note the glory that streamed downward . . . —anyone can do that beyond the ocean, but few can do it here" (II, 291).

The deceptive pleasure of enchanted memory operates by exactly the same principle of wishful selection as that at work in the picturesque set pieces like Twain's description of Gennesaret by starlight, in the popular or official legends that obscure original historic events, and in the general popular acquiescence to the old masters. In passages such as the ones quoted above, Twain exhibits his genteel qualifications by indicating his capacity for this sort of admiration. But the major implicit idea of every sort of affective palinode is to assert the new master—the priority of his satisfaction by his own authoritative version of illusion. Consequently the pleasures of an alchemic memory substituting for the fraudulent reality can be evoked in other tones, as a few pages earlier:

> Here was a grand Oriental picture which I had worshiped a thousand times in soft, rich steel engravings! But in the engraving there was no desolation; no dirt; no rags; no fleas; no ugly features; no sore eyes; no feasting flies; no besotted ignorance in the countenances; no raw places on the donkeys' backs; no disagreeable jabbering in unknown tongues; no stench of camels; no suggestion that a couple of tons of powder placed under the party and touched off would heighten the effect and give the scene a genuine interest and a charm which it would always be pleasant to recall, even though a man lived a thousand years. (II, 310)

But no satisfaction, not even the relief of humourously phrased vengeance, is permanent since it derives from conjurations without basis except one's ability to maneuver them in endless succession. It follows that there is the recurrent necessity for novelty, for "something fresh" as Twain's gang of Sinners, or Captain Stormfield, would phrase it; and it is as a "novelty in the way of excursions" that Twain had advertised the trip on the narrative's first page. The counterpart of his recurrent necessity for novelty is the equally marketable sentiment of impermanence—nostalgic celebration—which Twain employs as a way of substituting the private past of personal emotional time for the disappointingly recorded public past of history. In the book's closing pages, the historical sense is invoked only to be overwhelmed by a personal and carefully conventional nostalgic rendition. This emotion fittingly sounds in the narrative's last diapason ("vanished and been forgotten!") after the overarching novelty of the work, the entire pleasure pilgrimage, has been exposed as the necessary ruse that it is. "Such is life," Twain says earlier of an artificially created picturesque perspective, "and the trail of the serpent is over us all" (p. 286).

It also follows from the impermanence of satisfaction, as from the whole of *Innocents Abroad*, that a consideration of Twain's views, his "ideas," must first attend to his effort to find and authoritatively wield novelty by systematic contrast with whatever appears worn and defunct. The chameleon character "Mark Twain" acts as a rhetorical membrane, becoming whatever persona—politely sensible observer, credulous clown, ironic commentator—that suits the purposes of novel contrast. These contrasts not only are rhetorically authoritative but also constitute an attempt at achieving a "realizing sense," to use Twain's own habitual phrase. This contrast-centered *realization* of life is the sole endeavor possible in an evanescent world that Twain lacks confidence in, where value is keyed to literary negotiability —which is to say, for Twain, keyed to the inseparable notions of entertainment and adulation, picnic and pilgrimage.

II

Scholarship has shown that in composing *The Innocents Abroad* with an Eastern as well as a Western audience to please, Twain modified the original *Alta California* letters by adding many of the passages, like the second gondolier description, that reinstate the objects he had humorously or non-humorously reduced.[6] I have argued that this method of having it both ways is not adventitious but functional in the book's general scheme, which substitutes Twain's stylistic hegemony for the received authority, his created illusion for the official version. It is functional because of, not despite, its opportunistic basis.

In *Innocents Abroad*, Twain had anticipated audience response and adjusted his tactics accordingly. Upon reading the reviews of this immediately popular first book, Twain delightedly noted that for both Eastern as well as Western readers, "The irreverence of the volume appears to be a tip-top good feature."[7] Twain's second long book concerns an entire community that is, at least on the face of it, altogether irreverent by Eastern genteel standards, the official tenets of the literary world. The general tone and rhetorical strategy hinge upon this fact, which also determines the second book's difference from the first. In *Innocents Abroad*, Twain confronted alone a civilization's structuring of automatic reverence, so that his countering irreverence was militant. For this militancy his only moral support within the narrative was the small coterie of "the boys." However, in *Roughing It*, "the boys" provide the communal norm, and consequently the social order is not attacked but cele-

---

[6] See Leon T. Dickinson, "Mark Twain's Revisions in Writing *The Innocents Abroad*," *American Literature* 19 (1947), 139–57; Dewey Ganzel, *Mark Twain Abroad: The Cruise of the "Quaker City"* (Chicago: University of Chicago Press, 1968). For the original *Alta* travel letters, see *Traveling with the Innocents Abroad*, ed. Daniel M. McKeithan (Norman: University of Oklahoma Press, 1958).

[7] *Letters to Publishers*, p. 28. Typically, Twain added immediately, "though I wish with all my heart there wasn't an irreverent passage in it."

brated. Twain's celebration of the community is inherently and paradoxically an encomium of a certain kind of irreverence, and so eschews, with a few exceptions like the Tahoe episode and the detachable Sandwich Island excursion, both rigorous invective and rapt description. *Roughing It*, though it does not lack acerbity, is a much more serene work than *Innocents Abroad*; its mobility is that of leisurely whim, not excitable temper.

The perspective of celebration is most evident in the second volume, with its nostalgia for the "flush times" and the colorful "nabobs," but the first volume also discloses the basic attitude in the treatment of trickery. In *Innocents Abroad*, when the protagonist's expectations of the Old World were abused, the general insinuation, with a few farcical exceptions, was that the fraudulent older civilization was at fault. In *Roughing It*, when the tenderfoot protagonist is comically deceived, his naiveté is the comic target, and the old-timers' knowing communal experience is thereby positively supported.

As with *Omoo*'s rhetoric, the communal irreverence in question is not likely to be as sharply felt by the modern reader as by Twain's contemporaries. The irreverence can be summed up as *carelessness*—a carelessness not so much insisted on in itself as casually advanced in the pervasive details of Western life-style. The details principally concern matters in which carelessness is, by genteel standards, a synonym for social irreverence: clothing, money, and the truth. Western carelessness in dress is ironically introduced in the opening pages by an exaggeration of Eastern propriety and its negation. First the travelers mourn the "sad parting" from their "swallow-tail coats and white kid gloves" and from all such apparel "necessary to make life calm and peaceful." Then they strip to their underwear to enjoy the overland stage ride. Disreputable dress is thereafter the style of such representative men as Scotty Briggs and, for a time, "Mark Twain" himself. The importance of financial enterprise in the official national culture finds a dramatic parallel in the flush times of silver and gold mining, but the arbitrary luck that usually separates great wealth from hopeful scrounging, as well as the Western habit of spending sprees, completely flaunts the official morality of acquisition through orderly stages of work and capitalization through sober saving. As for social norms of truth, a relaxed attitude toward veracity reclines in everything from the artistic pseudo-lying of George Bemis' tall tale to "Mark Twain's" casual invention of news as a reporter and his inflation of mining prospects in exchange for "feet" of ownership.

The purpose of these devices is not to satirize Eastern mores; neither the book's offhand tone nor the scattered Eastern references are suited to such an aim. The purpose is to define Western life by Twain's favorite method of contrast in which Western novelty can have meaning only if periodically offset by what is accustomed and (in this context) seems outworn. As *Roughing It* presents them, the genteel mores are a cultural stylization of the principle that status is founded on meticulous effort and moral strenuousness; the Western are a stylization of potency allied with unstrained ease and laxity. The book's running joke, especially in the first volume, is that the protagonist confuses Western style with fact and repeatedly finds back-breaking labor in what had appeared easy.

The wholesale communal relaxation, amplified considerably by Twain's lounging, digressive rhetoric, belies Cox's notion that the book rouses the reader to skeptical questioning about truth. Cox attempts to clinch this idea, oddly enough, by citing Bemis' tall tale, accurately described as the defining form of the book. Bemis' story of a buffalo climbing a tree, like most literary tall tales, is a ritual play with the pose of lying—and with the pose of truth. In the Western communal ritual of the tall tale, the category of truth/lie is irrelevant literally. Veracity matters only because it has prestigious power outside the ritual circle and is therefore the more satisfying to manipulate by a feigned concern for it. Engaging in ritual questions at the story's conclusion extends the pleasure by a poker-faced sharing of implicit outlook toward the uses of truth and falsehood. The in-group pleasure is often heightened further by the inclusion in the audience of a neophyte who is really baffled or deceived by the tale. Twain's presentation is more subtle than this, however. Bemis' listeners are themselves all neophytes, travelers on the very point of entering the Far West region, and they are farcically uncertain about how to take such an extravagant report. The questions that they in fact ask serve as rhetorical approximations for the correct attitude, which is left for the reader to appropriate. That is, the absurdity of the story's events removes it completely from any real question of falsity *or* truth—we are scarcely going to worry about the objective reality of a bull making his plans, climbing the tree, and all the rest of it. But the fact that the represented audience persists in trying to think of Bemis' yarn in empirical terms make the pleasure even stronger. It is as if they ask in earnest skepticism the virtuoso questions that we, the superior audience, would have asked in mock solemnity. We are to be the old-timers, and the ritual in reality exists between Bemis and ourselves. Bemis' last reply to his interlocutors condenses the attitude toward literal truth and a whole Western posture toward experience: " 'I never saw anybody as particular as you are about a little thing like that' " (VII, 65).

To be in a really skeptical frame of mind about such a yarn as Bemis' is to be as much befooled as to be deceived by it. Similarly, to think with Cox that Twain's rhetoric later frames for us a genuine choice of biographical fact concerning the blind lead episode and Twain's claim to lost wealth is to confound the biographer's special curiosity (the records do not support Twain's assertion, Cox reports) with the ideal reader's concerns summoned up and delimited by the rhetoric. After all, a tall tale about searching for riches in the West would not be complete without such an incident of monetary wealth lost through *over*-carelessness. Even aside from the general tenor of the book, in the immediate context, when Twain says that his moment of wealth was a true event, he protests lest the reader think the episode a "fancy sketch" (VII, 325)—the same formula he had used earlier to protest the substantial accuracy of the hilarious "Mexican plug" swindle. In short, one is not supposed really to care one way or the other. Playing with caring is the point.

In the lawless West that *Roughing It* presents, most of the buffers of an established society are absent, and survival, much less success, means that the usual habits of internal censorship must be either abandoned or quickly transformed into a more rough-and-ready Virginia City analogue. One way to show the process of abandonment and transformation in such a community is *au tragique*, somewhat in the manner of Melville's *Redburn*. Here, whatever the rhetorical strategy, change must be given body in a coherent succession of genuinely transformational events featuring the protagonist. Twain's method in his second book has for its primary target the reader. The method is the rhetoric that puts the reader in the "Washoe" frame of mind by playfully relaxing a censor that is, in terms of Western communal life, too particular about "little things." We are to be, as Twain describes his audience in his preface, "the resting reader." As befits the audience of a tall tale, we are prompted to an attitude in accord with the governing narrative perspective: experienced relaxation expressed in amusement at the folly of the uninitiated and appreciative bemusement at the community's wild spirit.

With the most important implications for the course of his subsequent writings, Twain's overall stance is that of flexible authorial marginality. As author, he moves about familiarly over the depicted community without ever fully being of it, his tone generally taking its cue from the specific position of "Mark Twain" within the social hierarchy, and each social class in turn seeming to be the most attractive as he reaches it. On one page, the protagonist is one of "the boys," beating about the rocks and gullies of Nevada and California in search of instant riches; correspondingly, the authorial tone is genially egalitarian. On another page, the protagonist's fortunes temporarily improve, as when he first dons the boiled shirt of a newspaper reporter; and Twain's perspective also elevates a perceptible notch to regard a "stalwart" Scotty Briggs with genial superiority. The idea of social initiation is itself to be played with and made a joke, for to take it in any other fashion would imply that transformation *mattered* and would therefore be a barrier to the attitude required. In the random world of the book, the protagonist's "variegated vagabondizing" (vii, v) entails metamorphoses of outlook as facile as his transformation from miner to newspaper reporter by a change in costume and a lecture from his superior on confidence in his new role. Similarly, the reader is coached to take the proper attitude by a tacit assumption that, as in Bemis' story, he already has it.

All of Twain's rhetorical authority is bent toward fostering this insouciance; this posture is Twain's essential Western adventure, the Western community as experienced from within, and it is the book's fundamental import.

Twain's pleasure is to deliver his meandering yarn according to two casual tenets, one proleptically stated in the preface, and the second inferable from another defining tall tale, Jim Blaine's "Grandfather's Ram" story. Twain declares in his prefatory note that, although the book is intended to "help the resting reader while away an idle hour," the amount of information in it "could not be helped: information appears to stew out of me naturally, like the precious otter of roses out of the otter. Sometimes it has seemed to me that I would give worlds if I could retain my facts; but it cannot be. The more I calk up the sources, and the tighter I get, the more I leak wisdom. Therefore, I can only claim indulgence at the hands of the reader, not justification." Here facts are comically transposed from the realm of objective reality into the personality afflicting Mark Twain, and for the sake of the pun on "tight," facticity itself accedes to a metaphor in which calking a container makes it leak more. The way the author must do things "naturally" will determine the narrative method, and the comic apology only emphasizes the sovereignty of the authorial personality in Twain's claim that he himself is powerless before it. We are again reminded of this ironically self-effacing narrative mastery when Twain urges us to skip a factual chapter (VIII, chapter xi) if we wish and when he thinks better of apologizing for a forthcoming digression because "I digress constantly, anyhow . . ." (VIII, 87). The implied author is the first and most important character, albeit a virtual one, in the gallery of Western types whose dominant temperaments are allowed eccentric cultivation by the laxity of social and legal restraints. A comic version of restraint demonstrates what happens if a storyteller has his container calked: when a man is warned against inflicting the much-repeated Horace Greeley anecdote on the travelers, "In trying to retain the anecdote in his system he strained himself and died in our arms" (VII, 165).

The pun on tightness in the preface also foreshadows Jim Blaine's "symmetrically drunk" flow of memories, which "the boys" use to dupe the protagonist by playing on his expectation of orderly narrative. Blaine's maundering story compactly exaggerates Twain's leisurely recollections, in which each brief episode is as liable to be coupled to the next by a transitional "that reminds me" as by chronological advancement. The implied author of *Roughing It* is a creature of capricious memory as well as capricious facts, and both easily recurrent whims are rhetorical gestures of relaxation. We are invited to rough it by submitting the moral-perceptive censor to the gentle befuddlement proper to enjoying Jim Blaine's tale. This state is requisite as well for enjoying the fictive mining community's revel of speculative confidence, a whole social dis-order built on mutually negotiated illusions unfunded by little but imagination and crazy hope, yielding the euphoria that Twain celebrates. The book's unhurried sorting through strands of information and anecdotal memory at once comically offsets the feverish revel and enacts the relaxation of constraints that permits it. When, to the delight of "the boys," the protagonist is "sold" by his inappropriate expectations of Blaine's story, he is helping to ritualize the communal confidence game operating at all levels: the daily exchanges of trickery in which mines are salted, nonexistent "feet" are bought and sold, and newspaper puffery is the accustomed verbal counterpart of the general inflation.

With Blaine's story, Twain discovers a major theme that perfects the comedy of memory first performed in "Jim Smiley and his Jumping Frog." In the rambling stories as told by Simon Wheeler and Blaine, we are first of all engaged by the fictional narrator's own musing fascination with the world he recalls. What is persuasive, too, is the comic discrepancy between the narrator's wondering nostalgia (" 'I don't reckon them times will ever come again,' " Blaine begins) and the means he has for expressing it. Not far beneath the comic stylization, one senses the disparity between the hollow account of adventures and the meaningful feelings that originally accompanied the events and still attend them in memory.

Blaine's tale comically treats the process wherein imagination redigests memory in order to make events, in some final way, real. Specifically, the underlying act converted into humor is the attempt at achieving a realizing sense by investing events with the significant coherence of rank-ordering, thus making them sufficiently substantial to validate strong feeling. In *Roughing It* Twain discovers the comic possibilities of Providence, in this case as the significant ordering principle Blaine's inebriated memory struggles toward in slow motion through whatever was best or most extreme of its kind. Blaine's ruminating conservation of the past, taking the most surprising and comically inscrutable turns in the associative chain, farcically vindicates the moral he imputes to his history: " 'there ain't anything ever reely lost' " (VIII, 125) in Providence's mysterious linkages and appointed acts. Blaine's disorderly account and his drunken confidence in Providential order combine as a joke confirming the book's portrayal of a haphazard existence and the stance appropriate to it. The jest is sharpened by the realization that, given the absurd connections the story-teller both attributes to Providence and dramatizes in his technique, there is a suggested proportion of "order": Blaine's eccentric disarray of memories is to his story as Providence is to life.

The idea of Providence had been broached earlier to make a similar comic point about randomness as well as life-style. In the Hyde-Morgan hoax, Providence becomes the central device for duping the self-important Easterner, Attorney General Buncombe. Buncombe's defense of his client exhibits a moral strenuousness and an obtuseness to preposterous fun that are antithetical to the communal style. In his "impassioned effort" (VII, 269), he pounds the table and grandiloquently quotes every conceivable author-ity to defend Hyde against Morgan's pretended claim to his property because a landslide has allegedly moved Mor-gan's ranch on top of Hyde's. Buncombe cites every author-ity, that is, but the One that trumps in the judge's mock decision that the landslide was " 'a visitation of God' " for inscrutable purposes: " 'Heaven created the ranches, and it is Heaven's prerogative to rearrange them, to experiment with them, to shift them around at its pleasure. It is for us to submit, without repining' " (VII, 271). A second enlist-ment of Providence by Twain compounds the irreverence by further sporting with hierarchy. In his tale, Blaine sees a divine dispensation in a missionary's being eaten by cannibals, since despite the missionary's preaching " 'noth-ing never fetched them but that.' " Twain's rendition of the Providential chain of consumption operating in desolate Mono Lake allows him a glancing blow at the Indians: "Providence leaves nothing to go by chance. All things have their uses and their part and proper place in Nature's econ-omy: the ducks eat the flies—the flies eat the worms—the

Indians eat all three—the wild cats eat the Indians—the white folks eat the wild cats—and thus all things are lovely" (VII, 297).

Blaine's fable illustrates how generally effective a mask of authority naive humor is for Twain, indeed more effective a concealment than the ironies that call attention to their equivocality. This humor, broad though it is in one sense, is so delicately dependent on just the right trick of represented voice and manner, and conduces to such a responsively naive lowering of guard on the reader's part, that to speak (however correctly) of a ratio between Blaine's eccentric recollections and his drunkenly moralized Providence seems impossibly heavy. For part of Blaine's comic performance is his very attempt to be an exegete to Providence and in effect to his own tale—as by solemnly explaining how his uncle, not his uncle's dog, was appointed to save the falling Irishman because " 'the dog would a seen him a coming and stood from under. That's the reason the dog warn't appinted. A dog can't be depended on to carry out a special providence' " (VIII, 125).

Depending on the rhetorical scene that is set, such complacent idiocy can give rise to at least two different reactions in the listener. One is frustrated fury at the utterly impervious stupidity manifested; and a humorous counter to this incipient feeling is the unassumingly bland response that, as with "the boys" and the guides in *Innocents Abroad*, doubles back frustration upon the one who produced it. But Twain has combined move and countermove here: Blaine is the epitome of unassuming blandness who nevertheless doggedly, gently pursues his preoccupations.[8] Instead of the emphasis lying on Twain's sensitive reaction, we are placed face to face with Blaine, with only a frame-device mediation. When to this is added the farcical covert self-exegesis, in-

---

[8] After these chapters were written, Joseph Doherty pointed out to me that Kenneth Burke makes reference to Twain's general "bland strategy" in "Rhetoric—Old and New," *New Rhetorics*, ed. Martin Steinmann, Jr. (New York: Scribner's, 1967), p. 71.

tellectual frustration is defused because intellection is denied by the speaker's unassuming demeanor and unconscious exaggeration. As a Freudian account would put it, the energy economized by this quick arousal and denial of intellection is discharged in humorous pleasure. And, I venture to add, one finds Blaine "lovable" because he spares us the intellectual frustration of the confusion he pertinaciously fuddles through; we are psychically disengaged in regard to intellectual acuity and attendant bafflement, and we are engaged by the rhetor, Blaine himself. (All this is why, upon coming to a piece of criticism—any criticism—after having been freshly exposed to Twain's best humor, one is liable to feel "a condition bordering on impatience" worthy of Twain, at having to reengage intellect and tempt frustration.)

Thus the parody of exegesis blandly defends against our analysis at the same time that it comically anticipates the tale's own misconstruing by the hopelessly solemn language and viewpoint of discursive reasoning. This immediate but equivocal resistance is a major element of Twain's humor, which insulates itself in this fashion because its success depends upon instant intuitive perception, the lightning-flash effect Twain described in his letters and critical comments. This is also partly why Twain's writing must rely for its success on clearly delineated, easily accessible cultural conventions. A contrast in humorous strategy should help to make the point clearer. In *Moby-Dick*, the gamesome humor of Melville's narrator invited questioning and analysis in order eventually to show both their inevitability and their limitation. Twain's makes them seem superfluous yet ruefully predictable. Melville's is a strategy of inducing skepticism; Twain's disowns the inhibitions that make skepticism possible or necessary.

Blaine is the exemplary rhetor of the second volume of *Roughing It* as Bemis is of the first. If Bemis' narrative first encapsulated the rhetorical nature of the book and a posture suited to entering the Western community, Blaine's espouses the rewards of looking backward to praise. Look backward Twain does, as in Scotty Briggs' tribute to the deceased hero, Buck Fanshaw, and in the evocation of the old gold rush in Sacramento Valley, now a "lifeless, homeless solitude" depopulated of its "erect, bright-eyed, quick-moving, strong-handed young giants" in the "noblest holocaust that ever wafted its sacrificial incense heavenward" (VIII, 156–57). There is also, among numerous other instances, the re-membered anecdote in which this vanished all-male popula-tion encountered a woman "with the look of men who listened to a *memory* instead of a present reality" (p. 158)— Twain achieving a double-barreled nostalgia here—and Dick Baker's memories of his cat, Tom Quartz. This change in temporal perspective, frequently noted in criticism, is reflected at the factual level as well, as in the typical for-mula, "An extract or two from the newspapers of the day will furnish. . . ." In the second volume we have stepped backward from the immediacy of the Western community, and in that step back we discover the limits of Mark Twain's irreverence again. Indeed, we discover that the irreverence is in the service of benediction.

For, with all the carelessness of the Western communal style, the conventions of feeling are more than given their careful due. The second volume, analogous to the substi-tution devices of *Innocents Abroad*, is a reinstatement of important matters that may have been handled too roughly in the first; Twain knows that for his public as for himself this is primarily an issue of common modes of feeling, es-pecially involving the satisfactions of praise. Near the be-ginning of the second volume, Twain's refurbishment of easy sentiment in treating Buck Fanshaw's funeral is ac-complished by comically stylizing Scotty Briggs' testimony to his departed friend and contrasting it to the parson's equally exaggerated propriety of speech. The "stalwart's" language is a comparative novelty, but the rough heart-of-gold comradeship it glories in is an emotional cliché. Here Twain's disposition toward the vernacular, but not the sentiment, is condescending. Comic misunderstandings aside, the reverent parson and careless Westerner speak the same basic language on the most important issue. This is the reassurance Twain had already provided in the Sanitary Flour Sack auction; he continues to furnish it principally by variations on the tonalities of nostalgia.

The book's two concluding episodes round off the experience of the West, which is the experience of reading Twain's book. The first is the account of how "Mark Twain," now trying his hand at lecturing, triumphs over his initial audience. He does so with a trick that backfires, but still leads to success. Fearing that his first lecture will be a disaster, he arranges to have confederates in the audience, who at a given signal will laugh and thus trigger the mirth of the other listeners. The device works admirably throughout most of the talk.

> Presently, I delivered a bit of serious matter with impressive unction (it was my pet), and the audience listened with an absorbed hush that gratified me more than any applause; and as I dropped the last word of the clause, I happened to turn and catch Mrs. ——'s intent and waiting eye; my conversation with her flashed upon me, and in spite of all I could do I smiled. She took it for the signal, and promptly touched off the whole audience; and the explosion that followed was the triumph of the evening. . . . But my poor little morsel of pathos was ruined. It was taken in good faith as an intentional joke, and the prize one of the entertainment, and I wisely let it go at that. (pp. 330–31)

The point is not that the pathos of the lecture, or book, lacks sincerity according to the applicable standards: pathos is as much a performance as is the intentionally irreverent humor. The decisive point of the passage, as of the sequence leading to the audience's laughter, is the narrator's inability to suppress himself "in spite of all I could do." Yet this expression of his unreliable moods wins his audience, gains ascendency over its feelings and completely redirects them

into "the triumph of the evening." Formally, we are returned to the book's preface, in which we originally came
under the imaginative jurisdiction of the author's irrepres-
sible temperament. But we have never really left that
jurisdiction. The protagonist "wisely" lets both humor and
pathos go as they will, as long as the triumph is forthcoming.
Surely by the end of our Western adventure we should be as
wise. And the triumph is the redirection of all the book's
laudatory momentum to its true intended focal point, the
communal nexus, the performer himself.

This winning of an audience is the real end of the adventure, as the last episode shows. Whereas the lecture was
a trick that backfired pleasurably, the brief return to Washoe is terminated by a trick on "Mark Twain" that turns
completely sour. With the holdup hoax, the revels of "the
boys" are ended: "Since then I play no practical jokes on
people and generally lose my temper when one is played
upon me" (p. 338). We are back in the quotidian world
again. An authorial presence has emerged from its masks of
naiveté and insouciant chicanery to reveal a sober visage,
the very image of an authoritative personality who really
brooks no infringement of his dignity. At least this is the
impressive effect that is produced, consolidating Twain's
imaginative jurisdiction by a final reassurance that the
resting reader's moral relaxation was overseen by a responsible manager. The question is not whether this sober citizen
is "really" but another authorial mask; the point is that the
reader, for clearly functional rhetorical reasons, is encour-
aged to think that it is not, but that he has been reading an
author sufficiently confident of his own basic personal
propriety that he can afford to play entertainingly and with
bland equivocality outside its strict confines. The book
closes with the protagonist's departure on the *Quaker City*
for Europe and the Holy Land, where Twain does indeed
lose his temper and makes capital of the process. But we've
been there before.

Twain's authority is secured in *Roughing It* by the
fraudulently smiling, easy potency and superior mobility he

represents in one of the book's best-known sketches, the coyote outmaneuvering the town dog. The disreputable coyote, the totemic trickster, is the totem of the West Twain enacts and depicts. Yet the animal's cowardice and shameless scavenging make him for Twain a spiritual brother to the Indians. Like Lake Tahoe in *Innocents Aboard*, the coyote is a pivotal metaphor that allows Twain to be both eulogistic and dyslogistic in establishing a pyramid of superiority—or establishing a pyramid and then pivoting it onto its head, giving priority to neither pyramid nor inversion. The coyote has such confidence in his power that he can afford to play with it and, by deceitfully seeming to be less able than he is, trick the earnestly straining town dog. The book comically shows that the reverse is also true: a properly Western casual potency can derive from confident equivocality.

But without ceasing to be displaced into performance, the feared and desired qualities condensed in the ambiguous coyote are never very far from mind. When the protagonist is "scared into being a city editor" by the imminent prospect of humiliating scavenging if he does not take the job, he is lectured by the chief editor: " 'Never say "We learn" so-and-so, or "It is reported," or "It is rumored," or "We understand" so-and-so, but go to headquarters and get the absolute facts, and then speak out and say "It *is* so-and-so." Otherwise, people will not put confidence in your news. Unassailable certainty is the thing that gives a newspaper the firmest and most valuable reputation.' " And Twain agrees, "It was the whole thing in a nutshell . . ." (VIII, 19). This counsel of unassailable certainty and confidence is the same that the cub pilot "Mark Twain" will receive from his superior Horace Bixby. In *Roughing It*, the fledgling editor promptly goes out and wins the public's confidence by fabricating what news he cannot find, though he eventually becomes adept enough as a reporter not to depart "noticeably" from fact. He has written himself into being the writer who composes the book we are reading.

7

River Courtship: "Old Times on the Mississippi"

> ... *that gracious severity which knows that it is its mission to maintain the* order *of rank in the world, among things themselves—and not only among men.*
>
> Nietzsche, *Beyond Good and Evil*

In *The Gilded Age*, the genius of idolatry gave his period in history its fitting name. This is the book's social importance. Its literary importance is briefly expressible: Colonel Sellers. As a jointly authored work of the imagination, *The Gilded Age* will not bear much scrutiny. It is not, to the extent of Melville's third book, *Mardi*, an instructive failure, although it indicates a similar attempt at a more thoroughly fictive creation, and a fantastic one, after each author's first book of picturesque art and a second of picaresque. *Roughing It* was a literary tall tale, which is to say an entertaining pretense at trickery. Colonel Sellers provides a cognate pleasure in the continual failure of his transparent schemes. Sellers also represents an advance in Twain's practice of the palinode. Sellers may be called a palinode character, one who can exercise a propensity and simultaneously retract it in a rhetorical sense because he is harmless and unsuccessful. Into Sellers' creation goes Twain's device of reinstatement as well as the characters "Mark Twain" and Jim Blaine; eventually emerging from Sellers will be Tom Sawyer and Huck Finn. Twain clearly wants to see a manipulator of confidence like Sellers as innocent and lovable, in contradistinction to Senator Dilworthy, the despicable confidence man. Sellers' efforts at social climbing up to and above the Senator's level thus introduce in consecutive narrative form and in a manner purified of censurable wrongdoing, the notions of hierarchy and "court-ship" that dominate the remainder of Twain's career as fictional signatures of his authority. By fictional signatures I mean to suggest the shift of emphasis from direct perfor-mance by author and persona to the traditional devices of story. "Old Times on the Mississippi" presents the first complete flowering in Twain's novelistic development of what Kenneth Burke has called the hierarchical motive. Here we move, as in Twain's first two books, from an empha-sis on attack to a stress on celebration. We move from the Gilded Age to the Golden.

The first thing noteworthy about "Old Times on the Mississippi" is that it was not originally published in the subscription market. The second is that a particular respon-sive audience was in Twain's mind during the genesis of a concrete form and its full realization. The inception and development of the series for Howells' *Atlantic* is not an unfamiliar story, but it deserves brief recapitulation as an indispensable record of Twain's creative transactions.

In letters written in 1866 and 1871, Twain had alluded generally to a projected book about the Mississippi. He had written his wife in the latter year, ". . . I bet you I will make a standard work."[1] But when Howells approached him in 1874 for contributions to the *Atlantic,* Twain at first wrote that he could think of nothing to submit. Two hours later, Twain wrote again, retracting the statement: "For [the Rev-erend Joseph] Twichell & I have had a long walk in the woods & I got to telling him about old Mississippi days of steam-boating glory & grandeur as I saw them (during 5 years) *from the pilot house.* He said, 'What a virgin subject to hurl into a magazine!' I hadn't thought of that before. Would you like a series of papers to run through 3 months or 6 or 9—or about 4 months say?"[2] Pretty clearly what had

[1] *The Love Letters of Mark Twain,* ed. Dixon Wecter (New York: Harper, 1949), p. 166.
[2] *The Mark Twain-Howells Letters,* ed. Henry Nash Smith and William Gibson (2 vols.; Cambridge: Harvard University Press, 1960), I, 34.

not crystallized before was the specific focus and vantage point to govern what he had earlier merely called his "Mississippi book" and, with his eyes typically on glory before the book had any definite shape, "a standard work." The key phrases are "steamboating glory & grandeur" and "from the pilot house"; they evidence, in the context of Twain's yarning to Twichell, an inchoate artistic form. This incipient design is summoned not only by anticipation of a definite readership but by two mediating audiences, two "respectable" admiring friends, existing in clear relationship to that prestigious readership. But Howells is not only a mediator, he is the linchpin in the ensemble.

Howells' eventually close friendship with Twain was still in the late courting stage during the period at hand. What the courtship partly entailed is evident in Twain's acknowledgment of the complimentary review of *Sketches, New and Old* that Howells wrote shortly after the "Old Times" series ended:

> The newspaper praises bestowed upon the "Innocents Abroad" were large and generous, but somehow I hadn't *confidence* in the critical judgment of the parties who furnished them. *You* know how that is, yourself, from reading the newspaper notices of your own books. They gratify a body, but they always leave a small pang behind in the shape of a fear that the critic's good words could not safely be depended upon as *authority*. Yours is the recognized critical Court of Last Resort in this country; from its decision there is no appeal; and so, to have gained this decree of yours before I am forty years old, I regard as a thing to be right down proud of.[3]

To conceive a very rough approximation of the Twain-Howells relationship, it is as if Melville had had as a continuing confidant Hawthorne and Evert Duyckinck rolled into one. Melville had expressed "unspeakable security" at

3 *Ibid.*, pp. 106–07.

Hawthorne's private praise of *Moby-Dick* as well as despair of the public's approbation. By contrast, Twain's stress on the *confidence* and *authority* invested in Howells' "recognized Court" speaks volumes for the tight interdependency these notions had for him. Though Melville was strongly interested in popular acceptance, nothing in his letters or elsewhere shows that the expert authoritative response that mattered must have general recognition. Indeed, instead of Hawthorne's being anything approaching a recognized critical court during Melville's crucial period, it was Melville who as an anonymous reviewer had solicited public attention to Hawthorne's genius. None of this necessarily makes Twain or Melville "superior," whatever that would mean. But the difference between the courtships does go far toward describing Twain's creative persuasions to confidence.

The word *courtship* perhaps seems a bit theatrical. Nevertheless, it is the most exact possible term in every sense. It is suggestive that immediately before Twain submitted his first, nostalgic "Old Times" installment, he sent Howells a "letter" ostensibly meant for Olivia Clemens, consisting entirely of a mock-nostalgic literary performance featuring Twain, Howells, and other friends as comically aged, and socially arrived, courtiers—Lords and Ladies in the (Irish) Empire, formerly America. A few days later, Twain wrote Howells, "Oh, that letter wasn't written to my wife, but to *you*."[4] My intention is just the opposite of questioning

---

[4] *Ibid.*, p. 44. In his excellent chapter on Olivia Clemens, "The Muse of Samuel Clemens," James Cox points out how Twain's idolatry functioned to establish her as his self-appointed censor. When she protested that "it was unchristian to be so worshipped, he blandly replied that perhaps his idolatry might lead him toward her God. . . . Through all the reverence of his [courtship] style, Olivia was quick to sense the heresy of his courtly love." And Cox quotes one of Twain's letters to Olivia: "I have faith in you—a faith which is as simple & unquestioning as the faith of a devotee in the idol he worships." *Fate of Humor*, pp. 72–73.

In this context, Twain's humorously courtly letter to Olivia/Howells takes on additional significance—whether looked at as rhetoric or symbolic action.

Twain's real affection for the man whose letters began "My dear Clemens," to whom Twain almost always signed himself in an abbreviated nom de plume, "Mark." The point is that Twain's italics in the letter quoted above are of paramount significance for the literary approbation he coveted. Twain's courtship (which was by no means one-way) aimed at completely prepossessing an authority worthy of confidence, one whose value judgments were "recognized." The first sketch submitted to Howells was accompanied by this brief note: "Cut it, scarify it, reject it—handle it with entire freedom."[5] It can be no mere coincidence that the narrative weight of "Old Times" falls upon a closely comparable persuasion of authority and garnering of confident recognition and status. Thus when the young "Mark Twain" sees that he "must contrive a new career," he plans a "siege against" the eminent pilot Bixby to admit him to apprenticeship. The apprenticeship commences with Bixby's profane excoriation of the new cub, and its success hinges solely on this one man's public approbation of "Mark Twain."

For my purposes, it would be clumsy to proceed now by reading "Old Times" as an allegory of one phase in a biographical relationship. Even if correct, this would merely lead to Samuel L. Clemens. I wish to go in the opposite direction—to Mark Twain, at once performer and performance, for whom a sense of audience was a primary constitutive element of virtuosity. My view is that the relationship with Howells itself partly involved a semiliterary rhetoric, a "courtly" courtship directed by Twain's ambition for status. "Old Times," written for Howells as much as for the *Atlantic*, is consequently the product of Twain's doubled concern for questions of ascendancy and confidence. One reflection of this absorption is the directness with which he entertains these questions in the series. A second is the work's lucid sensitivity to every graduation of assurance and commanding status, a plotting of the comic hero's course in

5 *Twain-Howells Letters*, p. 42.

advancement and in progressively refined appreciation that makes "Old Times" akin to the standard nineteenth century novels of ambition. The very first sentence deals with the constancy of an ambition, and the first two paragraphs are dominated by the repeated key term. As for Twain's authority, it arises first in the special excitement of encountering a writer who has fully hit his stride for the first time. Yet to say, accurately, that "Old Times" contains Twain's best writing in nonvernacular prose clearly makes no absolute claim for the inspiration of the cultural saving remnant who, theoretically at any rate, read the *Atlantic*. "Nonvernacular" is plainly an important qualification, showing the book's limitation measured in terms of Twain's subsequent vernacular masterpiece, which would be written for a mass subscription audience.

As he composed the series, Twain continued to benefit primarily, not from Howells' explicit recommendations, but from a suggestive relationship that stirred Twain's deepest creative motives. Additionally, no small part was played by the receptive air Howells carefully maintained and the sense of immediate audience reaction he gave his prize performer. Thus, besides the comprehensive narrative concern for competent assurance in "Old Times," specific credit for the work's fresh stylistic conviction must probably be apportioned to the courtship between two talented writers and the redoubled awareness of position it bred. The conviction that Twain achieves is largely a function of his elevated, yet largely amiable, perspective regarding his material; the perspective not only gave Twain the confidence to deal crisply with "low" matters before his combined public-private readership, but, as I will show, served in several ways to make the work successful.

After receiving and praising Twain's first "Old Times" sketch, Howells wrote advice that defines the inside audience's salient attributes: shrewd editorial instinct for Twain's concerns, and strategic assurance of sympathetic reception: ". . . I should say, stick to actual fact and character in the thing, and give things in *detail*. *All* that belongs with old river life is novel and is now mostly historical. Don't write *at* any supposed Atlantic audience, but yarn it off as if into my sympathetic ear. Don't be afraid of rests or pieces of dead color. I fancied a sort of hurried and anxious air in the first."[6] However, this letter crossed Twain's letter of the same date, which suggested a conception of the work rather different from Howells'. It suggested, specifically, Twain's allegiance to the original formative concept, piloting, whereas Howells advocated something approximating Twain's first two books, or the "standard work" earlier contemplated. Twain wrote:

> Let us change the heading to "*Piloting* on the Miss in the Old Times"—or to "*steamboating* on the M in the Old Times"—or to "Personal Old Times on the Missi". . . .
>
> I suggest it because the present heading is too pretentious, too broad & general. It seems to command me to deliver a Second Book of Revelation to the world . . . whereas here I have finished Article No. III & am about to start on No. 4 and yet I have spoken of nothing but of Piloting as a science so far; and I doubt if I ever get beyond that portion of my subject. And I don't care to. Any muggins can write about Old Times on the Miss. of 500 different kinds, but I am the only man alive that can scribble about the piloting of that day. . . . Its newness pleases me all the time—and it is about the only new subject I know of. If I were to write fifty articles they would all be about pilots and piloting—therefore let's get the word Piloting into the heading. There's a world of freshness about that, too.[7]

After this stress on the work's novel personal authority, Twain later replied to Howells' reassurances:

> It isn't the Atlantic audience that distresses me; for *it* is the only audience that I sit down before in perfect

6 *Ibid.*, p. 46.   7 *Ibid.*, p. 47.

serenity (for the simple reason that it don't require a˙ "humorist" to paint himself striped & stand on his head every fifteen minutes.) The trouble was, that I was only bent on "working up an atmosphere" & that is to me a most fidgety & irksome thing sometimes. I avoid it, usually, but in this case it was absolutely necessary, else every reader would be applying the atmosphere of his own river or sea experiences, & *that* shirt wouldn't fit, you know.[8]

These selected exchanges, as well as the general drift of other correspondence, outline the rather differing conceptions each man had of Twain's aim and consequently highlight Twain's actual procedure. Howells' suspicion of haste was a canny guess at Twain's strong sense of audience, but it basically resulted from the editor's expectations of a more detailed local-color study, as another tactful comment on the first sketch further makes clear: "The sketch of the low-lived little town was so good, that I could have wished ever so much more of it; and perhaps the tearful watchman's story might have been abridged—tho this may seem different in print."[9] In fact, critics have generally followed Howells instead of Twain in the sense that they have given as much attention to the opening description of Hannibal as they have to the famous pilot-versus-passenger views of the sunset. Since *Life on the Mississippi* does turn out to be a broader cultural study, it is perhaps understandable that most commentators have neglected episodes like the watchman passage in favor of Twain's "atmosphere." But in 1875, the long book is still eight years away from publication, and our business is with the far superior "Old Times." Perhaps the watchman and his apparent contextual opposite, the mate, can be as revealing about this work as pilot and passenger.

"Mark Twain's" encounter with the sentimental watchman climaxes and terminates the first sketch (comprising chapters 1 and 2 of "Old Times," chapters 4 and 5 of *Life on the Mississippi*). It will be recalled that the protagonist had conceived the ambition of becoming a steamboat pilot, the "one permanent ambition" among the village boys being that of "steamboatman," and pilot being the most glamorous and powerful position. The first chapter ends with the rebuff of an initial meek inquiry after the pilots, and a rejection by underlings at that: "but I had comforting daydreams of a future when I should be a great and honored pilot, with plenty of money, and could kill some of these mates and clerks and pay for them." Later, "Mark Twain" is again cuttingly snubbed by a mate, but he still does not lose his admiration for the officer's profane style of giving an order: " '. . . *for'ard* with it 'fore I make you swallow it, you dash-dash-dash-*dashed* split between a tired mud-turtle and a crippled hearse-horse.' I wished I could talk like that." Then begins the courting of another stylist, but now at the comically lowest rung of officialdom. The episode, considering its neglect, deserves full quotation as a presage of the coming adventures:

When the soreness of my adventure with the mate had somewhat worn off, I began timidly to make up to the humblest official connected with the boat—the night watchman. He snubbed my advances at first, but I presently ventured to offer him a new chalk pipe, and that softened him. So he allowed me to sit with him by the big bell on the hurricane deck, and in time he melted into conversation. He could not well have helped it, I hung with such homage on his words and so plainly showed that I felt honored by his notice. He told me the names of dim capes and shadowy islands as we glided by them in the solemnity of the night, under the winking stars, and by and by got to talking about himself. He seemed over-sentimental for a man whose salary was six dollars a week—or rather he might have seemed so to an older person than I.

But I drank in his words hungrily, and with a faith that might have moved mountains if it had been applied judiciously. What was it to me that he was soiled and seedy and fragrant with gin? What was it to me that his grammar was bad, his construction worse, and his profanity so void of art that it was an element of weakness rather than strength in his conversation? He was a wronged man, a man who had seen trouble, and that was enough for me. As he mellowed into his plaintive history his tears dripped upon the lantern in his lap, and I cried, too, from sympathy. He said he was the son of an English nobleman—either an earl or an alderman, he could not remember which, but believed was both; his father, the nobleman, loved him, but his mother hated him from the cradle; and so while he was still a little boy he was sent to "one of them old, ancient colleges"—he couldn't remember which; and by and by his father died and his mother seized the property and "shook" him, as he phrased it. After his mother shook him, members of the nobility with whom he was acquainted used their influence to get him the position of "lob-lolly-boy in a ship"; and from that point my watchman threw off all trammels of date and locality and branched out into a narrative that bristled all along with incredible adventures; a narrative that was so reeking with bloodshed and so crammed with hairbreadth escapes and the most engaging and unconscious personal villainies, that I sat speechless, enjoying, shuddering, wondering, worshipping.

It was a sore blight to find out afterward that he was a low, vulgar, ignorant, sentimental, half-witted humbug, an untraveled native of the wilds of Illinois, who had absorbed wildcat literature and appropriated its marvels, until in time he had woven odds and ends of the mess into this yarn, and then gone on telling it to fledglings like me, until he had come to believe it himself. (IX, 51–52)[10]

A typical approach to such a passage would treat the "older" vision as that of the Gentleman patronizing the low-class fictive storyteller in the manner of several Old Southwest yarns.[11] Pertinent though this approach is, it usually fails to tell us what concrete rhetorical use the device is put to. Obviously, and very importantly, the method allows Twain to elevate his authorial stature by implying his superiority to the storyteller and his credulous audience. We are never permitted to forget for long the presence of Mark Twain, author. But just as significantly, the protagonist's own single-minded desire for status combines with the double perspective on style to very pointed realistic effect.

"Mark Twain" is put through familiar paces of misplaced sentimental confidence and disillusionment here, but never until now have the paces been so richly given and so functional in a developing story line. The richness is partly the special realism of contextual contrast: the realizing sense turning upon the genuine (literary) novelty of the mate's profanity versus the watchman's banal fairy tale. Lest we miss the implied general contrast, there is the older perspective to judge the watchman's inferior cursing ("so void of art that it was an element of weakness . . ."). The indirect discourse permits Twain to establish the double-edged point of view by inserting such comments. Offset by the mate's directly quoted commands, the indirect summary also concretely seconds the overt judgment by suggesting that the watchman's style would be too shoddy to warrant

10 I cite *Life on the Mississippi* in Twain's *Writings* because there is no separate edition of "Old Times." Twain used the original *Atlantic* sketches with few minor changes (negligible for my purposes) to comprise chapters IV–XVII of the subsequent work.

11 See Kenneth S. Lynn, *Mark Twain and Southwestern Humor* (Boston: Little, Brown, 1960).

fuller direct representation. Yet all these observations about
the role of perspective are backwards. The perspective is
not a subordinate artistic instrument, but the very vehicle
of realism. Let us readdress the passage.

If "Old Times" is considered in the line of Twain's development, the general narrative approach can be signified
in terms of projection and perspective—projection of the
earlier eccentric authorial personality onto the narrative
plane, and a firmly suggestive angle of vision on what is
projected. In his first book, Twain's authority rested largely
on his skillfully rendered shifts from invective to sentiment.
The second book purposefully dampened the cycle of emotional swings but by no means abandoned them. In the
present passage from "Old Times," this same emotional
juxtaposition is transferred from the personality of implied
author into a contrast of two characters admired by the
neophyte "Mark Twain." Set against the watchman's fraudulent burlesque, the mate's salty outburst, which effectively
is his character, seems at first glance the realistic touchstone.
But Twain clearly implies that the mate's novel "realistic"
imprecation is a performance as much as the watchman's
hackneyed sentimental fabrication. For the mate "felt all
the majesty of his great position, and made the world feel
it, too. When he gave even the simplest order, he discharged
it like a blast of lightning, and sent a long, reverberating
peal of profanity after it." The long discharge partly
quoted before is supposed to have been a mere request to
have a gangplank moved one foot forward. Further,
Twain's elevation above the mate's style is neatly, and
delightfully, exhibited in the protagonist's very admiration
("I wished I could talk like that"), with its politely inappropriate naive focus. It is also inferable in other ways, as
in the choice of the words "low, vulgar," which place more
than just the watchman. The realism of this section, then,
results not so much from the contrast between the mate's
inherently realistic style of speaking and the watchman's

meretricious style as from Twain's elevation above the two juxtaposed performances, objects of naive adulation that are graduated in virtuosity. The protagonist's naive delight prevents the elevation from being excessive and merely meiotic. The first-person point of view implies a sense of continuing firsthand intimacy with the experience, a continuity shown for instance in Twain's linking of sentiment to status and profanity to conversational power, as if in playful compromise with the novice's obsessions.

Although the characters are both almost stereotypically larger than life, from the authorial perspective they are *seen* as intentionally *performing* larger than life, and unselfconsciously and without undue emphasis are placed in a ranking of effective artistry. In effect, we see one man playing at "profane mate" and another, less deftly, playing at "sentimental night watchman." This makes all the difference between unrealistic stereotypes and comically alive creations. An unexaggerated, nonperforming realistic foundation for the performing characters is never overtly given. But the reader credits the author for it nevertheless because Twain's authoritative elevation combined with the firsthand response implies that since he sees the exhibition so vividly for what it is, and can even criticize its art, he could have provided the unfeigned substrata as well. In a sense he does so at the end by unmasking the watchman, but the terms are so general ("sentimental, half-witted humbug," etc.) that they would be insufficient were not the reader already firmly disposed to take the bare gesture toward unfeigned representation for the deed. The brevity of presentation permitted because Twain treats the two men as performers helps to create a strong sense of concisely visualized reality and of Twain's authoritative power to tick off with precision successive characters and successive strata for the cub's ambitious admiration. In sum, the heart of Twain's much praised realism is not a revelation immediately given in the contrast but the unsimulated lives with-

held from presentation yet seemingly inferable from the
lofty but experienced "pilot-house" view of masquerades.[12]

The contrast of watchman and mate differs from most
later episodes in "Old Times" in its extremely broad, bold
delineation, but not in essential technique. If we now follow
Howells' preference in the first sketch, we will see a significant variation employed for economically "working up
an atmosphere." The "low-lived" village at the beginning
of "Old Times" looms large in the reader's imagination,
but as Twain's careful editor hinted, there is really not
much description of it. To be exact, the town is directly
described within one sentence of about twenty lines of
print, one-fourth devoted to the Mississippi and the surrounding area and not the village proper. But detailed
physical notation concerning the town plays a minor, although still important, role in establishing the vivid reality,
which is a felt reality: what "Not only the boys, but the
whole village, felt . . ." (p. 43). They feel the cycle in
which both experiential time and the town's activity share
—each day first "glorious with expectancy" of the steamboat's morning arrival, then with its departure "a dead
and empty thing"; and the "dead town" momentarily
rousing, and then relapsing into somnolence once more.
Twain represents this experience by staging a drama that
is as much a drama of perspective as anything else. He
prompts our intuition of the usual day-long existence,
only hinted at by hogs in the street and a sleeping drunk,
by demonstrating its negation. He characterizes this largely
offstage reality in two related ways: the metaphorical statement that the town's very life consists only in admiring
the steamboat's theatrics, and the disclosure that this
simple, tawdry daily show is an endless novelty for the villagers, as if "a wonder they are seeing for the first time."

Twain's view is elevated above both performance and

[12] Cox also stresses the general importance of performance in "Old
Times," although from the angle of Twain's reconstructing his personal past.

spectators. But again the elevation is combined with first-hand intimacy;[13] if it is objectively detached, it is also largely amiable, "all in the family," so that the reader accepts the description as he might a criticism delivered by one family member about another. The village reactions are in effect those of boys, and Twain's nostalgic view of "When I was a boy" and the "old time . . . just as it was then" is qualified, for example, by his describing the communal center of admiration as a "cheap, gaudy packet." A few sentences later, Twain seems to abandon this difference of perspective in a passage that revives the substitution device of *Innocents Abroad*; in particular, the second gondolier description is recalled as the passage begins, "And the boat *is* rather a handsome sight, too. She is long and sharp and trim and pretty . . ." (p. 44). However, Twain's partial adoption of the villagers' viewpoint here only distinguishes his intimate elevation the more sharply, as it does also his relish in assuming a posture that extols a novelty. In this context, to say "And the boat *is* rather . . ." is to signal a conscious indulgence in memory's eternal present and its appropriate style, marked by subsequent words like "gorgeous," "gallantly," and "bravely." The elevation from which this remission descends is emphasized by Twain's *sotto voce* indication that he knows how a steamboat display is contrived: "a husbanded grandeur created with a bit of pitch just before arriving at a town."

Thus a creative transcendence operates at two levels. Twain provides a rounded sense of the town's low-lived existence by dwelling on the high-toned performance that briefly goes beyond it; analogously, he delivers the villagers' apperception of the spectacle in an indulgent stylization surpassing the limits of what they see. He offers both effects almost simultaneously, so that the illusion that we have been directly given the whole inferable day-long reality of contrasted town and steamboat, tedium and novelty, is

13 Smith, *Development*, p. 74, makes a similar point about Twain's having a mixed perspective on the opening scene.

even more convincing. As in the passage first examined, a socially graded, extravagantly admired theatrical reality is used to shade in the nontheatrical, a relative novelty to heighten the intuition of banality and hunger for an object of adulation; the knowing elevated perspective is employed as a voucher that we should and can infer the second reality from the first. No wonder a whole way of life seems to have lodged in our minds within the first two pages of the work. Again, realism is a product of represented pretense translated into precise authenticity by Twain's mixed angle of vision.

The villagers' avidity for spectacle and admiration is not introduced for an immediate purpose and then forgotten. Twain retains and refines the idea in the education of the apprentice pilot, and, by shifting the emphasis of the double-angled vision to his hero's perspective, entertainingly represents the cub's psychological reality.

The atmosphere Twain establishes on his river from the beginning substantiates and explains the protagonist's persistent naive confidence that style is substance, that entertaining impressiveness is knowledgeable skill. Since "Mark Twain" thinks that authority resides chiefly in brio, he attempts to imitate the impressive steamboat mannerisms the villagers admire and is repeatedly surprised to find the performance to be an insufficient qualification. This confusion is allied to a general failure of discrimination that must be overcome in his apprenticeship. The neophyte's predisposition is shown, like much else, in his response to the watchman's artistry, as "Mark Twain" eagerly drinks in the fraud's blithely indiscriminate creations—his supposed father "either an earl or an alderman, he could not remember which, but believed was both"; his school "one of them old, ancient colleges, he couldn't remember which"; and his whole narrative, which finally throws off "all trammels of date and locality." The language, partly reflecting

the cub's viewpoint, elaborates this sentimental running-
together of everything, from the phrase "melted into conversation," through the imagery of dimness and weeping,
and even to the term "lob-lolly-boy" (lob-lolly being a thick
gruel). Emotion itself is a matter of status since the watchman is said to be sentimental beyond his salary, so that if
one avenue of development clearly leads from this rightful
heir to the maudlin Duke and Dauphin in *Huckleberry
Finn*, another leads more immediately to the top of the
boat's hierarchy, the explosive Horace Bixby. The watchman is the comic obverse of Bixby, whose professional
calm is severely tested by his cub's indiscrimination. The
watchman idly names shadowy islands and capes as a pre-
lude to further rambling nocturnal entertainment; the pilot
expertly distinguishes among them. Yet this skill also becomes in effect a nocturnal show. We can begin to have
an inkling of the author's relationship with his protagonist
when we see that Bixby's greatest feat of discernment is
made the work's second greatest performance as well, and
the ostensible focus for the reader's highest admiration.

In his first two books, Mark Twain transmuted a world
into his performance of temperamental responses to it. That
is to say, he converted a world—the Old World or the
Far West—into personal, entertaining style. Yet simultaneously, his narrative persona was led into comic difficulties,
as he is in "Old Times," by habitually confounding stylization with substance, gesture with complete act (*act* in the
philosophical, not the theatrical, sense). In "Old Times,"
Twain the authorial performer is, relatively speaking, with-
drawn from the stage in favor of a consecutive narrative
development. But there is still a specific relationship between the author's absorption with style and telling gesture and his persona's. Just as Twain never makes the
pilot's apprentice abandon his airy dreams of grandeur
but has him put foundations under them by learning what
glory entails, so in his narrative technique Twain trans-
figures the novice's undiscriminating misdirection of con-

fidence. Twain accomplishes this, as we have noted in part, by locating meaning and interest in matters in which performance and genuine act are indeed made to converge.

One of these matters is profane rage, a frequent condition in "Old Times," and one whose potential evidently so possessed Twain that Howells felt obliged to request deletions of profanity from the manuscript. It is typical of "Mark Twain" that, having been entertained earlier by the watchman's list of geographical names, he cannot forbear applying the spectator's response to Bixby's first lesson in nomenclature. The pilot is livid at the cub's forgetfulness:

> "Look here! What do you suppose I told you the names of those points for?"
> I tremblingly considered a moment, and then the devil of temptation provoked me to say:
> "Well—to—to—be entertaining, I thought."
> This was a red flag to the bull. He raged and stormed so (he was crossing the river at the time) that I judge it made him blind, because he ran over the steering oar of a trading scow. Of course the traders sent up a volley of red-hot profanity. Never was a man so grateful as Mr. Bixby was: because he was brim full, and here were subjects who could *talk back*. He threw open a window, thrust his head out, and an eruption followed as I never had heard before. The fainter and farther away the scowmen's curses drifted, the higher Mr. Bixby lifted his voice and the weightier his adjectives grew. When he closed the window he was empty. You could have drawn a seine through his system and not caught curses enough to disturb your mother with. Presently, he said to me in the gentlest way. . . . (pp. 58–59)

The progress of emotion is familiar from *Innocents Abroad*: explosion followed by a calm continuation after the grateful venting of feelings. The target is principally a welcome convenience; the adequate relief is what matters. Twain has transferred his early rhetorical habit to the master pilot, whose authoritative position aboard the boat licenses him to invest himself freely and fully in commination, and whose responsive target is worthy of the investment. Whereas earlier the mate's constant ritual cursing was an intentionally impressive exhibition more than a spontaneous expression of feeling, Bixby's profanity is, by comparison, a genuine affective act.

But Twain turns it into a performance also. He accomplishes the conversion by using the cub's point of view, and in the process he also solidifies the characterization of "Mark Twain." In the passage quoted, although the cub now realizes from Bixby's anger that amusement is not at issue, he can no more resist getting a further rise out of Bixby by a mischievous provocation than the novice lecturer in *Roughing It* could repress the smile that incited an immediate dramatic response. When the expected result follows, the cub's report of Bixby's actions is filled with an imperviously appreciative, placid astonishment, shown in phrases like "I judge," and "Of course," and "Never was a man so grateful" as well as in the whole air of explanation and the madly precise metaphor of seine and mother. One almost expects the cub to crown his folly by applauding.

Such passages in "Old Times" brilliantly render the native sound of rooted self-complacency; they not only are very funny, but make excellent narrative sense. The complacency is "the easy confidence of my time of life," as Twain describes his persona's youth. It is an assurance that all difficulty is but a pretense belied by "the easy confidence with which my chief loafed from side to side of his wheel" (p. 54), a pretense calculated to set off the cub's hair-trigger instinct for worship. When Bixby explains that the entire river must be memorized, the "dismal revelation" quickly loses effect on the cub: ". . . I did not feel discouraged long. I judged that it was best to make some allowances, for doubtless Mr. Bixby was 'stretching'" (p. 59). The monumental naive assurance inherently embodied in the cub's point of view, then, has a double function. It furnishes Twain the means of transforming a character's vituperative rage into an entertaining performance. And it is also the focal point for the theme of education, the "easy confidence" that is to be converted from the cub's callow assumption into the pilot's mature possession. All along, the education is one in discriminating piloting skills; more profoundly, it is also in a discriminating appreciation of worthier objects of homage, built on the cub's bumptious persistence in admiring *something*.

The distance the cub must traverse is demarcated by two exhibitions of piloting, one by Bixby and the other by "Mark Twain." In the first, it is not chiefly the cub's perspective on Bixby that creates the effect of performance but Twain's staging. Bixby's adventurous Hat Island crossing is a show complete with an expert audience of visiting pilots, their cheers, and their vocal praise of Bixby's "calm and easy" expert style: " 'Oh, it was done beautiful—beautiful!' " (p. 68). The climax of the cub's education is staged in much the same way, but now the staging is attributed to Bixby as one of "various strategic tricks," a "friendly swindle" (p. 115), he employs to train his apprentice. Earlier Bixby has taught the cub a lesson by concealing himself to view the novice's complacency give way to panic. The purpose had been a specific lesson in reading the water's surface; now the test is to be general. It is to be an assay of confidence, with a reward of dramatic praise—or blame—by a hierarchically arranged audience. Approaching an extremely simple crossing in broad daylight, Bixby plants a seed of doubt in the cub and then leaves the pilot-house to assemble an audience pointedly including the very ranks "Mark Twain" originally hoped to rise above:

> The very tone of the question shook my confidence.
> . . . Presently the captain stepped out on the hurricane deck; next the chief mate appeared; then a clerk.

Every moment or two a straggler was added to my audience; and before I got to the head of the island I had fifteen or twenty people assembled down there under my nose. I began to wonder what the trouble was. As I started across, the captain glanced aloft at me and said with a sham uneasiness in his voice—

"Where is Mr. Bixby?"

"Gone below, sir."

But that did the business for me. My imagination began to construct dangers out of nothing, and they multiplied faster than I could keep the run of them. All at once I imagined I saw shoal water ahead! The wave of coward agony that surged through me then came near dislocating every joint in me. All my confidence in that crossing vanished. (pp. 116–17)

After the cub's busy panic culminates in the audience's "thundergust of humiliating laughter," Bixby drives home the point: " 'You shouldn't have allowed me or anybody else to shake your confidence in [your] knowledge. Try to remember that. And another thing: when you get into a dangerous place, don't turn coward. That isn't going to help matters any.' " The fact that this public confidence trick is chosen to clinch the cub's final lesson in *independent* self-reliance acknowledges the role that a public display of authoritative assurance nevertheless has had and will continue to have in his motivation.

Yet the cub's frenzy of unconfident, ineffective motions is a comically inverted definition of expert piloting as not only impressive performance but the epitome of individual act. It is act par excellence in the sense that its whole sanction is individual and internal. When the cub asks if he has to learn all the innumerable changing shapes in which the river can appear under different conditions of light and weather, Bixby replies, " 'No! you only learn *the* shape of the river; and you learn it with such absolute certainty that you can always steer by the shape that's in

237

your head, and never mind the one that's before your eyes' " (p. 72). Piloting is for Twain the perfection of act not only because it is a set of skills that become instinctive, working with the mechanical fidelity he often admired, but also because at a given moment it can become a performance that is fully conscious and fully volitional, virtually independent of external appearances. The act of piloting can resolve into a decision made in a governing mental landscape, but with empirical effect. To trust a shape in one's mind over the evidence of one's eyes means having a supreme confidence and an authority in a measure transcendently sovereign to the uncertain phenomenal world as well as to other men.

Thus Twain's paean to the "wonderful science" of piloting and the personal hegemony it brings has a great resonance; following the cub's final lesson, it climaxes "Old Times" by fully disclosing the pinnacle he has at last reached. Significantly, the cub disappears for good in the remaining two sketches (although in *Life on the Mississippi* he is pulled back onstage for a moment of vengeful triumph. over the sadistic Mr. Brown). For this is the point where "Mark Twain," the comic failure whom we have never seen do anything right, gives way to Mark Twain, confident, knowledgeable judge of distinctions: "If I have seemed to love my subject, it is no surprising thing, for I loved the profession far better than any I have followed since, and I took a measureless pride in it. The reason is plain: a pilot, in those days, was the only unfettered and entirely independent human being that lived in the earth." Twain goes on to discriminate the fettered powers of kings, parliaments, clergymen, and writers, and tops off the ranking with this conclusion: "writers of all kinds are manacled servants of the public. We write frankly and fearlessly, but then we 'modify' before we print. In truth, every man and woman and child has a master, and worries and frets in servitude; but in the day I write of, the Mississippi pilot had *none*. . . . So here was the novelty of a king without a keeper, an absolute monarch who was absolute in sober truth and not by a fiction of words" (pp. 119–20). This fiction of words is also the pinnacle of Twain's authority in "Old Times," and it has been prepared for thoroughly by a rhetoric that guides us, in parallel with the cub, in discriminating worthier objects of admiration.

Earlier, Twain had followed another crescendo, his famous lament for having lost his sense of the river's "romance and beauty," by directly asserting the novelty of the compensatory pilot's lore he does have: "I feel justified in enlarging upon this great science for the reason that I feel sure no one has ever yet written a paragraph about it who had piloted a steamboat himself, and so had a practical knowledge of the subject. If the theme were hackneyed, I should be obliged to deal gently with the reader, but since it is wholly new, I have felt at liberty to take up a considerable degree of room with it" (pp. 86–87). As Henry Nash Smith has wisely noted, Twain's claim to loss is contradicted by his own description of the sunset.[14] Further, the contention is a reverse compliment to himself, boosting him in the ranks of right feeling. To lament losing a power that is in fact displayed in a highly conventional sunset description certifies that one values the conventional norms of feeling. But the implication is even broader, since Twain goes from his lament to the justification quoted immediately above. In reality, Twain is claiming the common power plus an additional, unique resource founded on "practical knowledge." As in the opening Hannibal scene, and repeatedly with the cub, he has depicted a dramatic posture of adulation in order to show that his own awareness transcends it; in effect, he is implying that he can perform the commonplace sentiment, whether it concern Hannibal's admired steamboat or the *Atlantic* audience's worshiped literary sunset, and could—even if he does not actually—go it one better.

When he celebrates the absolute novel authority of the pilot, he is celebrating his own as well, and transcendently. The derogation of writing relative to piloting may be, as

14 Smith, *Development*, p. 80.

Brooks notoriously saw it, biographically confessional; but in context it is clearly tactical, a rather complicated form of litotes. The writer who composes "frankly and fearlessly" plainly has the courage that Horace Bixby advises, but since writing here is seen as an intrinsically public function, it is "modified" from pure private act into acceptable performance. As in Twain's sunset lament, his direct announcement of how the writer bows to propriety has the result of elevating him in social rectitude and simultaneously implying reserves of sophisticated awareness surpassing the very proprieties that are acknowledged. Since every member of the public is said to be "in servitude" as well, Twain is raised to the humble exaltation of sophisticated *servus servorum*.

Above all, if the pilot's unique condition no longer literally exists, the writer Twain is the one man who can with entire authority imaginatively recreate a condition of entire authority. Twain had wanted to end the series with the sixth sketch (so that he could "retire with dignity," he explained to Howells),[15] which closes by reemphasizing that piloting is "of the dead and pathetic past" (p. 140). We are in a position now to see how doubly well motifs of nostalgic pathos and loss can serve Twain. In *Innocents Abroad*, the recorded public past of the Old World had been an active rival authority to be displaced. In "Old Times," the past acts as a liberation, a clearing of the field for the author. The series stresses that the river's golden age, its glory and grandeur, are irrevocably gone with scarcely a trace. Twain's overt laments and his whole governing perspective banish them into the old time. But in the same breath Twain also reinstates and supplants them, for he has made them exist again from his own unique authoritative pilot's memory, which again masters the river's distinctions. Twain's work tells us that the old river and its sovereign pilots are no more; praise them. What we have is solely Twain's novel Mississippi, the shape in his head; praise him above all.

<hr/>

[15] *Twain-Howells Letters*, I, 85.

8

But I Never Said Nothing:
The Adventures of Huckleberry Finn

"Oh, this is the boss dodge. . . ."

The King

I felt good and all washed clean. . . .

Huck

In the years that lie between "Old Times" and *Huckleberry Finn*, most of them spanned by the slow, intermittent composition of the latter work, Twain embellished his courtier's art in interrelated juvenile books.[1] Behind these was "A Boy's Manuscript" (c. 1870), an early fragmentary story of infantile romantic courtship investigating the area of venerating attitudes to which Twain could both yield his fancy and yet be automatically superior. In *The Adventures of Tom Sawyer*, he developed in the child-hero an especially powerful potential for expressing the hierarchical motive. Tom, because he is both a child and a member of a "respectable" family, provides opportunities for the special view of the whole social pecking order that the marginal figure can give from his double position in the scale of social power. Alongside Tom, Twain discovered Huck Finn, destined in his extreme marginality to make Tom Sawyer in turn look solid and fixed. Such situations as Tom's memorable courtship of Becky Thatcher, his comic public recognition by Judge Thatcher to climax a graduated series of Sunday School showing off, and his eventual emergence as St. Petersburg's hero allow Twain to elaborate courtly

[1] For the most authoritative account of *Huckleberry Finn* in the making, see Walter Blair, "When Was *Huckleberry Finn* Written?" *American Literature*, 30 (1958), 1–25; and also his *Mark Twain and Huck Finn* (Berkeley: University of California Press, 1962).

and mock-courtly postures within the now-standard frame of nostalgic praise for the old time. Concordantly, he maintains the combination of authorial intimacy and elevation that, even more than in "Old Times," constantly suggests that the kindly author is above the top of any hierarchy envisioned within his fictional world. In *The Prince and the Pauper*, the courtly metaphor is literally exact. Twain, as he will later in *A Connecticut Yankee, Joan of Arc,* and *The Mysterious Stranger*, employs a setting and basic situation in which occasions for treating hierarchical authority, with all varieties of praise, derogation, and beseechment, constantly arise in the very nature of things. *The Prince and the Pauper*, like the other works named here, features a marginal figure who partakes of both the lowest and the highest ranks: the Prince-pauper (in the others, the commoner-Boss, the peasant-saint, and devil-deity), who is thus an individual epitome, or condensation, of an entire hierarchical chain.

The Adventures of Huckleberry Finn perfects these efforts in an art of indirection that is Twain's triumph of courtly decorum. Used to launch Twain's own boldly independent venture in subscription publishing, the Webster Publishing Company, the novel portrays one of the least ambitious heroes in world literature. At the very time that Twain apparently sought to end his marginal straddling of two worlds, to abandon the role of popular buffoon and enter once and for all the highest realms of the respectable wealthy by such adventures as his publishing firm and investments in kaolotype and the notorious Paige typesetting machine, his most famous character remains irrevocably marginal, with one foot in the "sivilized" world and the other in the pariah's. During the years of the book's composition, a whole set of such oppositions can easily be made between the author's endeavors, abject humiliations (the Whittier birthday speech), and glamorous conquests (the Grant reunion speech), and those of his fictional creature—oppositions that seem to testify yet again to the split personality commonly ascribed to Mark Twain. Rather than dwell on this critical truism, it seems to me much more useful to understand that *Huckleberry Finn* implicitly speaks against the very values that Mark Twain was reaching for by means of the book, and yet in the same breath celebrates the hierarchical motive itself, to which Twain was committed undeviatingly, whatever the circumstantial shortcomings of the social scale in which he must perforce operate. Or, stated with a different emphasis: the novel is an attempted imaginative purification of the motive dominating Twain's efforts, in which the novel was also a significant practical instrumentality.

I intend "purification" in the connected senses in which it attaches to the novel: a ritual to create what is morally blameless, and what is essential or unmodified by circumstance. The book is both an exculpation and exploration of what fundamentally moved Twain as he wrote it. In its language, genre, and structure, the novel is the ideal form of purification for Twain; it climaxes his efforts to enact and disguise, to say and unsay his motive with the bland demeanor that is also blandishment. This creative assumption is what his authoritative humor initially stipulates, equivocally forbidding our investigation beneath the mask, just before he turns us over to his narrative persona: "Persons attempting to find a motive in this narrative will be prosecuted; persons attempting to find a moral in it will be banished; persons attempting to find a plot in it will be shot. BY ORDER OF THE AUTHOR PER G. G., CHIEF OF ORDNANCE." The bland preemption of a possibility and implicit move to discover it, the combined overt "you musn't" and covert "but I dare you," is, even to its hierarchical framing, the defining form of the book. Like all forms of flirtation, it disavows what it compels to.

With Twain's notice as my warrant, I append this: the discussion that follows is lengthy, and systematically analytical in tone; this is required, I believe, by the very blandness of the book's simplicity, where the surfaces, like Poe's famous thief, conceal everything by displaying it.

I

Huckleberry Finn is a story of pure courtship first in the important respect that Huck admires "from afar": he admires what he is convinced he can never be a part of, and does not even desire for himself since it is not for the likes of him, not "being brung up to it." The fact that Twain has us frequently view with disenchantment the objects of Huck's appreciation, summed up in the respectable Tom Sawyer, who follows the best authorities, only confirms the purity of Huck's motive per se. Huck's affectionate tolerance of the ways of the "quality" is the more impressive because often they exasperate him personally. And his mistaken admirations seem the more courtly-gallant because of their innocent misdirections of focus, just as his famous decision to go to hell rhetorically purifies his moral choice of aiding Jim—that is, offers Twain's dramatic assurance to us that Huck's intent is as purely selfless as is imaginable. This is the significant point that Huck's deference to Tom in the concluding section reemphasizes: with whatever comic demurs, Huck defers to a socially superior respectability that he does not altogether understand and finds personally inappropriate. The weight that the essential motivation carries with Huck is explicit in his concern that Tom would be injuring his respectability by helping Jim escape, combined with an acquiescence to Tom's authoritative statement that he generally knows what he's about.

But the controversial Phelps section is unsettling largely because Twain insists on Huck's unchanging submission to Tom after two important effects climax in the moral decision Huck has just made. Huck has drawn our affectionate esteem because of his very humility, his certainty that he is inferior to the aristocratic class of Widow Douglas and the Grangerfords that keeps wanting to adopt him, whose God he is sure he offends. However, this same decorously expressed admiring humility has also been used to make us increasingly impatient of much that Huck feels to be superior. As a result, at the end we want Huck to cease being the humble courtier of Tom Sawyer and all that Tom represents, although it is this very disposition that has given Huck fictive stature and the book's social criticism its powerful and moving ironic edge. In effect, I wish to argue, the novel leads us *à rebours* to want Huck Finn to cease being Huck Finn; we unconsciously want a fundamental egalitarian or aristocratic transformation in a fiction whose profoundest logic denies such a possibility.

Recent commentators, rightly stressing the social criticism in the novel, have also tended to slight the intrinsic value of Huck's attitudes in favor of reading many of his approbations as a mere ironic translucency through which Mark Twain's really significant social disapproval can be seen. Even a reader as rewardingly sensitive to stylistic surfaces as Richard Poirier, to whose statement I want to return later, does not fully see the meaning of what he discerns in discussing the opening chapters:

> . . . we are uncomfortably aware of a gap between Mark Twain's position, his view, . . . and the more socially engaged and eager position of the hero. . . . The sound of Huck's socially involved voice first wavers, then nearly disappears, then returns as a sickly version of what we find in these opening scenes. Here, though, it is heard distinctly enough to make the metaphors amusing and affectionate, however damaging they become if one isolates their implications.
>
> The great difficulty for the reader in the opening chapters is that we feel no confidence in balancing the implications of style, its tendency to repudiate what is at the same time being affectionately rendered. . . . Put simply, it is predictable from the outset that the book must elect to give its attention either to the development

of the hero or to a review of the environment which forestalls that development. The two cannot be synchronized.

And Poirier goes on: "the novel discovers that the consciousness it values most cannot expand within the environment it provides, that the self cannot come to fuller life through social drama. . . ."[2] Poirier opposes concepts that are crucial for understanding the novel; his opposition of developing consciousness and social environment is one that the novel, through its ruses, tempts us to make but does not really sustain.

Huck, otherwise evidently the paragon of utilitarianism, admires and defers on principle, disinterestedly. It is as if—to begin with an ultimate model—the perfection of homage were dramatized by showing the damned in hell worshiping God. (In fact, it is characteristic of Huck that immediately after deciding that he will go to hell and live a life of wickedness, he announces as he approaches the Phelps farm that he will trust in Providence to put words in his mouth.) This suppositious model would evidence the more forcefully the human need for some form of courtly behavior if at the same time the Deity were shown as venial and unworthy. For then the hierarchical motive per se is unmodified by circumstance and is therefore capable of being felt in its purity: this ironic, or negative, model would show a courtship unaffected by the unworthiness of the

[2] *A World Elsewhere: The Place of Style in American Literature* (New York: Oxford, 1966), pp. 187–88, 195. For similar views, see Smith, *Development*, 113–37; and Alan Trachtenberg, "The Form of Freedom in *Adventures of Huckleberry Finn*," *The Southern Review*, 6 (1970), 954–71. In his book, Cox appears to me to finesse the issue by reducing everything to a question of sociological conscience (Tom Sawyer equals "Northern conscience") and the triumph of the pleasure principle. *Fate of Humor*, pp. 156–84.

In addition to these works, Paul De Man's *Blindness and Insight* (New York: Oxford, 1971), a fine metacritical study that does not deal with Twain, has helped me to crystallize my ideas about the novel.

entities occupying the hierarchical positions or by any hope of individual advancement up the scale. The principal of the scale is seen as suasive in itself; the hierarchical motive, thus ironically uncircumstanced, would be felt in its inevitability and perfect reality as a constituent of human action.

This model is intended to be illustrative, but it is approached in the book's treatment of Providence, prayer, and cognate matters. Students of *Huckleberry Finn* have dealt with these ideas almost wholly in thematic terms that neglect Huck's persuasive habits both as protagonist and narrator. The connection is a key one, for the book marshals rank upon rank of persuasive order—including magic, prayer, confidence trickery, and personal-social "style"—in which the *adventures* of the book's title take their complete meaning.

Huck's introduction to the rites of civilizing in the first several chapters has a strongly religious complexion, but the definitive religious act, prayer, is set within the context of a practical rhetoric, magic, identified with socially inferior status. When Huck is first introduced to prayer, he regards it as if it were magic, of a piece with the prophylactic and coercive actions one performs when one has killed a spider or wishes to make a hairball prophesy. Thus Huck is quickly disappointed in his attempts at praying when "nothing come of it" (XIII, 28). But "superstitious" magic is also given a broader frame of analogy. From the first, Huck has impressed upon him the near-magical properties attributed by everyone to correct "style," a word recurrently on the lips of Tom Sawyer as well as Huck. The world portrayed in the first scenes is charged with manneristic significance: Huck's gaping and stretching is interpreted by Miss Watson as stylistic misbehavior to be countered by threats of hell; his unintentional killing of the spider is particularly terrifying because he feels stylistically helpless, knowing no specific ritual counter to ward off bad luck, and so "hadn't no confidence"; the juvenile gang and its games are established according to a detailed outlaw style determined by the mysterious ordinances of Tom's precious books; Tom's genie must be summoned in the correct way; Jim's hairball only reveals its secrets if properly approached; Pap Finn is as outraged by his son's new upperclass dress and behavior, and by the style of an educated Black, as any punctilious guardian of the social ladder would be; and so on through Jim's lessons in folk magic on Jackson Island.

In short, each social class is carefully identified with the style in which it has confidence and in terms of which it understands its own persuasive authority, properly circumscribed in relation to that of classes above and below. This is the fictive world of summoning, coercing, blandishing, and threatening in which the fittingly named Duke and King will make their way by mimicry of pertinent manners, and in which the ribald Royal Nonesuch is tailor-made by the Duke: "So the duke said these Arkansaw lunkheads couldn't come up to Shakespeare. . . . He said he could size their style" (p. 200). Given the cultural obsession with degree and appropriate and impressive sets of decorum, "style" threatens to become solely constitutive of act, subsuming all considerations of will and intention into graduated performances acceptable according to certain conventions. *Huckleberry Finn* is in its own way a symbolic investigation of the classical courtly dilemma, represented in the Renaissance for example by the machiavel type: in a community where stylistic decorum and hierarchical suasions are predominant values, what will keep Iago and those who smile and smile from making everything subservient to empty shows? The problem is only exacerbated in a democratic, ostensibly egalitarian society, for "Degree being vizarded,/ Th' unworthiest shows as fairly in the mask" (*Troilus and Cressida*). Pap's redneck version of this fear is manifest in his double-edged complaint that he is a wealthy man ("worth six thousand dollars and upwards") brought low by the "govment" while a mulatto professor walks freely about with fine clothes. From here the path is plain to the Duke's lament about being "fetched . . . so low, when I was so high" (p. 167) and the steps the two confidence operators take to right this hierarchical injustice, nonetheless real for being only rhetorically alleged. In part, Twain's reply to the dilemma is traditional, as in aristocratic Colonel Sherburn's coordination of style and the courage to back it up. But this particular answer raises more problems for Twain than it solves. Another reply, also troublesome, is Huck Finn himself, with his "good heart" and his calm assertion as he first assumes the role of our narrator: "I never see anybody but lied."

Huck's confusion concerning prayer is, therefore, broadly instructive. For Western man at least, genuine prayer is traditionally at once the opposite of coercion and a true instance of style-as-act. Nor is it fundamentally a petitioning, although it may frequently take such a form, for the petitioning presupposes what the prayer must essentially enact: a resolve to align oneself with the divine will. Prayer is formulaic and persuasive, but the object of persuasion is not one's Audience. The stylization, however subtly denoting a shift in linguistic or tonal registers, functions as a *self*-persuasion to the pious end of subordinating the private will to the deific. The supplicant's freshly self-formulated desire must be, "Thy will be done," his courtship above all an act that reaffirms the hierarchical coordination. Will, intention, and formulaic style all become one in the ideal; that is, words that give witness only to the Word.[3]

Huck first comes close to the genuinely prayerful feeling when, after his pragmatic grousing about praying for a selfless concern for others, he describes his marginally dualistic response to supreme order:

> Sometimes the widow would take me one side and talk about Providence in a way to make a body's mouth

---

[3] This discussion of prayer, besides drawing on Kenneth Burke, is also indebted to Irwin C. Lieb, *The Four Faces of Man* (Philadelphia: University of Pennsylvania Press, 1971).

water; but maybe next day Miss Watson would take hold and knock it all down again. I judged I could see that there was two Providences, and a poor chap would stand considerable show with the widow's Providence, but if Miss Watson's got him there warn't no help for him any more. I thought it all out, and reckoned I would belong to the widow's if he wanted me, though I couldn't make out how he was a-going to be any better off then than what he was before, seeing I was so ignorant and so kind of low-down and ornery. (p. 29)

In this quintessentially comic vision, Twain draws from Huck's humble pragmatism ("how he was a-going to be any better off") an unexpected but entirely credible nascent piety, a desire to "belong . . . if he wanted me," before which Miss Watson's forbidding deity and even the widow's mouth-watering version look inadequate. The language here solicits us to observe the kinship between the Providential view and the pragmatic, both emphasizing the purposeful order in which every meanest detail is valued for its use—an assumption implicit in Pap's apologia for chicken stealing on the grounds that someone else could always use the chicken if the thief cannot, "and a good deed ain't ever forgot" (p. 96). I will want to return later to consider language and prayer further. For now, we can see that Huck, self-consistently, is able to view himself in the light of his potential usefulness to a comprehensive pragmatic scheme, though he is very doubtful of his serviceable qualifications.

The next time we actually observe Huck attempting prayer, as he prepares to make his climactic choice, the ideal verbal act is again clearly inferable from Huck's discovery that he cannot even utter the necessary words:

. . . I about made up my mind to pray, and see if I couldn't try to quit being the kind of boy I was and be better. So I kneeled down. But the words wouldn't come. Why wouldn't they? . . . I knowed very well why they wouldn't come. It was because my heart warn't right; it was because I warn't square; it was because I was playing double. . . . You can't pray a lie—I found that out. (pp. 277–78)

Not only does Huck's failure underscore the interdependence of will, intention, and words in prayer's pure courtship; but it helps to distinguish the other two chief modes of persuasion, folk superstition and confidence trickery, that dominate respectively the first and second halves of the book.

The world order, and inevitably the persuasive rationale, inherent in prayer is the inverse of that in both magic and trickery, where effective stylization is detached from and substitutes for what is in the heart. In the superstitious view, which incorporates a stoic wisdom regarding a large experiential domain, certain apparently trivial deeds are held to have adverse consequences, so that one is made accountable for inadvertencies just as if they were willed choices; motion, or mere deed, is promoted to act. But the promotion, though seemingly masochistic, is really the first step in a meliorative cycle that, ideally, promotes something in order to usurp its power. One negates one's accountability by ritual deeds whose magic efficacy (in *Huckleberry Finn*, at any rate) is no more dependent on one's heart being right than was the significance of the original inadvertency. One achieves a stylistic authority over disturbing psychological realities by conceiving in ritually controllable form the kind of elusive fears that Huck feels at the end of chapter one: ". . . I heard an owl, away off, who-whooing about somebody that was dead, and a whippowill and a dog crying about somebody that was going to die; and the wind was trying to whisper something to me and I couldn't make out what it was, and so it made the cold shivers run over me" (p. 18). In this view, the order of reality and morality is basically formal; power and rectitude

reside in knowing the stylistic secrets required for interpretation, coercion, and prevention. In order to calm one's
inner life, one assumes an external calm, a bland poker
face, or equivalently some merely formal demeanor, while
one transfers all activity into externally prescribed manipulations of words or objects. In principle, the view supposes an unfixed, or provisional, scale of power, in the sense
that provided one knows the proper forms one can rise to
higher levels by stylistic coercion. In practice, and especially
in *Huckleberry Finn*, the hierarchy ultimately maintains
its supreme stasis because the number of imponderables and
rank-ordered inimical forces is incalculably large. This
calls for the underlying informed fatalism Jim manifests,
in which ritually bland demeanor becomes stoic outlook.

Twain uses this suasive order in a combined eulogistic-
dyslogistic fashion typical of the novel, and of superstitious
magic itself. For instance, he uses it to give Jim stature:
Jim's command of superstitious lore expresses his particular
wisdom and his firm maintenance of an area of self-identifying, self-respecting expertness. But Twain uses superstition
also as a vehicle for minstrel-show comedy and as an implicit parallel derogating stylistic fanaticism like Miss
Watson's.

In confidence trickery, too, reality is viewed as controllable by the properly bland blandishments, but the
world in question is overwhelmingly human. With this
proviso, what was said concerning superstition's "heartless"
promotion in order to usurp clearly applies *mutatis mutandis*. In addition, whereas the benign, defensive trickster
Huck discovers that he cannot pray a lie, the Duke and the
Dauphin twice discover—at the camp meeting and in the
Wilks adventure—that the King's ability to simulate piety
is the "boss dodge" (p. 221). The King deserves his name
because his most characteristic sort of trickery has the highest, and most remunerative, reach in the trickster's parodic
scale of persuasion so that even theatrics are advertised as a
"Shaksperean Revival" (p. 186). For all their important

differences, the book suggests that prayer and confidence trickery can be treated in comparable terms of self-persuasion, and can even coexist in a sense that is only partly ironic. The formulas of prayer are a means of arousing self-conviction designed for self-subordination; in the confidence game effective performance is a self-persuasion designed for convincing and subordinating others. As Huck says of the King at one point, "he warmed up and went warbling right along till he was actuly beginning to believe what he was saying *himself* . . ." (p. 262). What marks the effective con man, like the habitual liar, is his ability to give consent not so much to what he is saying as to *his saying* it. His performed personality, as the focus of his ego-expansive belief, thus also dominates over the communicated matter to which an entirely truthful person would direct his entire credibility. As a symbolic enactment of the private personality's sovereignty over the objective or communally perceived, this is a malign analogue to the pilot's masterful reliance on his mentally internalized river in "Old Times."

A corollary in *Huckleberry Finn* similarly shows Twain's transposition of his narrative practice, from *Innocents Abroad* through "Old Times," to the frauds' knavery. The ludicrously stylized worshipful roles the con men take, whether of reformed pirate, Shakespearean actor, or English clergyman, vividly spotlight the transactional ground—that is, adulatory performance itself—toward which both performer and audience direct their confidence. Once the con men find the proper key to each community's style, the villagers' most prominent trait is their enthusiasm for being in awe. Nor do the charlatans, who immediately use their art to establish a miniature courtly ranking when they board the raft, lack a god-term appropriate to the ultimate height of their hierarchy. The King's strong advocacy of trusting Providence to provide swindling opportunities (as if such trust were essentially beneficial, overriding one's other intentions) is a brilliantly parodic trickster's version of prayer. It comically testifies to a knave's courtly trust in a comprehensive notional order of trust: if Providence didn't exist, the King would have to invent it. " 'Thish yer comes of trust'n to Providence,' " he assures the Duke as they look at the Wilks fortune. " 'It's the best way, in the long run. I've tried 'em all, and ther' ain't no better way.' " The next ironic sentence makes clear the compensatorily abstract purity of this notional order, in consonance with that of the whole novel: "Most everybody would a been satisfied with the pile, and took it on trust; but no, they must count it" (pp. 220–21).

If Providence is an ultimate concept required by both the Widow's and the King's world orders, Tom Sawyer is effectively the necessary god-term for Huck. The point must be insisted on because critics, attentive to the book's important theme of freedom, have often spoken as if Huck could, or in fact did, escape from his subordination to Tom. The mistake is fundamental since this claim overweights the theme of freedom by improperly removing it from the hierarchical fabric in which it alone has meaning. From first to last, the book plays variations on a three-term modular hierarchy—Tom/Huck/Jim—capable of further refinement into a number of conceptual graduations. Just as each socially authoritative style can be defined only in terms of higher and lower styles in the scale, so Tom, Huck, and Jim each have meaning only in terms of each other and the scalar positions shading off above and below. Tom, of "respectable" but not aristocratic stock, in persuading Huck looks up toward aristocratic romances and acts in their name; and Jim, whether tricked by the boys or persuaded to be freed in Tom's style, is thereby awarded precedence over the "other niggers," whose reverence for him is referred to at the beginning and the end of the work: "he was more looked up to than any nigger in that country" (p. 22). Tom's lieutenancy to his books awards him the advantage of doing homage to a loftier term that gives him identity and simultaneously purifies his authority

with the selfless inevitability of "principle." " 'Why blame
it all, we've *got* to do it,' " he can say. " 'Don't I tell you
it's in the books?' " (p. 25). And again: " 'The thing for us
to do is just to do our *duty*, and not worry about whether
anybody *sees* us do it or not. Hain't you got no principle
at all?' " (p. 344). (This last to the marginal waif who
epitomizes admiration on principle.) Similarly, Huck acts
in the name of Tom to convince Jim to board the *Walter
Scott* and, more generally, during the several times he
wishes Tom were with him to do things correctly or bless
Huck's own plain-style contrivances. And Jim (in one of
the book's most embarrassingly ineffective closing moments) legitimizes his decision that Tom must have a doctor
for his leg by appealing to the top of the immediate order
as Tom would call on his books: " 'Is dat like Mars Tom
Sawyer? Would he say dat? You *bet* he wouldn't! *Well*, den,
is *Jim* gwyne to say it?' " (p. 353). The rhetorical device of
appeal to authority, from the novel's famous first words,
is so pervasive in word and deed as to constitute the predominant means of being of most of the characters, Colonel
Sherburn comprising the major and very significant exception.

The frequently noted fact that Huck several times plays
Tom Sawyer to Jim's Huck means more than that Huck
Finn is shackled by Tom's viewpoint, or embodies Sawyerish
traits in his own character—or even that Mark Twain is
sacrificing consistent characterization to stage his standard
comedy routines with what Franklin R. Rogers helpfully
terms a character-axis.[4] The fact gives us a way of determining what such observations themselves basically mean in the
novel's own terms, once the hierarchical motive is seen with
its full force. Huck's playing Tom is a means of reestablishing the whole modular "court" made incomplete by
Tom's absence; it is especially proper that in the most fully
given instance (chapter XIV) Huck not only call upon Tom's

4 *Mark Twain's Burlesque Patterns* (Dallas: Southern Methodist
University Press, 1960), *passim*.

superior resource, books, but that the discussion center on King Solomon and royalty in general: "how much style they put on, and called each other your majesty, and your grace, and your lordship . . ." (p. 110). Huck first introduces himself by invoking Tom's name; blithely renounces Miss Watson's heaven in favor of being together with Tom Sawyer in the other place; is relieved from his acute lonesomeness at the first chapter's end by Tom's call; and immediately, with their first joint act, must serve as witness to Tom's trickery of Jim. As the mediate, marginal figure in the social triad of high, middle, and low, Huck must somehow supply the insufficiency when Tom is missing, in order to be Huck Finn. For he is, even more than the others in the novel, a term among terms in a hierarchy. This is the literally and figuratively inescapable formal logic of his being a truly marginal figure, a character who exists "nowhere" in the social structure and yet in a sense "everywhere," tugged between belonging to two different Providences, and pulled between the Widow and Pap over the issue, as Pap says, of "who was Huck Finn's boss" (p. 44).

In a word, Huck's identity in every respect is conceived by Twain as psychosocial. Tom and Jim are objectifications and elaborations of what Huck is by his marginal nature; he necessarily implies them—implies, that is, a modular hierarchy in his straddling two extremes. Everything in the novel, it might be said, is exfoliated from this datum. Huck's characteristic chronic lonesomeness, his recurrent desire for "some company," signifies his pregnant incompleteness in himself; he requires the objective realization of the bounding identities inherently potential in his interstitial existence. Consequently, when Huck and Jim are momentarily free on their raft, Tom Sawyer is with them as a reference point of Huck's deepest imagining. Their freedom can only exist within the entire miniature hierarchy because they themselves can have no meaning, no existence, outside it. There is never any real question of opposing the symbolic raft, or Huck's consciousness, to shore society except as more or less harmful versions of the same reality. "Society" is always aboard the raft: its other name is Huck's consciousness.

As for Twain's customary technique of juxtaposing "high" matters to "low" incomprehension, first with regard to Tom and Huck, then Huck and Jim, this staging is yet another reflection of courtly sensitivity, the same eccentrically heightened authorial concern that in *Innocents Abroad* set a laudatory deific analogue to Lake Tahoe directly over against reductive images of grasshoppers and grubbing savages. Twain's is an art of indulging in the satisfactions of praise and yet intimating that the object of one's praise is not really worthy of it. Seen in the broadest context of Twain's fictive enterprises, it is a way of being the grandest courtier by implying that the quality of one's worship far exceeds the quality of the court itself. *Huckleberry Finn* is nicely poised between the self-satisfaction and the despair, neither ever far from Twain's awareness, inherent in this state of affairs. Thus, however one initially views Huck's playing Tom, whether from the perspective of moral crisis or as another evidence of Twain's usual joking, functionally the one dominant hierarchical motive constellates character, theme, and habitual comic device in a single fictional system.

II

Huck's consciousness, then, from first to last remains hierarchically motivated, and in the novel's action it is refined increasingly regarding trust and its abuses within this psychosocial order: regarding what is owed others and, inseparably, oneself. But a modern confusion of liberty and fraternity with equality has influenced many readers either to deny that any real development takes place or to claim too much for Huck's growth. A largely unwitting preconception about what development must entail in a social bond has caused misconception about what development means in *this* novel. Even aside from humane or political habits of mind, one of two major tendencies in a hierarchy, particularly as it must be presented in a democratic environment, tempts to this confusion. In the ideal courtly dynamic stasis, there exists an ordination of degrees securely graduated, yet interpersuasive, to that extent interidentifying, and thus mobile in imagination. As against this ideal, the hierarchy may collapse in one of two similar but distinct ways. Either all the ranked terms may be imperiously summoned into the god-term (a providential Tom Sawyer), or there may be a thorough egalitarian leveling to some lower common denominator. Twain exploits both tendencies masterfully for purposes of purification: to make the basic courtly issues salient and to pretend simultaneously that they are not; thus the right hand can do vigorously what the left hand does not know. An examination of hierarchy's tendency to collapse in the direction of equality, because it requires primary consideration of Huck's development, calls for rather tenacious pursuit of ancillary ideas before the other tendency—the imperial summons—will again claim our attention. One investigation leads us to the novel's pivotal action, the other to its end.

I have in mind first, of course, Jim. Jim is the repeated focal point of Huck's internal struggle; and Huck's apparently callous relationship to him in the concluding section has usually either been explained away as Twain's blunder or as not meaning what it seems to, or else used as conclusive evidence that Huck's "growth" was nonexistent after all. The truth is, between themselves Jim and Huck achieve a comic and poignant kind of liberty and fraternity, but not equality. Huck's much-discussed statement that no one was killed in a steamboat accident (" 'No'm. Killed a nigger.' ") is not simply indicative of Huck's perhaps harmless failure to generalize from his earlier revelations about Jim. Nor is "nigger" when directly applied to Jim simply a term wholly neutralized by its common generic usage: " 'Ain't them old crippled picks and things in there good

enough to dig a nigger out with?' " Huck incredulously asks
Tom, who is intent on promoting Jim to State Prisoner (p.
314). Jim is, in fact, usually "my nigger" to Huck. Yet this
is the proprietary air not of slave possession but of loyal
noblesse oblige toward a friend who is nevertheless a social
inferior and never has ceased to be after carefully attaching
himself to Huck in exactly that combination of terms.
When Huck apologizes to Jim for tricking him at the end
of chapter xv, Huck is entirely aware that it is "a nigger"
to whom he is apologizing. His apology does not alter his
consciousness of relative status but if anything impresses it
on him, because Huck despises above everything having to
feel "low-down," "humble," and "mean," as he typically
does whenever he is troubled.

The books tempts us to misread precisely by playing up
such tensions and resolutions as those in the apology scene,
as a condition for making the courtly motive manifest
dramatically but hidden linguistically and socio-morally.
(Even here, however, we will note a double effect.) As hierarchies create themselves by an endless structural drama of
symbolic and actual transgressions, resistance, and resolution, so Twain depicts status-defining tests of authority accompanied by apology, praise, and demonstrations of loyal
confidence. To understand both Huck's development and
Twain's purifying equivocation, we can proceed at once to
the major turning point of the novel, the trickster Huck
Finn's remarkable assertion at the end of chapter xv: "I
didn't do [Jim] no more mean tricks. . . ." The assertion has
the rhetorical status of a promise, apparently foreclosing a
troublesome possibility. But it seems to be a true promise
to the reader only if it is interpreted rather narrowly, since
Huck subsequently engages in at least three contradictory
actions commonly cited as showing that he has not really
matured his perception of Jim: he does not tell Jim that the
Duke and the King are frauds, he acquiesces in their binding Jim and dressing him in a comically demeaning "King
Lear" costume, and he cooperates with Tom's similar ex-

ploitation of Jim on the Phelps farm. If we examine both the immediate and the general contexts, however, the matter appears in a different light, and in turn illumines the rest of the novel.

First, the remainder of the quoted sentence reads: "and I wouldn't done that one [i.e., trick] if I'd a knowed it would make him feel that way." Nothing in the three later actions indicates, either to Huck or the reader, that Jim's feelings are hurt by his treatment. Jim, like Huck, at last comically protests the physical inconveniences involved in Tom's proceedings, but there is no sign that his dignity or *amour propre* are touched, as they are in chapter xv by what might seem a much less significant transgression against him. Exactly like Huck, Jim yields to higher authority at the end: "Jim he couldn't see no sense in the most of it, but allowed we was white folks and knowed better than him; so he was satisfied . . ." (p. 321). Shortly after this, Jim farcically apologizes to Tom for briefly rebelling against the further burdens Tom sees as opportunities for glory.

Second, the sequence of events leading up to and away from chapter xv demonstrates that what is at stake when Jim does stand up for his dignity as an individual is the hierarchically appropriate area of stylistic authority that signifies his identity. Huck's trick climaxes a running battle over sovereignty in superstitious magic. Huck acknowledges Jim's lore ("Jim knowed all kinds of signs"), but he is also covetous of it and seeks to debunk it. Although the novel shows that there is an overlap of socially decorous stylistic power here between slaves and lower-class whites, and although there is a natural tension in Huck because of the ambiguous relationship of dependency between a white child and an adult runaway slave, the conflict of dominion also manifests Huck's stylistic hunger. By this I mean that Huck, existing on the margins of divergent classes, and concomitantly possessing a sensitive, frequently troubled consciousness, is exceptionally avid for stylistic devices that seem to have calmative power internally and externally. At the same time, his debunking habit not only is an attempt to neutralize and resist potentially threatening stylistic powers, but more importantly is a reflection of his intense disappointment at finding that the allegedly potent device is yet another lie, that his hunger has been teased and not fulfilled. He is "all in a sweat" to try out Tom's magic lantern and to raid the magically transformed Sunday School picnic, as well as (for Huck) strongly denunciatory on discovering each to be just another "one of Tom Sawyer's lies" (p. 32).

The trick Huck plays after he and Jim have been separated in the fog is one that causes his companion, as Huck knows it will, to interpret omens according to the black man's rightful powers. Huck expects the trick to debunk Jim's alleged potency by turning it into an object of fun. So intent is he on this courtly competition-*cum*-entertainment, his instinctive but confused resistance to "egalitarian collapse," that he fails to see that the trick transgresses against the interconnected loyalty of friendship—making light of Jim's worry over Huck's disappearance—and the dominion marked by the structural subordinate as rightfully his. Although Jim may incidentally dispute about Solomon and the French language, he repeatedly stresses, either in explicit statement or in a tactful silence whose force Huck feels, the accuracy of his magical predictions regarding snakeskins and other such emblems. Thus in the concluding chapter Jim's only derived moral from his captivity and Tom's payment "for being prisoner for us so patient" is that this wealth corroborates Jim's earlier prediction: " 'signs is *signs*, mine I tell you. . . .' "

In chapter xv Jim speaks his rebuke as a man of a social class that knows the sting of the word "trash" for Huck: " 'Dat truck dah is *trash*; en trash is what people is dat puts dirt on de head er dey fren's en makes 'em ashamed.' " In effect, Jim is urging Huck not to act like white trash in seeing a black man's suitable area of dominion as a threat to his own, as would Huck's Pap. Indeed, the firm implication is that the only way for the two escapees to be friends and to have their joint liberty secured is for Huck to cease viewing Jim's identifying dominion as competitive—that is, as existing on an equal plane where it must be countered or co-opted. In the context of Huck's sharply felt humiliation before a friend and "nigger," Jim has proscribed *mean* tricks in both senses of the adjective. Metaphorically speaking, Huck must not only learn to render unto Caesar what is Caesar's but unto Lazarus the Beggar what is his—a universally harder lesson perhaps. Jim is telling Huck, "don't do that"; but every such negative supposes a positive, a "do that instead." The positive injunction is immediately forthcoming in the next crisis. Jim's scornful use of the loaded word "trash" is the obverse of his epithet, "white genlman," in the following scene, in conjunction with the pivotal concept of trustworthy friend. Whatever Jim's conscious intentions, both statements are received by Huck, and function in the dramatic situation, as suasions to the same end: Huck must not abuse Jim's confidence because of the intertwined obligations of friendship and a variety of *noblesse oblige*.

As Huck leaves the raft intending to betray Jim now that the enormity of the slave's liberation seems clear, Jim's rhetoric of praise states as fact a result in Huck that is desired, just as his preceding reproof ritually described a condition that was not wanted. The blended progression of appeals to liberty, fraternity, and finally courtly non-equality demands full quotation:

> "Pooty soon I'll be a-shout'n for joy, en I'll say, it's all on accounts o' Huck; I's a free man, en I couldn't ever ben free ef it hadn' ben for Huck; Huck done it. Jim won't ever forget you, Huck; you's de bes' fren' Jim's ever had; en you's de *only* fren' ole Jim's got now."
>
> I was paddling off, all in a sweat to tell on him; but when he says this, it seemed to kind of take the tuck all out of me. I went along slow then, and I warn't

right down certain whether I was glad I started or
whether I warn't.

And then Jim delivers the courtier's ultimate: "When I
was fifty yards off, Jim says: 'Dah you goes, de ole true
Huck; de on'y white genlman dat ever kep' his promise to
ole Jim.' Well, I just felt sick" (p. 127).

The passage evinces Twain's purification-by-equivocation
by portraying extreme courtliness but disguising it in Jim's
extreme stereotypically "nonpolite" dialect. Once stripped
in imagination of its "low" dialect distortions, the passage
is disclosed as a near-feudal hortatory celebration. Its use of
the decorous intermixture of grammatical persons enacts the
desired combination of friendship and reverent hierarchical
naming, casting "Jim" and "Huck" (" 'Huck done it. Jim
won't ever forget you, Huck' ") as actors in an inevitable
drama of potency and consequent praise. While acting in
a face-to-face situation—me-and-you, if not I-Thou—the
speaker repeatedly summons the revered focal third person,
climactically as the "true" Huck. He then, in an admiring-
soliciting apposition, defines that the true Huck, whatever
the appearances, is a white gentleman, one defined in relation to an implicitly powerless Jim and further distinguished in being the only gentleman true to that relationship. And this last reminder of obligation is delivered
clearly over fifty yards of water, in a manner that bespeaks
the intimate distance designated in the words.

Consequently, when Huck is accosted by the men in the
skiff, for one of the two crucial times in the novel he tries
to speak, "but the words wouldn't come." Both here and
in the famous parallel episode in chapter xxxi, the identical
formula signifies a moment when Huck has been put in his
place in regard to Jim—once when Jim beseeches him and
again when Huck tries to beseech Providence. Both times,
Huck's failure of speech is allied to Jim's verbal triumph
of praise, for Huck explicitly recalls Jim's earlier gratitude
as the climactic memory leading to his "low-down" but

noble decision for hell. Here in chapter XVI, Huck can do nothing but tell the men in the skiff a low-down but noble lie.

My argument should not be understood as saying that Huck is even momentarily deceived into thinking that he is really a gentleman, either in the social situation at large, or "at heart" in an absolute sense. But Huck's place is nevertheless that of gentleman in regard to Jim, for two reasons. One is the rather minor, obvious, but still important fact that Huck is Jim's social superior in every way but age (this of course does not ennoble Huck, but in this scene we are reminded, as elsewhere, that there is a quantum-jump from one level to the other simply because Huck is white, Jim is black). The second, and fictionally major, reason is that Jim's rhetoric situates Huck in a superior and ennobled role much more because Jim wants and needs it to be so than because Huck consciously does. Huck would have been content with stylistic sparring that, however defensively, would neutralize and appropriate Jim's manner of identification. Jim, who is stylistically secure, knows the obligations of place and coaches Huck to see them also by praises and condemnations that are at once recipes for speech and prescriptions for role.

Moreover, Huck's two key failures of speech are decisions not to trick Jim, not to betray his trust in the name of society's law or what Huck takes to be divine precept. The decisions are reached not because Huck has ceased to be a socially involved being but because Jim's yoked dyslogistic and eulogistic terms have renamed Huck's uneasy psychosocial marginality; they manifest the better sense in which Huck should be above Jim and condemn the lesser. Jim has laid his finger on Huck's lips by instinctively touching Huck's vital marginality and transforming it, refining it in relation to Jim. The repeated passive construction ("the words wouldn't come") coupled with Huck's verbally resourceful lying in the first case and verbally energetic "I'll go to hell!" in the second, indicate the active-passive psychosocial equilibration, which is a restriction on the one hand and an enabling freedom on the other. Jim is simultaneously a person and an internal necessity that has revealed itself. Before this, Huck has shown that he knows much about what is above him; with his trickster's apology to Jim and his trickster's defense of him, Huck begins also to discover what is "below." Nothing in the book is quite the same after this point.

When the book goes ashore after Huck's courtly lie (with the steamboat collision, the Grangerford adventure, and our subsequent survey of the river villages under the tutelage of the Duke and the King), we are not abandoning the basic issues of developing consciousness for the sake of divergent social satire. Instead, we are exploring further with Twain the implications of Huck's marginal being, and collaterally, his promises to Jim and to us. We are being led to understand what Huck has decided for and against, and will have to decide again and again in the refining of his hierarchical consciousness even as he attempts to evade full awareness. Jim's relative placing of Huck as white gentleman initiates a motif that the narrative develops: "Col. Grangerford was a gentleman, you see. He was a gentleman all over; and so was his family." Our narrator's unwittingly comic generalization is carried over in its generic perspective into the physical description: "he had the thinnest kind of lips, and the thinnest kind of nostrils, . . . and the blackest kind of eyes . . ." (p. 146). Grangerford is also seen as a white gentleman, in Jim's confidence-oriented sense: "He was as kind as could be—you could feel that, you know, and so you had confidence." Huck's, and Twain's, relish in describing the family's courtly bearing and behavior with one another, especially in the breakfast ceremony, is not somehow canceled out by the satire of the house-beautiful gimcracks or of Emmiline's sappy sacerdotal Naming (" . . . the sacred name / Of Stephen Dowling Botts"), or even of the feuding that murders children. Rather, the feudal postures stand out the more dramatically

in their positive manifestation and in turn make the sentimentality and cruel waste respectively the more comically
and pathetically telling as inherent temptations, self-perver-
sions of the hierarchical motive. Similarly, the antics of the
Duke and the King in the villages and on the raft are a
"purifying" parody of genuine *noblesse oblige* spelled out at
comically inventive length to demonstrate the constant pull
toward disintegration in the attitude. Says the Duke to the
other vagabonds, " 'I will reveal [my identity] to you, for I
feel I may have confidence in you' " (p. 167). He and the
King then proceed to betray each other and everyone else
with a fine calculating indiscrimination that sets off the
benign and outwardly directed trickster hierarchy of Huck
and Jim, and also amplifies the inevitable tendency within
it.

In this regard, it is certainly true that the novel presents
a conflict between Huck's and Jim's "community of saints"
and society ashore.[5] But it is also axiomatic that in order for
the conflict to be meaningful there must be some common
issue between raft and shore communities, or else Twain is
indeed guilty of the elementary compositional error of mix-
ing apples and oranges—failing to establish some common
ground ("comparison") within which a conflict ("contrast")
is significant either dramatically or rationally. It has often
been criticism, rather, that has treated conflict without
thinking very hard about some unity that must underlie it.
In effect, however, we have already located this ground in
the combined courtly relationships of bad faith and good
faith between Huck and Jim that are brought to a head in
chapters xv and xvi. These relationships are given extended
development in the scenes emphasizing the shore society's
hierarchical suasive dramas of trickery, self-deception, and
good faith (as for example the mutual fidelity of the
Grangerfords evidenced in both benign and malign forms
of courtliness and feudal loyalty). The irony of the mixed

[5] The famous phrase, of course, is Lionel Trilling's, in his introduction to the Rinehart edition, 1948.

dramas on shore exists under the fictive rubric of the raft-community *quid pro quo*: that in order not to betray Jim's trust, Huck must trick almost everyone else he meets. The question is not universal trust, but where one tries to draw the line of hierarchical loyalty and institutionalized betrayals. In other words, it is always the question of one community of presumable saints defined in contradistinction to another of non-saints. One answer is the Grangerfords versus the Shepherdsons, with intrafamily loyalty and interfamily ambushes. As for trust within the family, there is the elopement of Sophia Grangerford and Harney Shepherdson; and there is the Wilks episode to show what can come of trusting "uncles." The Phelps family is of course Twain's comment on the "classless" society within a pseudo-democracy: the lovable and ineffectual farmer Phelps who trusts everyone, and imprisons Jim.

With the issues unfolded in all their combinations in the society whose Providence still conditions Huck's mind, we return again at the climax to the central courtly issue, which is always and always will be alive, of good and bad faith between Huck and Jim and what deceptions and adjustments in courtly resources each crisis of confidence entails.

It is now possible to conclude with full understanding that Huck's earlier statement is correct: he will connive against Jim in the manner of a benign hierarchical superior and in a way that Jim does not object to in principle, but he will play on Jim no more mean tricks—again in the double sense of *mean*. The important thematic arrangement has equally significant consequences for narrative tone. Given this circumscription of Jim's dignity, Twain feels free to have Jim behave with impervious comic resilience, as in the novel's closing episode. Jim, like the other major figures, can thus act both pathetically and comically precisely because of a hierarchically graduated role. Further, Huck's several statements that he will shove something completely out of his mind and not bother about it anymore, like his rhetorical promise, are to be taken with a courtly qualification. In line with Huck's habit, he implicitly shoves Jim out of his mind during their first separation, and then on encountering him stresses, not his own relief and pleasure at seeing Jim alive, but the expectation of his "courtier's" manifest devotion: " . . . I reckoned it was going to be a grand surprise to him to see me again, but it warn't. He nearly cried, he was so glad, but he warn't surprised" (pp. 153–54).

To put the matter bluntly, Jim must be shoved out of mind periodically because Huck discovers that he means trouble; and "trouble" is Huck's fated burden, evaded only to be resumed. The relationship between Jim and Huck is consolidated around this disclosure. Yet this is a special, crucial case of the book's hierarchically enclosed repetitive design, wherein each thing that is a solution to troubled consciousness also turns out to be a source of renewed trouble: at the end of the first chapter Huck's situational discomfort is doubled by elusive fears having to do with lonesomeness, and Tom Sawyer is welcomed as a deliverer; then Tom's energetic stylistic punctiliousness and exposed lies become a bother and his gang collapses, so that when Pap steals Huck away he feels a welcome release in lazying away the day in accordance with "Pap's style"; then Pap's cruelty and his fearfully haunted consciousness become intolerable and nearly fatal; after Huck's Sawyer-style escape, Jim relieves Huck's loneliness on Jackson Island and seems an idyllically "comfortable" companion; but Jim and Huck compete for stylistic authority, and finally Jim becomes the epitome of troubling consciousness while still remaining the objectification of inner idyllic peace; and the rest of the book alternates between separating Huck from Jim and reuniting them joyfully, so that Jim functions primarily as dramatic relieving presence until the con men's betrayal reestablishes him as the primary emblem of deep disturbance.

If Jim begins to introduce Huck to a knowledge of his

lower boundary, the confidence game that Huck becomes involved in with the King and the Duke explores this boundary as having its own pleasure-seeking yearning for unconsciousness. Huck's lovable and dangerous habit of shoving things out of his mind is both true to his kindly, circumspect nature and a temptation to the implicit self-betrayal of betraying Jim and the painful conscious life. Twain depicts this type of betrayal, as he had in *Innocents Abroad*, in the anonymous mobs of spectators whose entertainments reciprocate the casual cruelty the charlatans practice on them. Here the pleasure principle of unconscious self-indulgence exists with a vengeance; and here, of necessity, Huck's perspective elevates above the sleep of consciousness: "There was empty drygoods boxes under the awnings, and loafers roosting on them all day long, whittling them with their Barlow knives; and chawing tobacco, and gaping and yawning and stretching—a mighty ornery lot" (p. 187). We recall Huck's own gaping and stretching, stylistic misbehavior unjustly countered with threats of hell; but Huck's later perspective is seen as a contradiction only if we fail to recognize contextual differences. These "loafers," persistently seen by Huck with the same generic perspective he had applied to the Grangerfords, are those who had sportingly given the Duke and the King a lead in order to chase them with dogs; who in the immediate context torture dogs and pigs in the streets for entertainment; who turn the murder of Boggs into an entertaining reenactment by the man in the tall white hat; and who finally, to the sounds of pans and bells, turn the two rascals into "monstrous big soldier-plumes" (p. 299) for entertaining punishment. No matter who tricks or is tricked by the other, the con men and their audiences expose the tyranny of the pleasure principle, the rule of unconsciousness. Huck's kind of trickery is offset sharply as an elementary act of survival by his increasingly disapproving view of the charlatans, even while their betrayals underscore a corrupting potential inherent within Huck's relation to Jim. In exactly the same fashion, Huck's superior angle of vision on the somnolent, untrustworthy Deep South culture distinguishes both his shared potential and individual difference. We fail to see the nature of Twain's narrative art unless we can understand that the development in both narrative and narrative consciousness is the refining definition of a given marginal existence that can never be otherwise than marginal. Huck's earlier and later perspectives will appear contradictory if we can recognize what Poirier calls social involvement only in one form because of the "egalitarian" confusions noted before. Or, equivalently: only if we fail to see that the difference is explained by the very advancement of consciousness Poirier also must deny.

The Colonel Sherburn episode, it follows from this reasoning, is not the anomaly that some readers have thought it to be. For Sherburn's aristocratic height conclusively defines the mob's lowness, and the other way around. On the one hand, Sherburn is intolerable: an aristocrat whose coolly conscious control, reflected in his every deliberate word and movement, also involves him in the cold-blooded murder of a helpless old man who is fleeing him. Twain's revulsion is plainly shown by the emphasis on Boggs' physical harmlessness and on his weeping daughter. Yet Twain's sympathy is also with the Colonel's disgust at his inferior's gross impropriety to him, as is shown in the next scene, when the Colonel's conscious verbal skill embodies his courageous, knowledgeable superiority over the mob. Twain can put final confidence in neither high nor low—neither in full linguistic, moral, and perceptive consciousness, which he sees allied to a rigid code devoted to the tyranny of the god-term; nor in comfortable unconsciousness, which he sees allied to vacuous boredom or entertainment devoted to the tyranny of the devil-term.

Sherburn is pure autonomous authority, deliberate act contrasted to the blindly motion-ridden mob surging through the streets. Huck dodges the mob for his life, and then stands without comment, "silently" before Sherburn as if nearly mesmerized before a fire or a snake that seems to be only one thing, monolithically powerful. This is a king's authority, not a courtier's; and it is both envied and feared as Twain presents it, in a striking variation on the rhetoric that maintains the sense of hierarchical dynamic stasis. To understand this means to see that Huck's narrative perspective changes subtly in order to show variations of the same reality. Again, if the book's fundamental focus is a psychosocial reality, to examine shore society means to investigate Huck's essential psyche in all the potentials it confederates. Huck's troubled choices, in turn, are an individual vitalization of mechanical cultural balances, isolated through Huck's marginally dualistic response to them, which is never able to stay either conscious or unconscious for very long. Thus, after confronting Sherburn, Huck immediately heads for the circus; but here his thoughtless pleasure must contest with his worry about the bareback rider.

III

In his calmative aspect, Jim is in the passive voice, accompanying Huck's idyllic peace in the Jackson Island cave, and during the Mississippi nights that "swum by," and in the famous river sunrise scene. Tom is in the active voice, allowing aggressive action by renaming trouble eulogistically as *adventure*. " 'He'd call it an adventure,' " Huck says in the name of Tom to persuade Jim to board the *Walter Scott*. Here Huck anticipates the Phelps section, where the recurrent ideas of trouble and adventure perform an antic dance around each other as Tom tries to transform the first into the second by main verbal force. The power of Tom's naming satisfies Huck's stylistic hunger by giving his protean marginality a way to "act" in order to act. But it also constitutes danger. At this juncture we return, after following the idea of egalitarian collapse through its consequences, to the second previously noted tendency of a hierarchy, to summon all the ranked members into the pinnacle term.

Huck's marginality accounts for both his sensitivity and his insensitivity. To be marginal is to be uncertain of where one's ties of obligation exist and, conversely, what responsibilities others owe oneself. In the largest perspective, it is to be anxious concerning the pertinence of events to the self and vice versa, and thus to be alert and perceptively vulnerable to them. Marginal acuteness thus covers the wide range indicated by these instances: Huck's fear of haunting night-sounds; his acute delight at a river sunrise scene, which nevertheless includes notation of a deceptive woodpile and rotting fish; and his singular concern for a circus rider. This consciousness is what Huck and Twain mean by "conscience," the free-floating scrutiny that, unconfident of any stable accountability, projects personal obligation when cruel suffering is perceived, although one's moral choice has not caused the pain. To recall the vocabulary instituted earlier: "conscience" is a property of consciousness like superstition, promoting deed into act, but without the ameliorative ritual. And we can now understand that this exaggerating consciousness is profoundly concordant, generally, with Huck's trickster talent for "stretching," and specifically, with his habitual self-portrayal as a waif beset by calamity, as a means of disarming others. All this is summed up when Huck says, as he sees the King and the Duke punished by being tarred-and-feathered and ridden on a rail, " . . . I warn't feeling so brash as I was before, but kind of ornery, and humble, and to blame, somehow—though *I* hadn't done nothing. But that's always the way; it don't make no difference whether you do right or wrong, a person's conscience ain't got no sense, and just goes for him *anyway*. If I had a yaller dog that didn't know no more than a person's conscience does, I would pison him. It takes up more room than all the rest of a person's insides, and yet ain't no good, nohow. Tom Sawyer he says the same" (p. 300). What Tom Sawyer typically says comprises a way of hypnotizing the moral imagination. Tom's style is to make discomfort the obligatory, manneristic stuff of adventure. In a burlesque perversion of conscious ingenuity, Tom labors at the gold-leaf distinctions (Huck's term) that the literary authorities demand. By contrast, though Jim's presence is recurrently troubling to Huck, the trouble is transmuted by Jim's courtly descriptions and proscriptions into a clarifying stipulation of confidence. Yet Tom's systematizing of clear-cut but illusory obligation is so much more comprehensive in what it seemingly accounts for and confidently clinches in place that Huck finds it irresistible. The book ends by rescuing Huck with the frontier metaphor that embodies his cultural status. The novel breaks off, that is, with Huck's reestablishing his tense marginality, preparing to escape to the borders of civilization "ahead of the rest," but not before Twain has indeed almost collapsed everything into Tom and his aristocratic play. If we look ahead to clarify the implications of this tendency, we see that *A Connecticut Yankee in King Arthur's Court* does collapse all into one consciousness that reveals its psychosocial reality in a courtly dream-vision fictionally poising the objective and subjective. For the protagonist the dreamfact of identity is intolerable and is attacked and destroyed self-destructively. From here it is only a very short step to "Which Was the Dream?", "The Great Dark," and the confused manuscripts Paine palmed off as *The Mysterious Stranger*. This last pseudo-tale is broadly symptomatic, for it really exists as a dislocated ending that Twain, perhaps self-protectively, could not find creative ligatures for among several inadequate narrative alternatives: the solipsistic collapse of everything into a solitary ruling thought.

Huck's language works against this strongly seductive summons of the god-term. It is in Huck's language, after

all, that we sense him most firmly; and it is in his language
that many of the best readers of Twain have tried to discover the old true Huck amid his renewed marginal pullings
and driftings. Huck's language resists a dangerous hierarchical mounting not only in a general vernacular lowness
but in two features that can be isolated within his vernacular. One is the often-remarked negative flair of his vocabulary, his constructions, and his outlook, which also signifies
in other related ways: as an attempt to flatly negate "trouble," for instance in the formula he uses to trick Jim with
an alleged dream ("'I hain't seen no fog, nor no islands,
nor no troubles, nor nothing.'"); and as a reflection of the
relatively unfixed identity that makes Huck, within his
marginal boundaries, a protean, stylistically avid, trickster.

Huck's other linguistically resistant trait may be termed,
to recall the prior discussion again, his anti-prayer. That is,
Huck's narrative speech placidly digs in its heels against
changing linguistic registers to comport with the dignity
of its subject matter. On the opening page of the narrative,
for example, the unwitting irreverence at once overtly acknowledges the social distinctions—Mr. Mark Twain, Judge
Thatcher; and Aunt Polly and the Widow as possible exceptions to universal lying—and speaks of everyone and
every action, high or low, in the only language Huck knows.
The pleasure the language furnishes is precisely the fresh
sense it gives of the hierarchical shibboleths by innocently
failing to do them linguistic obeisance. Huck's anti-prayer
effortlessly refuses to acknowledge that now the Judge, now
the Widow's charitable adoption, now the investment of
significant funds, is being treated. According to Huck's report, the Widow "allowed she would sivilize" him much as
Jim Smiley allows he will train the best jumping frog in
Calaveras County. Even when Huck clearly wants to praise,
the language seems to go its own way, as in his enthusiastic
pronouncement on the King's Shakespearean performance:
"It seemed like he was just born for it; and when he had
his hand in and was excited, it was perfectly lovely the way

he would rip and tear and rair up behind when he was getting it off" (p. 185). "Perfectly lovely" tells us which way the speech seems to want to go by gesturing toward fragile upper-class locution; but the subsequent phrasing refuses to budge, in comic counterpoint to the sort of uplift it describes. Another, longer example, dealing with Mary Jane Wilks' promise to pray for Huck, can provide its own commentary in collocating ideas of prayer "for its own sake," flattery, and equivocal nonflattery ranging from the obvious to connotative nuances like "lays":

> Pray for me! I reckoned if she knowed me she'd take a job that was more nearer her size. But I bet she done it, just the same—she was just that kind. She had the grit to pray for Judas if she took the notion—there warn't no backdown to her, I judge. You may say what you want to, but in my opinion she had more sand in her than any girl I ever see; in my opinion she was just full of sand. It sounds like flattery, but it ain't no flattery. And when it comes to beauty—and goodness too—she lays over them all. I hain't ever seen her since that time that I see her go out of that door; no, I hain't ever seen her since, but I reckon I've thought of her a many and a many a million times, and of her saying she would pray for me; and if ever I'd a thought it would do any good for me to pray for *her*, blamed if I wouldn't done it or bust. (pp. 250–51)

Huck's admiration for Tom indicates a love of "style" for its own sake to which Huck blinds himself (as the Connecticut Yankee will do later) whenever he implies that he is totally pragmatic. This delusion helps to maintain the hierarchical distinction between what one admires and therefore to an extent identifies oneself with, and what one nevertheless resists becoming wholly. In this sense, Huck's language, in enacting Twain's purifying concealment, is also partly a self-concealment, or benign repression, for Huck. The language refuses to go the whole way with

Huck's admirations. Like his grumbling even as he submits to Tom's domination, it is a form of foot-dragging to
maintain the coherent continuity of one identity—a resistance to that with which Huck identifies himself and yet
refuses to become identical.

Nevertheless, though the language is courtly resistant in
its inability to change registers, within its register it is not
deluded at all, but is characterized by such adjectives as
noble and *grand* at one extreme, and *low-down* and *ornery*
at the other. The result is a courtly tension of high and
low in the set of hierarchically loaded terms, so that Huck
can speak of a "noble good lot" of rats and yet provide this
sort of verbal placing: "Well, when Tom and me got to the
edge of the hill-top we looked away down into the village
and could see three or four lights twinkling, where there
was sick folks, maybe; and the stars over us was sparkling
ever so fine; and down by the village was the river, a whole
mile broad, and awful still and grand" (pp. 22–23). The
effect is dependent not so much on the commonplace complimentary adjectives as on the simple stateliness of rhythm
accompanying the discriminations of place. Another passage,
eschewing all fine adjectives but instead employing language like "creeping" and "monstrous big," is even more
elegant in its rhythm of placing:

> I went up and set down on a log at the head of the
> island, and looked out on the big river and the black
> driftwood and away over to the town, three mile away,
> where there was three or four lights twinkling. A mon-
> strous big lumber-raft was about a mile up stream,
> coming along down, with a lantern in the middle of it.
> I watched it come creeping down, and when it was most
> abreast of where I stood I heard a man say, "Stern oars,
> there! heave her head to starboard!" I heard that just
> as plain as if the man was by my side. (p. 60)

For all the economical effect of the passage, it allows for
unobtrusive stylistic elaborations of location that are "in-

efficient" in the most courtly way, the sound and rhythm celebrating the easy release of intimate distance: "away over to the town, three mile away"; "coming along down"; "as if the man was by my side." With this kind of beguiling lucidity, it is difficult to notice that Huck is presented as both sitting and standing.

The excitement of Huck's language, as we begin to find out not very far into the novel, is that the slouching manner is a spell cast over a subsurface of insistent disturbances. Its defensive function for Huck in maintaining his distance from the upper and lower boundary terms, Tom and Jim, also appropriately gives his narrative speech its courtly circumspection, as in his habit of saying, "but I never let on," or "but I never said nothing," and his formulaic "no matter" and "no harm" regarding some apparent human failing. This is the rhetoric of comfort, more exactly the coziness that hearkens back to *Innocents Abroad* in creating the sensation of comfort sharpened by the threats encompassing it. As narrative action and rhetorical enactment proceed, comfort becomes not a negative state but an achievement that attracts our sympathy with Huck's restless escape toward rest. The opening pages negotiate a tacit understanding with the reader to the effect that Huck's discomfort, as it is stylistically transformed and shielded, will produce our own feeling of relaxation. It "ain't no matter" whether we know or not who Huck Finn is; there is "no harm" meant by Huck's behavior or the manners of his "dismal regular and decent" captors. "That is nothing," that Mark Twain lied in *Tom Sawyer*; we all lie, and it was mostly a true book anyway. And it does not matter how one talks, for the seemingly careless chaos of grammar appears to get the job done very competently, inviting us simply to enjoy the language's swift energy since the "matter" of just who and just how does not appear to demand much concern. This assurance of comfort, renewed periodically, acts as a buffer for every disturbing event that follows (modern critics have counted up the murders and other cruelties).

Otherwise stated, this is an assurance that the title of the book is trustworthy, that we will be reading *the adventures of* . . . , with all this promises for the treatment of disturbance as excitement, and mayhem as challenge. Like Huck's promise of no more mean tricks, this rhetorical assurance must be understood as a definitively ambivalent statement.

The novel as a whole is formally designed to arouse and preserve the deliciously cozy feeling of Jim and Huck snug in their cave watching the storm. In the light of this conservation of feeling, which must renew a threat and turn it adventurously into something new and strange, we can elucidate the "problem of the ending." Or rather, we can observe how it elucidates itself. In the closing section, Huck feels "easy and comfortable" (p. 290) on finding that he is supposed to play Tom Sawyer once more. But we are now naggingly bothered because for the first time at any length the book presents us with an untransformed trouble that we sense the more sharply because the three major characters sweat and contrive before our eyes to make it into adventure, even as Twain also now labors to find his culminating, all-transforming "snapper" of an ending. Now it is apparent that not only alchemic adventures but base-metal difficulties themselves must be fabricated, as Tom strongly complains. Tom supplies the reason as well: the people are too trusting (see especially pp. 308, 343). This implicit denial that there is real trouble to be encountered and countered is, paradoxically, disturbing, because our comfort has been constructed on the basis of the very real troubles that the book's adventures disclose and buffer. We are like Huck and Jim in their cave, watching, instead of a storm, Tom/Twain doing an interminable rain dance. And the troubles that we have seen have arisen exactly because people are too trusting in one sense and treacherous in another. Thus at the very time that Tom complains of a lack of difficulties—the complaint itself partly an indication of difficulty—we increasingly recognize several: Huck's bowing to Tom; Jim's mistreatment; and, making both of these disturbing in a way they otherwise would not be, Twain's drastic diffusion of language and invention in a joke that goes on far too long as it strains to end itself satisfactorily. Yet the near-collapse of the ending carries its own diagnosis in the play of the boys with Jim. The "failure" is more interesting than the successes of most writers, in analyzing the basic matter of the book by a pretended pretense that "it ain't no matter." The transformational labors that until now have been brilliantly successful unmask themselves. But retrospectively we can see that, throughout the work, a subsidiary theme has been the impossibility of fundamental transformations, reformations— as with Pap Finn and the new judge, the King at the camp meeting, and Huck's attempt to be a better boy by the prayer that would allow him to betray Jim. The attempts at making new by renaming are pretenses that are consequential in refining hierarchical perceptions, and in causing peace or discomfort for a time, but leave things unchanged in *essentials*. They are transformations, but they do not amount to transubstantiation. The redundancy of such attempts is summarized in Huck's exclamation near the end: "all that trouble and bother to set a free nigger free!"

This disclosure is also recapitulated in the repetitive adventure-structure of the book, signifying that Huck will always have "been there before" precisely by evading adoption to flee to the margins of society "ahead of the rest." Huck, in other words, is a genuinely marginal, not a liminal, figure—his interstitial existence is not temporary or probative, leading to a reconsolidation with a secure social order, but instead fundamentally constitutive of being. Nevertheless, though no essential change can take place, we have seen that Huck's consciousness does develop in a firmer awareness of the external and internal realities it embodies. His freedom is also his necessity: to evade between his bounds, and to refine his perception of what tricks and burdens they elicit. The farcical quality of the ending does not deny or negate this troubled understanding but seeks to manipulate it by an overt caricature, usurping its high power according to the book's operational logic, and thus making climactic adventure. The attempt is not to laugh it away but to make it, once and for all, gay. But at the same time, being true to itself, the novel must diagnose the impossibility of doing this in any final sense by verbal conjurations, the tricks of nomenclature.

The end is therefore predictably an attempted transmutation that laughs in part at its own failure to transubstantiate, inseparably from the effort Tom directs. Huck quits writing because he needs a rest, not because he has found an end. We are left with the fundamental trouble: as Huck says, the trouble it is to make a book; to purify a troubling motive by inventing both fictional difficulties and the ruses that convert them into adventures; to call into existence a court and a fantastic "democratic" set of kings, dukes, and other courtiers and turn it all into equivocal elucidation and concealment. Yet, besides this revelation of fundamental trouble, we are also left with Huck's reference to the adventures he anticipates with Tom and Jim in the Territory. The two components face each other in an unresolvable, but endlessly self-refining, dialectic of hierarchical consciousness: trouble and adventure, Jim and Tom; with Huck the mobile diacritical mark between them.

Everything ends in a game, but Twain has nearly had a king's immunity all along. Huck's disclosure of fundamental trouble is of course a revelation not of his, but of Twain's, basic efforts. Huck's final complaint of discomfort—the Author to His Book in an inverted envoy—is a self-dismissal and a last gesture of comfort toward us, making us smile in permissive affection at Huck's characteristic language. With this pleasure we consolidate conclusively a shared adult vision with the real fabricator of these adventures.

Like Twain's initial notice, the closing section is preemptive. Whereas initially he had equivocally forbidden investigation, now Twain outbids our diagnosis of "failure" by himself being diagnostic. This affective distinguishing is after all the function of the courtier. Indeed, as Henry Nash Smith has pointed out, it is primarily Twain's voice we hear over Huck's during the concluding episode,[6] though Twain had led up to this dominance in Huck's increasing sentimentality regarding the Wilks' girls. Turning a mirror on the novel, Twain shows how it has not only depicted but woven transformational spells that smuggle into our perception one self-refining, circular motive of action. By making this situation the theme of parodic adventures, Twain gets us to forgive everything in uneasy amusement at seeing the difficulties showing through the adventures. The mirror, however, is not one but many since what is revealed is a self-reflexive contraband communication. Twain's longstanding device of the concluding palinode is thus perfected, for the implied mirror-sequence endlessly retracts, and withdraws retractions. I have said we are left facing adventures and troubles. This also means we are left with the authority who put up the warning notice in the first place; and who preceded it in the original edition by setting his sternly aristocratic likeness, from the new bust by Karl Gerhardt, directly facing Kemble's pen illustration of a ragamuffin Huckleberry Finn.

Huck is Twain's greatest creation, one of the greatest in literature, and the greatest usurpation by Twain. The self-wrenching, book-wrenching diagnosis purifies Twain of his purifier. Thus retracting its prize palinode, Twain's art reaches its height and effectively ends there.

This palmary authority that diagnoses and forgives itself dictates an underlying scholarly response to Twain that one critic has manifested bluntly in this way: "Of course a vision and the verbal means of its realization and execution are virtually inseparable. Mark Twain saw the world the best he was able to, given his special verbal resources."[7] The book itself of course provides the means of saying this kind of thing, even to the phrase that the critic might have

6 *Development*, pp. 130–34.
7 Trachtenberg, "Form of Freedom," p. 970.

used but did not: "a prisoner of style" (p. 344). If Twain is a prisoner of style, his style is lucidly conscious of it; and he is, at least in *Huckleberry Finn*, a prisoner as Jim is, making the most of being a royal prisoner as well as a "free nigger." Such criticism is, in its way, a perfect response to Twain, one he engineers with the alternate glee and despair of a lonely courtier who lacks a court. It is the response, fundamentally, of one interested in abstractly conceived "vision," what things "boil down to," and it is clear that this impulse has Twain's own blessing. Only, Twain was afraid that he knew what things did boil down to; and near the end of his career he wrote the knowledge as an ending that he could not reach, but bequeathed through a subordinate as an authoritatively inspired literary trick, *The Mysterious Stranger*, in a marvelously self-diagnosing act. The alternative was writing courtly elaborations that cannot find the end that is feared, but flirt toward and retreat from it, all the while pointing rhetorical vectors toward it: Mark Twain alone. The pleasures of this hierarchical round and the illuminations of psyche and society special to it are what too many searchers for literary *Weltanschauung* tend to derogate unwittingly in trying to pierce through the mask of rhetorical stances. But here the response, though it is invited, is not perfect, for Twain did not, could not, derogate in this fashion. He must keep putting between himself and the solitary "microscopic atom in me that is truly *me*" (as Hank Morgan calls it in *A Connecticut Yankee*) the lucidly revealing and lucidly concealing surfaces of his prose. In this reflexive resistance, the unended fragments and the fictionally unmoored ending of the last years are desperate versions of his earlier courtly successes. Mark Twain alone, is both joy and horror.

This is why, although Huck Finn is correct when he says in conclusion that there is nothing more to write, he is also correct in implying that further adventures would be forthcoming. These subsequent works by Twain seem to lie directly in the avenue of the present study, but they are really peripheral. From *A Connecticut Yankee* on, his writing makes no advances in rhetoric even as its thematic concern becomes more overt in situation and story line.[8] Thus the "Yankee of Yankees" becomes Boss as, in the name of democracy, he cons Arthur's court, destroys it, and then looks back with yearning, ostensibly toward the papier-mâché wife Sandy, but really toward the courtly world Twain creates and tries to transcend. And there are *Joan of Arc* and *Pudd'nhead Wilson*, both about the punishment, martyrdom, and rise of low-lofty figures, one tale accompanied by the maudlin praises of the aged French courtier-narrator and the other accompanied by a detached matrix of farce concerning aristocratic Italian twins.

The less Twain equivocates, the less he is fictively creative. Instead of courtly equivocation, there is a bifurcation between works. Twain's eulogistic impulse goes one way, into the hagiography of *Joan*. His dyslogistic impulse goes another, into the diatribes of Mark Twain in eruption. They remain together as coordinates only in the tired travel book that comes to Twain's financial rescue; or in the detective stories—one of them built feebly on "a confidence game"[9]— that displace formal praise and blame from ancient or modern courtliness into legal courts, and suffer badly from the attenuation. Lacking a court and needing one—that is, lacking a final god-term for his worship and an acceptable form of praise in a Gilded Age in which, for historical reasons directly related to Twain's dilemma, adulation was widely contaminated with bad sentiment—Twain must become a one-man court, performing all the functions of status discrimination. No wonder the exacerbated sense of his own troubled, clamorous, restless consciousness, the exasperation and increasing sense of mental pain. No wonder the gestures of calm giving way in the final years to fragments whose form and matter tell the story: the respect-

[8] For a powerful criticism of *Connecticut Yankee*'s failure of style, see Cox, pp. 198–221.

[9] *Tom Sawyer, Detective, Writings*, II, 141.

able man who is found out to be a cowardly knave; who is dominated secretly by a powerful inferior or by a Superintendent of Dreams in a slouch hat who is knavishly tricky; whose inner life becomes a dream life confused with the external world, both marked by merciless power struggles and vacant loneliness.

Correspondingly, in all the late completed works and the late fragments and philosophizing, there can be observed the splitting of Twain's psychosocial emphasis into separate absolutes: on the one hand, Twain's official philosophy of relentless social determinism, and, on the other, the psychological solipsism implicit in *A Connecticut Yankee* and explicit in the ending of *The Mysterious Stranger*. But in fact, as Paine jerrybuilt the latter tale from the manuscripts in which Twain wisely lost his way, the competing doctrinal attitudes dominate, respectively, the body and conclusion of the piece, with critics consequently attempting to join conceptually what Twain had fictionally put asunder. Earlier, Twain could fictively harmonize contradictions by mobile hierarchical arrangements of precedence and subordination. Untune that string, and hark the scholarly discord that has followed.

During the final part of his career, Twain wrote to Howells, "I suspect that to you there is still dignity in human life, & that Man is not a joke—a poor joke—the poorest that was ever contrived—an April-fool joke, played by a malicious Creator with nothing better to waste his time upon."[10] Twain of course could top this magisterial trickster's jape with a better maneuver; or, as he had put the matter more simply years earlier in another letter to Howells after the disastrous Whittier dinner jest, "Ah, well, I am a great & sublime fool. But then I am God's fool, & all His works must be contemplated with respect."[11] A courtier without a court could say no more, and no less.

[10] *Twain-Howells Letters*, II, 689.   [11] *Ibid.*, I, 215.

PART THREE

Nathanael West

Perhaps this is where we shall still discover the realm of our invention, *that realm in which we, too, can still be original, say, as parodists of world history and God's buffoons—perhaps, even if nothing else today has any future, our* laughter *may yet have a future.*

Nietzsche, *Beyond Good and Evil*

9

Trick or Trash

"There's a game we want to play and we need you to play it.—'Everyman his own Miss Lonelyhearts.' "

Miss Lonelyhearts[1]

IT is a fantastic, densely suggestive vision Shrike offers the hero in this mocking party invitation, though perhaps at first glance it does not seem remarkable in a book with more obviously fantastic events on every page. Everyman his own Miss Lonelyhearts—the modern priest, as Shrike calls him, the mediator supposed to alleviate individual suffering by refocusing it in the transformational perspectives of a culture's popular wisdom. If everyman is his own Miss Lonelyhearts, in a triumph of secular and religious Protestantism, then the role of all mediators, all cultural transmutation of suffering, is open to radical interrogation. Yet Shrike's words, since they are addressed to Miss Lonelyhearts himself, do maintain the necessity of a mordant play-role for the mediator: that of a cynosure, formal and empty in itself, but activating and activated by the responses of an audience. If Shrike's statement is designed both to undercut the protagonist's role and reveal its necessity as stimulus, the mockery also undercuts in every direction. For the audience's role too is clearly that of player—player at Miss Lonelyhearts. And the play thus collapses all distances, except tenuously willed play-distances, between audience and mediator, who share a negative status: precisely that of inability to be a Miss Lonelyhearts, either for oneself or for others.

This collapse of distance is fundamentally that between

---

[1] *The Complete Works of Nathanael West* (New York: Farrar, Straus & Cudahy, 1957), p. 132. Hereafter cited in the text.

a culture and its cultural mediator, the artist. It is the thematic *donée* giving rise to the main rhetorical contravention in Nathanael West's fiction. In West's compact body of writing as a whole, the thematic action is the fictive audience's resolute refusal to keep its place, because of either an impervious assumption that it already "understands" the performer, or Shrike's kind of superior presumption that he sees through him, or the audience's desperately vengeful crossing into the performer's space. The rhetorical counteraction is West's re-stimulation of distance with his own audience, the repairing of a precondition for art and culture. Condensing move and countermove, West described all his fiction when he called his first novel "a protest against writing books."[2] The initial work, indeed, presents the equivalent of West's primal scene, as a writer symbolizes his relation to his public in an obverse image of Shrike's mocking game:

> Some day I shall obtain my revenge by writing a play for one of their art theatres. A theatre patronized by the discriminating few. . . .
> In this play I shall take my beloved patrons into my confidence and flatter their difference from other theatre-goers. . . . Then, suddenly, in the midst of some very witty dialogue, the entire cast will walk to the footlights and shout Chekov's advice:
> "It would be more profitable for the farmer to raise rats for the granary than for the bourgeois to nourish the artist. . . ."
> In case the audience should misunderstand and align itself on the side of the artist, the ceiling of the theatre will be made to open and cover the occupants with tons of loose excrement. After the deluge, if they so desire, the patrons of my art can gather in the customary charming groups and discuss the play. (pp. 30–31)

[2] In an interview by A. J. Liebling, "Shed a Tear for Mr. West," *New York World Telegram*, 24 June 1931, p. 11.

The problem, for all its comically drastic statement here, is that of Melville and Twain, and again is converted into a searching theme: finding a distance from which an audience can be engaged and creative work can be done. Now it is the audience's over-familiarity, not (as with Melville a century earlier) the artist's, that is the crisis; and the writer, generalizing, sees in the threatened obliteration of distance the arch-anxiety and basic contamination of a civilization. Whenever an interpersonal distance is closed in West's fiction, there is frustration, impotence, or violence as the triad of possible results. There is no intimacy, for there was never a distance negotiable by the small unprecipitate gestures that respect a difference between persons and thus surmount it. There are only the alienations abridged by violence, or at the other extreme the facile familiarity that closes like an avalanche. To cite *Miss Lonelyhearts* again, the sexual scenes of engulfment with Fay Doyle are the counterpart of the anonymous punch the hero receives in the bar. The overarching model is found in the mutual titillation of performer and audience, an endless, sterile foreplay without issue except in abortive accidents like Miss Lonelyhearts' death, or dreams of consummating, purging violence such as end *The Day of the Locust*. With this model, *performer* becomes a loaded concept, and scenes of performance and attempted cultural mediation carry an overt sexual charge that communicates the teeth-clenched impotence of orgasm too often and too long denied. In brief, there can be no satisfying connection because one part of the population smugly assumes that the performer's connection has already been made—and "of course one knows all that"—and because the other part stolidly, hopelessly yearns for an impossibly transcendent connection. The common ground of these cultural moieties is existential deadness, and the common need is cultural regeneration after a deadening betrayal by a surfeit of mere novelties, the travesty of originality. West's work burns with a cold, sometimes self-scornful incandescence against smugness, and it moves with the tersely hurrying pace of a writer voicing his most feeling anxieties about hopeless, suffering inertia.

For approximately the last fifteen years, West has attracted his share of admiring criticism. But even his best commentators, I believe, have often praised him on misleading grounds.[3] One influential critical portrait is an intriguing Daumier creation: West as an exotic plant on our shores whose genus is really the Continental Decadent-Existentialist family of literature (represented, say, by the major Dostoevsky-Rimbaud-Celine branch). There is a great deal that is accurate and suggestive in this classification. But it seems to me that such a categorization is primarily significant because it is a response to something underlying the Continental label. It essentially identifies in West's fiction a crisis of confidence that is not exotic but indigenous. If confidence is the American Way, West saw that the modern failure of confidence is a national as well as an individual catastrophe, the wholesale contempt of familiarity that leaves no breathing space for mutual faith. He saw that the attempted American Way Out (as Shrike would say) of a schizophrenic debasement of selfhood is a game of confidence that easily becomes a confidence game. Like Melville and Twain, West found in the linked possibilities of confidence man and man-of-confidence the prototype of both the traditional American and the creative artist. But West's modern American exists primarily as a diminished variation of the prototype: he is the conned-man, the conned-artist, the unconfident confidence man.

West was part of a literary movement for which internationalism was a premise, not a program for writing. What

[3] West has had some able admirers, including F. Scott Fitzgerald, Edmund Wilson, William Carlos Williams, Josephine Herbst, and Daniel Aaron. Perhaps the best single book on West is Randall Reid, *The Fiction of Nathanael West* (Chicago: University of Chicago Press, 1967), which draws heavily from James F. Light's solid inaugural work, *Nathanael West: An Interpretive Study* (1961; rpt. Evanston, Ill.: Northwestern University Press, 1971).

West emphasized in his own comments on fiction were the native attributes and concomitant literary forms. His comments are focused on the overall cultural datum that allows for brief, concentrated effects that in turn enact the lack of foreground and sequel in accelerated American lives. Thus he wrote, directly on the question of appropriate form:

> Lyric novels can be written according to Poe's definition of a lyric poem. The short novel is a distinct form especially fitted for use in this country. France, Spain, Italy have a literature as well as the Scandinavian countries. For a hasty people we are too patient with the Bucks, Dreisers and Lewises. Thank God we are not all Scandinavians.
>
> Forget the epic, the master work. In America fortunes do not accumulate, the soil does not grow, families have no history. Leave slow growth to the book reviewers, you only have time to explode. Remember William Carlos Williams' description of the pioneer women who shot their children against the wilderness like cannonballs. Do the same with your novels.

West's next comment in this context, although it may seem unrelated to the desire for concentrated form, really treats one important means of attaining it:

> Psychology has nothing to do with reality nor should it be used as motivation. The novelist is no longer a psychologist. Psychology can become something much more important. The great body of case histories can be used in the way the ancient writers used their myths. Freud is your Bullfinch; you can not learn from him.[4]

This resource of cultural myths, in the possession of at least the "discriminating few" West was most concerned with reaching, allowed for the artist's vivid illustration of a

---

[4] "Some Notes on Miss L.," *Contempo* 3, 15 May 1933, 1–2; rpt. in *Nathanael West: A Collection of Critical Essays*, ed. Jay Martin (Englewood Cliffs, N.J.: Prentice-Hall, 1971).

society's revealing typologies, unimpeded by exposition on "motivation." The connection with brevity is made more explicit in a parallel set of West's comments on another, and general, cultural a priori of communication:

> In America violence is idiomatic. . . .
> What is melodramatic in European writing is not necessarily so in American writing. For a European writer to make violence real, he has to do a great deal of careful psychology and sociology. He often needs three hundred pages to motivate one little murder. But not so the American writer. His audience has been prepared and is neither surprised nor shocked if he omits artistic excuses for familiar events.[5]

Although West is using the term "motivation" in the special writer's sense of establishing a credible preparation for an event, it is still true that he is much less interested in individual case histories than in the one general malaise, the national mythic truth, appearing in different individual symptoms. For West, it is exactly the vastness of the contagion that permits him to delineate it concisely, in the short-breathed narrative rhythms that act out the terrible lucidity of a culture watching itself approach madness.

I

"Life is a pic-nic en costume; one must take a part, assume a character, stand ready in a sensible way to play the fool."

The Confidence-Man

The Cheated was the original title of West's last book, *The Day of the Locust*. All of West's characters have been cheated of self, whether they belong to the frenetic group of performers West calls masqueraders, or to the faceless, uneasy mob whose appetite for a vital identity is served by the masquerade. As Tod Hackett reflects, the anarchic

---

[5] "Some Notes on Violence," *Contact*, 1, no. 3 (1932), 132–33; rpt. in Martin, ed., *Critical Essays*.

audiences who throng Hollywood's cinema openings are the cream of America's madmen because they realize that they have been betrayed by the promise of life for the free individual. Con men have beckoned them to the "Road of Life," the national Dream culminating at the frontier's end in movie-set façades and the millennial expectations of the Church of the Third Coming ("Come Redeemer" beseeches the music at Harry Greener's funeral). As in Melville and Twain, the relationship between cheater and dupe is profoundly symbiotic. But in West, distinctive emphasis is on the state of being cheated—the given existential condition of a culture. The society's cheaters and façades are both symptom and result, created on demand: "the group of uneasy people . . . stood staring at the performers in just the way that they stared at the masqueraders on Vine Street. It was their stare that drove Abe and the others to spin crazily and leap into the air with twisted backs like hooked trout" (p. 264). West's characters are poorly made creatures, all fundamentally like Homer Simpson, because all that remains of real identity is a vestigial self felt as a restless desire for completion. The audience's demand that they be furnished with a full, authentic existence is insatiable, so that they are always ready to provoke and then to follow "the necessary promise" of a new con man into the violence that makes them feel alive. The growing recognition runs throughout West's work: the dissolution of self makes the existence of individual, artist, and nation three dependent coordinates of a con game.

The failure of cultural mediation envisioned by West means that he concentrates unremittingly on the limits of symbolic transformation. We do not discover these bounds, as in the writings of our previous authors, but we are always up against them. And to be in this situation is to confront violence repeatedly. The sole recourse left for the elisions and purgations previously accomplished in ritual process is the last-ditch mode of violence. One attacks those who suffer when it is unbearable to discern their agony anymore;

or, alternatively, assaults those pretended hierophants whose manipulations are blatant failures in the relief of suffering. We can see West's fiction as an ironic illustration of Kenneth Burke's philosophy: where Burke is guardedly optimistic respecting symbolic transformations, West pessimistically sees a directly opposite result. Burke might be construed as saying that a total awareness of ritual role-shifting in language will conduce to peace. His grand comic vision is of the human race meeting in a great dialectical circle to find, through this awareness, the common ground underlying their differences instead of murdering in their name. In contrast, West sees such a consciousness in the face of ubiquitous pain as either conducing to self-conscious catatonia, to even more vicious, thin, and self-blinding fictions, or to a violence idealistically aimed at shattering everything—fictions, fiction-makers, sufferers, and suffering—once and for all. When West says that "In America, violence is idiomatic," he means it exactly. After language fails, as it must with all distances short-circuited, violence must do the work of communication. One of West's bizarre instances can stand for all: in *Miss Lonelyhearts*, the Supreme Pontiff of the Liberal Church of America plans to offer prayers for an executed murderer "on an adding machine. Numbers, he explained, constitute the only universal language. [The murderer] killed Joseph Zemp, an aged recluse, in an argument over a small amount of money" (p. 73).

West's first novel, *The Dream Life of Balso Snell*, is set in the bowels of the Trojan Horse, which is "inhabited solely by writers in search of an audience . . ." (p. 37). As another character explains, " 'Art is a sublime excrement' " (p. 8). The book's studiedly clever protective coloration should induce, not block, our awareness that West is dealing with his own precocious crisis of confidence as a writer; and even before he encountered the frustrating neglect for which Melville's career provides the type.

Art is an excrement in that it seems to be a waste, a by-product, of the fundamentally selfish yet symbiotic relationship of artist and audience: the audience needing the stimulating illusions of the artist in order to feel that it exists and the artist needing someone to see his illusions for the same reason. The epitome of this alliance is one artist's relations with his mistress Saniette ("exactly those of performer and audience"). The casualness of her responses "excited me so that I became more and more desperate in my performances." But because of the excited extravagance of his complaint to her, "Saniette was able to turn my revenge into a joke. She weathered a second beating with a slow, kind smile" (pp. 25–30). The secondary, by-product nature of art is further indicated by the book's repeated explanation that creativity is a vehicle for sexual conquest and by the frequent suggestion that the content of art is inconsequential as long as it seems excitingly portentous; standing before his "cringing audience," another performer climaxes his act "by keeping in the air an Ivory Tower, a Still White Bird, the Holy Grail, the Nails, the Scourge, the Thorns, and a piece of the True Cross" (p. 56). The thesis that art must be a self-defensive act of aggression fulfilling the ulterior needs of performer and viewer is chiefly borne out in the long literary leg-pull of the book. We begin by entering the anus of the deceitful Trojan Horse, and after complicated stories-within-stories-and-dreams that explode in our faces after asking to be taken seriously, we finally come to a conclusion that defines the whole book as an excremental act, a wet-dream. There is little doubt that the excrement of West the con artist is aimed at the "discriminating few" who persist in aligning themselves on the side of the artist by reading *Balso Snell*.

The Dream Life of Balso Snell, which is a sketchbook of all West's preoccupations, begins his career by interdicting the possibility of direct regeneration, in a parodic journey to a cultural source. The book displaces the generative act, at any level of meaning, to the eliminatory. As in the bowels of the wooden horse, everything in West's fiction claustro-phobically presses upon individual or artistic *Lebensraum*, and an inventive variety of images and events dramatizes the need for a purgation to relieve the suffocating excess. This is the precondition for any recovery of generative function, for the deep source of culture is foully contami-nated—human interchange is a Trojan Horse, a treacherous "hidden imposthume" seen in West's type of ceremoniously savage comedy instead of tragedy. Once we understand this, we can see the important point obscured by critics who have frequently made, and often forced, comparisons be-tween West's fiction and Eliot's *The Waste Land*. The precise meaning of *waste* for the later artist is clearly given in the first novel and is redesignated thereafter in terms that amplify the idea without fully abandoning its initial grossness. West's Waste Land takes on the crucial difference of meaning that dominates much contemporary writing: refuse, trash. The polluting detritus of a civilization, rather than its barrenness, is the emphasis, sharply reversing the order of stress in Eliot's famous piece. In West and his successors there is not the spiritual desiccation of the desert, with its immediate potentials for leading Elijahs to internal springs of faith, but the overburdened, thick dehydration of a general hangover. To abandon parables: Eliot's desert is fundamentally a time-honored mediate ground, a liminal stage in the process of rebirth. Eliot's ruins are to be shored up, if only by fragments of regenerative memory; West's ruins and fragments both have been macerated into baser stuff, and must be somehow cleared away before even a spiritual desert is possible.

To read West and the contemporary writing he antici-pated in the by-now nostalgic light of the Modern Tradition is to miss the exact problem that is being addressed and the reason for important shifts in tone. In brief, the equiva-lent of cultural constipation, fatal but embarrassingly ri-diculous, calls for purgation by an anxious, painful comedy, not by tragic solemnity. West's apprentice novel foreshadows its own kind of menacing, ridiculous, yet close-retained waste in a long line of comic or picaresque successors: "the junk that memory had made precious" (*Miss Lonelyhearts*); the "surfeit of shoddy," imaged in the Grand Canyon filled up with razor blades (*A Cool Million*); "the final dumping ground," the "dream dump" of Hollywood, where the god of love lies fallen in old newspapers (*The Day of the Locust*); and, beyond West's fiction: Bellow's Chicago junkyard of "the gyps of previous history," "like a terribly conceived church of madmen . . . where worshippers crawl their carts of rags and bones" (*Augie March*); the "firm cloacal grip on life" of Donleavy's rogue (*The Ginger Man*); Pyncheon's bizarrely haunted sewers, and conspiracy of W.A.S.T.E. (*V* and *The Crying of Lot 49*); Barthelme's farcical entrepreneurs, who boast that they are "the leading edge of this trash phenomenon" (*Snow White*)—and countless other metaphors for the duplicitous traffic in mass contagion. Everything, West foresaw, is used up in the perfected stereotypes and pseudo-familiarities of an accelerated modern communication; the hyperbolic dreams intended to compensate turn out to be only more rapid means of using up the world and the self with human handling. In a vast circular system, facile masquerades of stereotypes answer to the exaggerations of illusion: the culture is thus defined as a confidence game, with its transactions in the medium of trash. Haplessly, the Trickster's catabolic function has been institutionalized and trivialized. Symbolically, the aspiring artist of confidence can only ironically elaborate the waste representing the dissolution of all boundaries, and thus attempt to re-distance his audience, to re-create mediation.

West knows that the general cultural dissipation does not dissipate, but only collects further waste. His career after *Balso Snell* is a high-wire act carried out in large measure as a dramatization and defiance of the recognition that Melville's *Pierre* puts in these words: "Like knavish cards, the leaves of all great books were covertly packed. He was but packing one set the more . . ." (book xxv, chapter iii). The "modern" art that, at base, attacks art has few more distinguished examples than West's second novel, *Miss Lonelyhearts*. The third work, *A Cool Million*, is almost ruined by another outbreak of West's scorn, though it is less shrill than that of *Balso Snell*. In *Miss Lonelyhearts*, however, Shrike serves as a lightning rod that draws off from the novel itself West's coruscating desire for parody and delivers it as stunning irony directed at Miss Lonelyhearts' realization that he can no longer play a joke with the real sufferings of his readers.

In both *Miss Lonelyhearts* and *The Day of the Locust* West extends his inquisition of the art-game to an exhibition of the art by which everyone lives. Human life is exposed as a set of tricks and defective rituals by means of which one person asks another for assurance, with the implied promise that confidence will be returned if the other cooperates in the game. People exist by inducing others to trust roles. Miss Lonelyhearts and Tod Hackett both make repeated, knowing attempts to stimulate themselves by concentrating on the artifice of existence: "[Miss Lonelyhearts] tried to excite himself into eagerness by thinking of the play Mary [Shrike] made with her breasts. . . . One of her tricks was to wear a medal low down on her chest" (p. 90); "She thanked him by offering herself in a series of formal, impersonal gestures . . . and there was something clearly mechanical in her pantomime" (p. 94). Tod's paintings are completely inspired by trickery: Faye Greener's "elaborate gesture[s] . . . so completely meaningless, almost formal, that she seemed a dancer rather than an affected actress" (p. 304); Harry's masklike face and intentionally burlesque devices; and the countless charades of Hollywood, where even the landlady's interest in Harry's funeral "wasn't morbid; it was formal. She was interested in the arrangement of the flowers, the order of the procession, the clothing and deportment of the mourners" (p. 341). But the roles West's characters put on display are inordi-

nately unconvincing. The players lack sufficient selfhood to
act confidently; the poses are transparent, obviously secondhand, loose-fitting, as if originally intended for someone
else. In West's extravagant comedy, the very lizards of *The
Day* are inept, "self-conscious and irritable" (p. 297).

The supreme form of confidence, religious faith, is the
dramatic center of *Miss Lonelyhearts*. Christ, the ultimate
Miss Lonelyhearts, is the sovereign conferrer of belief;
and West's protagonist, once he finds it impossible to betray
his readers' trust anymore, is forced to search for a self that
will give validity not only to his role but to Christ's. The
design is basic West. A tormented, cheated mob forces a
man to attempt to fashion an authentic self that will make
his role effective in giving the mob authenticity in turn. Miss
Lonelyhearts must play the part that the shadowy Dr.
Pierce-All does in *The Day*. He must indicate the road to
life. Such is the interdependence of all of West's huddled
artifacts—people, animals, and things in a continuum of
gaudy sterility—that one has the awesome sense that if
anyone in this world came to genuine life, Miss Lonelyhearts' whole "world of doorknobs" would indeed follow
suit miraculously. Christ is the answer, Miss Lonelyhearts
knows, but he is also aware that for him Christ is another
trick, a "hysteria" in whose "mirrors . . . the dead world
takes on a semblance of life" (p. 75). However, tricks and
mirrors are all that is available, so in a grimly comic parody
of the existentialist hero's quest to create himself, West's
hero willfully attempts to indulge the deception to the
hilt. As Shrike says, " 'the Miss Lonelyhearts are the priests
of twentieth-century America' " (p. 69).

The hero's dreams begin to reflect the shamanistic magician-priest's role that is part of the trickster's basic reper-
toire: "he found himself on the stage of a crowded theater.
He was a magician who did tricks with doorknobs. At his
command, they bled, flowered, spoke." But when he tries
to continue by leading the audience in prayer, he fails: "no
matter how hard he struggled, his prayer was one Shrike

had taught him and his voice was that of a conductor calling stations. 'Oh, Lord, we are not of those who wash in water, urine, vinegar. . . . Oh, Lord, we are of those who wash solely in the Blood of the Lamb' " (p. 76). For most of the novel Miss Lonelyhearts is the unconfident confidence man whose rituals are impotent and whose world remains stubbornly dead. West's "Drummond light" does not give even the illusion of working—nothing starts up to it.

Skeptical of his own roles and the illusions on which they are built, the West hero is vulnerable because of his inability to cloak himself completely with a façade, even the falsely protective kind others adopt. Desiring to find a believable role and yet despising the lies of which roles are made, he maintains an envious love-hate relationship with those who have apparently achieved invulnerability through manipulation of illusions—Shrike and Betty in *Miss Lonelyhearts* and Faye Greener in *The Day*. Betty and Faye share the "power to limit experience arbitrarily" (p. 79), Betty to the order bounded by gingham apron and party dress, and Faye to the mental screen where she projects a bright confetti of fragmented film strips.

Just as Miss Lonelyhearts is an eviscerated con artist, Shrike is a joke at trickery. His mockery is open. He is a papier-mâché Satan for our times, his dead-pan trick and his patter about a goat and adding-machine religion pointedly derived from the cinema and newspapers. He is the master player in the novel, admired, emulated, and feared because his game is to destroy games. Other people are poor, unpersuasive players; Shrike's exaggerated pretense at pretense establishes him as an expert at being unconvincing, and his superlative shoddiness doubly mocks their ineptitude. His dead pan fleers at their deadness. His complementary simpleton act ironically reflects the shams by which everyone asks for confidence: "While talking, he kept his face alive with little nods and winks that were evidently supposed to inspire confidence and to prove him a very simple fellow." Yet even Shrike is not wholly invulnerable. As he tells about his sterile relationship with his wife, "the dead pan broke and pain actually crept into his voice. . . . It was Miss Lonelyhearts' turn to laugh. Shrike tried to ignore him by finishing as though the whole thing were a joke" (p. 92). There is apparently a limit of tolerance for everyone in a world of tricks when the joke is no longer funny and one can no longer fool oneself sufficiently. At the moment this limit is reached in West, we teeter precariously between apocalyptic outrage and terrible laughter. The moment of laughter is particularly horrifying, for the sound is an automatic hedge against a crushing self-knowledge, and it resonates mechanically with the emptiness it seeks to shield. In traditional comedy the grace of laughter descends to dissolve difficulties in the end. West's comedy is black because it says that laughter is not enough, not nearly enough. Shrike's anti-game says the same thing of the specious assurance that has no foundation except mutual complicity.

Shrike's transparent simpleton's pose is a parodic version of the fool-character that fascinates West, who exhibits his diverse clowns, from Peter Doyle to Harry Greener, with the connoisseurship of a collector. Miss Lonelyhearts too tries at times to play the fool in a desultory way, but the paramount role he eventually tries to perfect is that of the Holy Fool, the Pauline fool in Christ. The traditional energy and dominion available to the fool-role is evident in the literary convention and religious paradox that identifies ultra-simplicity with divinely inspired wisdom. In the trickster's search for power, the fool-pose is ideal because it disarmingly tends to elicit a responsive simplicity from others. As Melville's hero advised, one must learn to play the fool in the human masquerade. In West's fiction the fool-role is crucial above all because it represents a way of dealing with a diminished self; in this sense, we may say, all of West's characters are fools.

Miss Lonelyhearts is thus more successful as the Holy Fool than as the magician-priest. In fact, in the transformation that takes place in the last pages of the novel he seems to achieve his desire to become a man of confidence. The inner sureness and stability that he suddenly comes to possess are unshakeable when Shrike fetches him for the sport intended as the paradigm of Miss Lonelyhearts' hapless cheating: " 'There's a game we want to play and we need you to play it.—"Everyman his own Miss Lonelyhearts." I invented it, and we can't play without you' " (p. 132). The sturdy rock that Miss Lonelyhearts has within him has made him invulnerable to Shrike, whose mock party game he ignores in order to play a "real" game with Betty. "The party dress had given his simplified mind its cue," and he finally becomes like the instinctive con man, responding accurately and effectively to the needs of his audience, manifested in its poses: "He was not deliberately lying. He was only trying to say what she wanted to hear. . . . He begged the party dress to marry him, saying all the things it expected to hear. . . . He was just what the party dress wanted him to be: simple and sweet, whimsical and poetic, a trifle collegiate yet very masculine" (p. 137). Miss Lonelyhearts' religious experience and his murder follow with inevitable logic from this successful artistry.

The rock upon which all these phenomena are founded is West's ironic summation of modern selfhood—a compromise between schizophrenia and a catatonic state. In simpler words, it is little more than Betty's ability to limit experience arbitrarily. "He did not feel. The rock was a solidification of his feeling, his conscience, his sense of reality, his self-knowledge" (p. 138). Earlier, he had felt that his confusion was more significant than Betty's order, although when he tried to pretend that his confusion was "honest feeling . . . the trick failed" (p. 79). But he also reflects that "Man has a tropism for order" (p. 104). The tropism at length dominates his confusion, which is a function of his painful awareness and sensitivity. When these precipitate out into his private rock, he becomes another stone object, congruent with the "enormous grindstones" (p. 101) that are Fay Doyle's buttocks and the obelisk in the park "about to spout a load of granite seed" (p. 89). In short, he has not revitalized the world but has become more solidly a part of what Balso Snell called the mundane millstone.

Miss Lonelyhearts' final return to his bed is a continuation of the illness that had prostrated him earlier: "he realized that his . . . sickness was unimportant. It was merely a trick by his body to relieve one more profound" (p. 111). The pronoun *one* hangs provocatively between the antecedents *sickness* and *trick*. With the arrival of fever, which "promised . . . mentally unmotivated violence," the ironic revelation and martyrdom of Miss Lonelyhearts commences. The vision is of everything the protagonist lacks, a light-source that rays out life to the world: the transcendent Miss Lonelyhearts, Christ, "is life and light"; he is a "bright fly, spinning with quick grace" to which "the black world of things" rises like a fish. Anticipating the image of performers writhing like fish before their inert captors in *The Day of the Locust*, the metaphor encapsulates the absurd possibilities of being thus hooked by the bait: frenetic activity winding down to absolute rigidity. In West's fiction, energy is a performer's desperate gambit, and it is that of frenzy; where all mediation is absent, there is no transitional state between this and the dramatic entropy of incipient inertia, the condition of a stone or waste. The same simplified, limited ordering of experience that causes Miss Lonelyhearts to hug his internal stone makes him mistake Peter Doyle's cry of warning for a cry of help. The hero rushes to perform for his last audience—Desperate, Sick-of-it-all, and all the rest—with fatal, and false, confidence. As he had told Betty earlier, he is really the victim of a joke, not its perpetrator.

II

One major attribute of West's self-doubt as an artist, his haste to laugh at himself before we do, gets the best of him in his next novel, *A Cool Million*. It is a bit like listening to the runaway laughter of Harry Greener. In the parody of Alger that turns into a self-travesty, West yields again to the con artist's aggressive temptation to flaunt his props and mechanisms. In *The Day* Tod is charmed by Faye's amateurish artificiality: "because he saw the perspiring stagehands and the wires that held up the tawdry summerhouse . . . he accepted everything and was anxious for it to succeed" (p. 316). The triumph of urgent need over acting skill that captivates West as it does Tod has an obvious ironic counterpart in Shrike's simulations. Yet West is unable to bring off a satiric work that gets stuck in a grey monotone somewhere between the amateurish charm of Faye's artifice and the expert counterfeiting of Shrike's. West can neither make us share a "camp" interest in Horatio Alger's sweating stagehands nor a savage bitterness in response to the Algeresque chicanery of the American Dream. Nevertheless, *A Cool Million* is not merely regressive; seen in the context of West's career, it represents his progressive generalization from the self-doubt of the artist to an understanding that this provides a key insight into a national as well as a personal malaise. Whenever West has a new or deepened perception his first instinct is to parody it. Thus *A Cool Million* bears much the same relationship to West's last novel that *Balso Snell* does to *Miss Lonelyhearts*. It is West's version of *The Gilded Age*, as *Balso Snell* was of *Innocents Abroad*.

Although con men, frauds, shysters, and masquerades abound in comic plenty on every page of *A Cool Million*, the novel is built on a simple sequence of proportions with three major terms: the patriotic con man Shagpoke Whipple is to the nation, as the literary con man Sylvanus Snodgrasse is to the Chamber of American Horrors, as Nathanael West is to the novel.

The confession of faithlessness by Snodgrasse is a setspeech bit of hyperbole that asks to be discounted: "Like many another 'poet,' he blamed his literary failure on the American public . . . and his desire for revelation was really a desire for revenge. Furthermore, having lost faith in himself, he thought it his duty to undermine the nation's faith in itself" (p. 238). West is clowning at himself and the truth. The book's ridiculous over-stylization itself is revenge enough on the reader, and the nation's confidence is not undermined but exposed and found to be rotten. Although the massive national fraud, the "surfeit of shoddy," is burlesqued to the point that the indictment loses force, in places the power of West's own doubt isolates the native virus sharply. " 'We accepted [the white man's] civilization,' " orates an Indian chief, " 'because he himself believed in it. But now that he has begun to doubt, why should we continue to accept? His final gift to us is doubt, a soul-corroding doubt' " (p. 232).

Over against this secret modern doubt is set the absurd confidence of traditional American iconic figures like the "ring-tail roarer" Missourian, which are made into flat stereotypic pop-up targets for satire along Lemuel Pitkin's picaresque road. The chief target is Shagpoke Whipple, ex-President, cracker barrel expounder of faith in America, enemy of "sophistication," Fascist dictator, and confidence man from first to last. Lemuel Pitkin, the stock-fool, is conned, beaten, or otherwise exploited by everyone in the book. His adventures touch on every kind of fraudulent victimization in the whole American Chamber of Horrors. Finally, after his dismantling and martyrdom, he is apotheosized as the American Boy and held up as an icon and mirror to Whipple's followers in order to fleece them further. The moral is shouted at us so loudly it is a sneer: the *schlemiel* Huck Finn's trust in the American dream of success means betrayal for himself and triumph for the native confidence game.

The suspicion that somehow, some unnameable agent has cheated them of something valuable hangs like the smell of smoke in the empty personalities of *The Day of the Locust*. West's ability to capture this mood is perhaps the most remarkable quality of the novel, but the book also has a certain diffuseness everyone has noted. In *Miss Lonelyhearts* plot was coterminous with meaning; the flesh and bone of *The Day* never quite connect, in part because West makes his most ambitious attempt to deal with the individual, artistic, and national crises of confidence that he feels are interrelated. The three threads of plot weave in and out of each other in the sort of disquieted ballet performed by the masqueraders and the mob that watches.

West's heroes have already lost their innocence but still attempt an open-eyed, desperate, fool's indulgence in resplendent fakery—Miss Lonelyhearts in the hysteria of the Christ-dream, and Tod in the sex-fantasy centered on Faye Greener. If Beagle Darwin in *Balso Snell* talks like "a man in a book" (p. 47), Faye is a girl out of a movie, personifying and acting out Hollywood's virgin-bitch-goddess role. The destructive force of this sexuality is plain ("it would be like throwing yourself from the parapet of a skyscraper"), but Tod needs the artificial stimulation as badly as anyone in the novel: "he would be glad to throw himself, no matter what the cost" (p. 271). Toward the end of the novel he begins to suspect that he too suffers "from the ingrained, morbid apathy he liked to draw in others. Maybe he could only be galvanized into sensibility and that was why he was chasing Faye." Tod's paintings of Faye at first had been the sublimation of his desire for sexual stimulus; once he sees the truth, he turns again to art as a saving game. He uses "one of the oldest tricks in the very full bag of the intellectual," which is to tell himself that he had drawn Faye enough times and to seek new models in Hollywood's insane religions. "It was a childish trick, hardly worthy of a primitive witch doctor, yet it worked" (p. 365). Tod escapes temporarily into art from Faye's attraction; but, for all his intellectual awareness of affectation, perhaps he is never capable of the deeply buried horror Homer Simpson instinctively feels at the small "dirty black hen" hidden within the statuesque blond sham. For Homer there is no escape at all.

Tod's (and West's) reaction to Hollywood is also his reaction to Abe Kusich's "grotesque depravity": indignation
coupled with an excitement that "made him feel certain
of his need to paint" (p. 264). Neither Abe the bookie nor
Hollywood come off as really depraved, however, nor are
they meant to. There is no evil in West's fiction; there are
only voids and needs. The suffering that is everywhere
seems the result of a vast scheme of raking violence. But
despite the omnipresence of suffering it seems sourceless—
no locatable evil has produced it. Depravity is a pose inseparable from an original warp of the soul, the same trick
of creation itself that made Homer a defective automaton.
Yet where is the Trickster? Melville's "metaphysical scamp"
bears the obvious yet ambiguous trappings of sacrality, both
divine and diabolic. Lacking such a figure, West's fiction
has no cosmic targets for resentment. When Miss Lonelyhearts searches the sky for a target, it "looked as if it had
been rubbed with a soiled eraser. It held no angels, flaming
crosses, olive-bearing doves, wheels within wheels" (p. 71).
Later when he again examines the sky "for a clue to his own
exhaustion," it is merely "canvas-colored and ill-stretched"
(p. 100). The gods have departed, addresses unknown, after
untidily erasing a few mistakes and putting up a covering
that fools no one.

However, Miss Lonelyhearts does find a clue to his personal exhaustion in the skyscrapers that rear up around
him: "Americans have dissipated their radical energy in
an orgy of stone breaking" and in building a civilization
of "forced rock and tortured steel" (p. 100). *The Day of
the Locust* elaborates the idea of radical exhaustion in
image after image of somnolence, impotence, and sheer
tiredness. The god of love lies facedown in a pile of old
newspapers on a movie set; Homer Simpson sleeps as if after
centuries of stone breaking that have left him a hulking,
tired shell; the betrayed mob stands listlessly about with
shabby clothes and worn personalities. The dissolution of
core vitality that is the individual's existential condition is

also his national heritage, a social-hereditary strain of spiritual debility. The energy that broke stones can now only construct fairy-tale edifices of lath and paper, a fantasy culture that in turn dupes and eviscerates its creators in an endless mechanical cycle. Melville's trickster offered to sell lots in the New Canaan on the frontier's edge, but West's Second Jerusalem has already been bought, built, and sold out; and it now threatens to collapse like the Waterloo movie scenery. It is already time to anticipate the next millennium in the Tabernacle of the Third Coming.

As William Carlos Williams indicated, West is the artist of city existence[6]—an enclosed world in which everything reflects only the human back to the human, in two complementary forms: "the paraphernalia of suffering" (p. 104), and the ludicrously blown-up and trivialized symbols of transformation that jade everyone. The world is alien because it is too familiar; humanity can find no opposite to measure itself by—Miss Lonelyhearts imagines that flowers smell like human feet; and animate and inanimate things interchange with and frustrate each other: "The decay that covered the surface of the mottled ground was not the kind in which life generates" (p. 70). Faye Greener holds out the essential promise of vital process—"She looked just born, everything moist and fresh, volatile and perfumed" (p. 314)—but she is only the sum of movies she has seen, parts she has mimicked. And it is significant that West can only present confidence tricksters as burlesque puppets (Shagpoke Whipple), failed or inverted con men (Miss Lonelyhearts and Shrike), or disembodied symbols (Dr. Know-All Pierce-All). Mock tricksters alone are possible in a culture that is itself a perpetual-motion swindling device; there can be no master manipulator when everything has already been too much handled. There is no Trickster; but there is, at

[6] "A New American Writer," *Il Mare* 11, 21 Jan. 1931, 4; and "Sordid? Good God!" *Contempo* 3, 25 July 1933, 1, 8; both rpt. in Martin, *Critical Essays.*

the end of West's fiction, an odd, seemingly perverse dream of one.

The Third Coming is really but a scatological joke. Tod Hackett's climactic vision of apocalypse is, as West says, "his escape," a mental painting of a symbolic Trickster who could purge the nation by incitement to violence: "A super 'Dr. Know-All Pierce-All' had made the necessary promise and they were marching behind his banner in a great united front of screwballs and screwboxes to purify the land. No longer bored, they sang and danced joyously in the red light of the flames." Tod pictures the last scene with zestful delight because it is *conclusive*, a terminal violence instead of the unbearably inconclusive back-and-forth surging Tod is literally caught up in with the rioting mob. What he imagines would be, precisely, artistic, with the meaning of intensified finality, closure: "to make his escape still more complete he [mentally] stood on a chair and worked at the flames in an upper corner of the canvas, modeling the tongues of fire so that they licked even more avidly at a corinthian column that held up the palmleaf roof of a nutburger stand" (p. 420). In thus seeking a final outlet for what suffocates him, Tod's apocalyptic vision is just as specious as Miss Lonelyhearts' dream of Christ. The super Dr. Know-All Pierce-All is much more a thing of desire than fear, for he constitutes the imagination of a really effective trickster performer who can replace the inept ones, including Tod himself, fleeing from the mob in Tod's painting. Tod's mental act is not an external, clinching comment by West; it is conclusive solely as the summary of the general malaise, as when Tod mimics the police siren. Tod's presented art cannot escape the condition it depicts; but, by being clear about the shared apocalyptic hunger for purgation, West places its seductive danger before us, double-framed within Tod and his imagined scene.

West once said that his writing was unpopular because it offered nothing to root for. Contemporary criticism, however, apparently has found something, in a way that fulfills West's prophecy ironically—for though he was clear about the status of Tod's vision, our critics generally have not been, and thus have been deceived by the dangerous hunger for the conclusive unburdening, all-revealing violence that is the most revealing thing West has to tell us about ourselves. West, to his credit, can find no such ending, but in presenting a last image of the disaffected audience, he leaves us with a beginning: with ourselves. The real con man of the novel is Nathanael West, the artist of unconfidence.

III

*Surely, and truly I honour them . . . and for that very reason
I make bold to be gamesome about them. . . . The fools and
pretenders of humanity, and the impostors and baboons
among the gods, these only are offended with raillery. . . .*

Pierre

In understanding how West makes a convincing art out of unconfidence, we may begin by considering his bizarre characters. West's characters, unconvincing in their daily shams, are modern men with a diminished radical integrity, yet they do not much resemble the attenuated presences who whisper and gossip hollowly in the fiction of Beckett and Sarraute. Because West's characters are still urgently trying to have life, to redeem the promise of which they have been swindled, they are gaudy and violent, like Melville's and Twain's more accomplished masqueraders. The elaborate exactness with which West catches their grotesquery is a skill that manages to be at once extravagant and austere. It is that of a practiced liar dealing with people whose lives are lies.

West is a confidence trickster not primarily because his style sometimes leers heavily at us but because his writing becomes a game of confidence that makes writing possible. His bitter self-doubt, activated by the role of magical guru the modern artist is asked to play, turns instinctively to the ludicrous strategies of make-believe. The game takes its strength from the confidence it seeks to win from us, the audience. Anticipating that confidence (this is the crucial initial "leap" of faith in the game), the artist first tricks himself into commitment to his work. It is as if the writer by his tone must never fully admit to himself, at least while the pen is in his hand, that he is trying to tell the truth, for he hasn't sufficient confidence for that role, and the realization would make art impossible for him. Like Tod Hackett, he must remind himself ironically that he is a painter, not a prophet. He commits himself to art as a trick to win confidence in the face of doubt, beneath which is a need for belief. Having admitted that art is a trick, he can allow himself to have faith in it insofar as it is an enticing game, and his skill both expresses and preserves that precarious conviction. West's artistry thus becomes a mental judo that makes the force of doubt lend momentum to confident creation. Solid images change surreally from one thing to another, natural facts bend like rubber artifacts, metaphors are absurdly reified, and pretense and reality blend into each other and dissolve. The fictional world is fantastic and full of ironies to remind one level of the writer's consciousness that a trick is being played, but the surreal world must be made vividly, exactly, with disciplined craft because it must also convince, win belief. If the writer is intelligent, perceptive, and lucky, then his bizarre lies will coincide with and betray the lies that exist in our lives. And this is the con artist's truth. This is West's delight in meticulous tall tales that circle around the doubt that feeds them.

It may be objected that every artist is in a sense a confidence man who tries to win our belief in his illusions of reality. And further, Schiller has told us that all art is a game. But not every artist has a radical self-doubt that is so close to the surface, and so much "compensated" by a bravura of fantasy and trickery, both stylistic and thematic. The account of West's genius that I am attempting to give is the same account of the artist that his work dramatizes; it is one of his central subjects, and the bizarreness of his presentation is as acute as his intimate self-awareness. Neither is a reductive description. If we are all tricksters, then art can be one of those tricks that illumine instead of darken our knowledge. Literature is a fabrication, a tissue of words, lies told in the service of truth—that complacent cliché becomes fresh, the tired phrase becomes vivid insight again in West's four brief novels.

Whatever wider applicability the wound-and-the-bow parable of art has, it is exact in regard to West. The crisis of doubt can produce, to be sure, a low-grade parody that winks at itself in the men's-room mirror. But when West plays his game most skillfully, the self-protective tendency toward a tone of austere detachment gives his judgments an impressive strength. It is not an exaggeration to say that West's distant perspective, close to the vanishing point of disinterestedness, gives that sense of life's impersonal balances to which Kitto has applied the term *diké*.[7] As with Greek tragedy, West's epiphanies of cruelty in their purity and exactness make us see, unable to avert our eyes, the inhuman, remote face of inexorable balances. This can be achieved in brief scenes: shears cutting through a quail's breast, a conquering fighting-cock eating the eye of a gallant, grotesque bird that we know is really the dwarf Abe Kusich. Or it can be the cumulative impact of a whole book, *Miss Lonelyhearts*. The austerity of West's attitudes has been a crucial matter of praise or blame for his critics; it can serve as a final focus of summation.

[7] H.D.F. Kitto, *Greek Tragedy* (Garden City, N.Y.: Doubleday, 1954). It is not difficult to see why West was such an admirer of Euripides. See his early statement, "You cannot touch it [the *Bacchae*] anywhere without having the desire to write and never stop writing." Quoted in Light, *Nathanael West*, 2nd ed., p. 30. See also Reid, *Fiction*, p. 34 *et passim*.

In the modern vein, Natalie Sarraute has written brilliantly of the way new visions of reality must render themselves in style, in the face of the mutual suspicion between writer and reader. *The Age of Suspicion*, trans. Maria Jolas (New York: Brazillier, 1963).

The effect depends upon a relationship between creator and creation that may be clarified by an analogy involving two famous versions of the supreme Creator. Dante's Maker is superior to Milton's, whom everyone hates, because Dante's is closer to the Greek feeling for life. For all Milton's classical erudition, his God is the (in every sense) personal Deity, who strikes the reader as a peevish, condescending old man whose "feelings" seem personally involved in both punishment and whatever compassion he may show. Milton's justification of God's ways suffers precisely because He is not remote enough, because His compassion and anger are not sufficiently removed from our individual quotidian whims. In the *Comedy*, on the other hand, Dante deals with a genuine Absolute, a Cosmic Being whom the poet admits he can only hint at in man's poor metaphors of circles of fire and light. The remotely iridescent Symbol successfully stands for the ultimate Good, the poem's undergirding Platonic concept, whose universal operation causes joy or suffering as evenhandedly as a gravitational pull causes waves. Milton's God is merely aloof; Dante's is truly remote. There is no more point in questioning Dante's Absolute than there is in questioning the fact that if a child innocently touches a high-voltage wire he will be killed. Such an execution outrages an untragic concept of justice; but it is *dikê*—a boundary is crossed, the scales of life are upset, if ever so slightly, and they will be righted. We can be sure of it, and our own undistracted, compassionate awareness, grounded in a conviction of accurate truth, is thereby released.

The point of the illustration is not to defend an "impersonal theory of art," or a tragic one. There are doubtless many ways of achieving the pure vision to which I refer. Nor is it a matter of Jamesian point of view and technical authorial absence from the work that is at issue. The question I am addressing concerns an extreme remoteness of tone, a positive chill, that readers have often misunderstood or criticized not only in West but in the later Melville and the modern "black humorists." The suspicion arises that these writers are really *ill*-humored. The truth is of course that West and the others are capable of being, and sometimes are, as peevish and as aloof from their creations as Milton's God. This is the West of *Balso Snell* and *A Cool Million*. But in his best writing West sustains a detachment from the infernal regions he depicts that is remote in the way Dante's sphere of Light is remote. Then in West's chill tonal brilliance the shears close on the quail and a bright drop of blood hangs on a feather-tip; Homer Simpson watches lizards eating flies and is himself hooked down by the mouth to be torn apart; the letters come in relentlessly about an idiot girl's rape, about aching kidneys and a demonic husband staring out from under the bed. The judgments, the cruelty, are *pure* and, it seems, self-actuating; and so, therefore, is our compassion.

But it is a strange feeling. There is no catharsis. Laughter is not enough, we know, and tears, real or metaphorical, seem excessive. Instead of being self-transcending, the compassion is finally reflexive. To speak of emphasis, though all three elements interpenetrate to some degree: in Melville, "what remains" as we complete his works is *caritas*; in Twain, the authorial presence; in West, the reader's presence-for-himself. The conclusions of West's superior works produce an effect as if a dead-pan audience or a large camera were suddenly turned close by to face us. Our consequent uneasiness is a groping toward that secret interior place where we keep our selves hidden from view, to see whether the secret is still safe, or even is there any more. The search is unsettling, yet is also oddly detached; for if the artist has communicated, over a great distance, his self-doubt to us, he has also loaned us an impersonal compassion toward what we find.

The camera faces us now, the audience stares its old dead stare and waits. And so we go into our act. . . .

Or do we?

Coda

EVERY statement pays its price, in a progression of narrowing possibilities and widening exclusions. This is as true for a sentence or a novel as it is for the thickened and extended statement, the total interwoven system of communications, called a culture. Every statement precludes in its duration and form some other thing that might have been said. In the largest sense, only one thing can be said at a time, no matter how polyphonic the utterance; the idea's specific formulation, sound, and rhythm delimit other possibilities for what comes next. Words move one at a time, in process, in actual speech or on the page. No matter what one's talent for gestalt, since "no man [or critic] can be coextensive with *what is*" (Melville), and since time must have a stop, each statement pays this price: it is its own limiting condition for expression. The longer one thinks about style, the more it seems clear that, at least for the accomplished writer, something must be said in a certain way in order for anything to get said at all. And further, in order for something not to get said. What a great writer can do is to make the inclusions and preclusions of utterance mutually enabling for his art and mutually enlightening to us.

One way to create this resonating silence of a price paid, the sense of what else might be said (but no less, thought and felt) on a subject, is to play against our customary categories, our associative and especially our dissociative necessities. It can't be that the slippery, insinuating, diabolical Confidence-Man is engaged in the dialectics of love. It can't be that Ishmael the symbolic alien is analogously engaged, and with us. It can't be that Huck Finn, with his lovable

315

self-abasement, is the central instance in a penetrating study of psychosocial hierarchy and obligation. Nevertheless, it is so, for when we do attend to a writer's interposed, pregnant silence, we find that it means he has come up on our deaf side by offering what we take to be incongruous combinations that do not observe our boundaries of thought and perception. Thus surprised, we are tuned to a fresh sense of what is irreducible and axiomatic in human action. We are teased, if not out of thought, then into a generative *lieu de passage* where the forms of the irreducible are disclosed as both an intercontingent whole and, in each individual case, as necessarily exclusive of other simultaneous forms. That is to say, we feel the living pressure of human time and identity in both their aspects of contingency and exigency.

Imagine a spectrum of response to human action, at one end of which is the conceptually unambiguous and morally judged view, and at the other end, the incongruously refreshed, ironically toughened view. Wayne Booth's invaluable book, *The Rhetoric of Fiction*, calls attention to the price paid when a literary work moves along the spectrum from the judged and received toward the irreducible; when, that is, an author does not take as unambiguous a moral stand as possible vis-à-vis his world and its presented values. The price is, simply put, the danger that many readers (especially, of course, those habituated to look solely for such doctrine) will misread the work, see only a confusion of competing nihilisms, and so experience a weakening of moral fiber. It is plain that any work characterized by subtle, scrupulous discriminations of attitude is very likely to be misread, as witness the many who, ironically, misread Booth's own powerfully inclusive, sophisticated book. And perhaps with a weakening of critical fiber. Booth is exactly correct: "we must never pretend that a price was not paid." But it is clear that a tremendous price is also paid in traversing the other way along the spectrum. To speak only on Booth's ground: the great danger at his favored end of the continuum is the rhetorical effect of moral complacency. The misreading likely here, with author and reader perched in unmistakably shared judgment above their world, is a chummy, downward-looking version of Starbuck's great immoral refusal: " 'that horror's not in me.' " It will be recalled that the conscious refusal of connection with the horror Ahab painfully suspects only makes Starbuck the more vulnerable to Ahab's hold, which grapples onto the profound self-potentials Starbuck will not acknowledge. In reading fiction, the moral vulnerability of such complacency, such easy reception of a literary decalogue without the original's burning Sinai or iconoclastic lawgiver, need not be labored. No doubt, to use Booth's manner of arguing, careful reading of the great writers in the period of literature central to him will reveal a subtle moral exercise being conducted rhetorically to forestall complacency. But then, this means that the problem is basically one of careful reading along the whole range of the spectrum. It is difficult to choose between moral temptations involved in either extreme of misreading. However, I grant that, though objectively presented moral ironies are directly provocative, complacency is always more difficult to recognize—and also perhaps more insidious in its working.

Above all, besides the equal and opposite dangers, there is the question of what positive value is sacrificed for what. At one terminus, the author's judgmental perspective implies: thus and so should happen, whatever my story shows. These are works with real conclusions, a solid sense of an ending. At the other, the author's "non-judgmental" perspective implies: thus it happens, just as my story persuades you. These may be works with repeated origins, a sense of a beginning. At one extreme of excellence, there is the value of urbanely insightful certitude, moral and aesthetic pungent crispness—the value of a decalogue, which in the hands of a Jane Austen is an immense positive contribution indeed. The other extreme has this: an irreducible human minimum, a beneath-which-not disclosed in an incongruous perspective that makes us see it new again. So human life touches its source, not at a set of precepts offered, but at an experiential given that must and does operate in peril and uncertitude. Here we have an ethos from which all decalogues will come, and surrounded by a palpable expressive limit—an awareness of costly exclusions. As any powerfully undertaken imaginative testing italicizes the tested resources, whether of self or rhetorical transaction, so this linguistic self-awareness of how strait is the gate of even the richest expression puts us in special re-possession of our shared language, with which we partly make and by which we are partly made. Instead of experiencing communication as a finished construction, we experience it at the molecular level of the rhetorical act, in the sharply distinguished— because problematic—elements of speaker and listener, performer and audience. A writer indeed makes his readers. Some do so by offering us a moral *telos*; and some do so by returning us to originative *ethos*, and showing the necessary de-creation and unrealized creations that every making exacts, without exception, for making itself is in question.

Every statement has its price. Let us not pretend that it is not to be paid. Some statements know their own cost, as part of their deepest knowledge of starting points and first things. Our writers have learned, and teach us. In their greatest works, human confidence discovers its exactions and its possibilities in enacting an eternally original process.

Selected Bibliography

(on the Trickster, play, and related concepts)

Abrahams, Roger D. "Christmas and Carnival on Saint Vincent." *Western Folklore,* 31 (1972), 275–89.

Babcock-Abrahams, Barbara, ed. *The Reversible World: Essays on Symbolic Inversion.* (In press.)

Bateson, Gregory. *Naven.* 1936; rpt. Stanford: Stanford University Press, 1958.

———. *Steps to an Ecology of Mind.* San Francisco: Chandler, 1972.

Berne, Eric. *Games People Play: The Psychology of Human Relationships.* New York: Grove, 1967.

Brown, Norman O. *Hermes the Thief.* New York: Random House, 1947.

Caillois, Roger. *Man, Play, and Games,* trans. Meyer Barash. Glencoe, Ill.: Free Press, 1961.

Campbell, Joseph. *The Hero with a Thousand Faces.* 1949; rpt. Princeton: Princeton University Press, 1968.

———. *The Masks of God: Primitive Mythology.* New York: Viking, 1970.

Cohen, Albert K. *Deviance and Control.* Englewood Cliffs, N.J.: Prentice-Hall, 1966.

Douglas, Mary. *Purity and Danger: An Analysis of Concepts of Pollution and Taboo.* London: Routledge and Kegan Paul, 1966.

Dumézil, Georges. *Loki.* Paris: Maisonneuve, 1948.

Evans-Pritchard, E. E. *The Zande Trickster.* Oxford: The Clarendon Press, 1967.

Festinger, Leon. *A Theory of Cognitive Dissonance.* New York: Row, Peterson, 1957.

Games, Play, Literature. Yale French Studies 41, 1969.

Geertz, Clifford. *Person, Time, and Conduct in Bali: An Essay in Cultural Analysis.* Southeast Asia Studies, no. 14. New Haven: Yale University Press, 1966.

———. "Deep Play: Notes on the Balinese Cockfight." *Daedalus* (Winter 1972), pp. 1–38.

Goffman, Erving. *Encounters: Two Studies in the Sociology of Interaction.* New York: Bobbs-Merrill, 1961.

———. *Interaction Ritual.* Garden City, N.Y.: Anchor Book, 1967.

———. *Relations in Public.* New York: Harper, 1972.

———. *Stigma: Notes on the Management of Spoiled Identity.* Englewood Cliffs, N.J.: Prentice-Hall, 1963.

Gombrich, E. H. *Art and Illusion.* Princeton: Princeton University Press, 1961.

Gluckman, Max. *Order and Rebellion in Tribal Africa.* London: Cohen & West, 1963.

Herskovits, Melville J. *Dahomey: An Ancient West African Kingdom.* 2 vols. New York: Augustin, 1938.

Hobsbawm, E. J. *Social Bandits and Primitive Rebels: Studies in Archaic Forms of Social Movement in the 19th and 20th Centuries.* Glencoe, Ill.: Free Press, 1959.

Huizinga, Johan. *Homo Ludens: A Study of the Play Element in Culture.* 1944; rpt. Boston: Beacon, 1955.

Hymes, Dell. *Reinventing Anthropology.* New York: Random House, 1969.

Jung, C. G. *Symbols of Transformation.* The Collected Works of C. G. Jung, vol. 5. New York: Pantheon, 1956.

Kaiser, Walter. *Praisers of Folly.* Cambridge: Harvard University Press, 1963.

Laing, R. D. *The Divided Self: An Existential Study in Sanity and Madness.* Harmondsworth: Penguin, 1965.

Layard, John. Rev. of Radin's *The Trickster, Journal of Analytical Psychology,* 2 (1957), 106–111.

———. "Note on the Autonomous Psyche and the Ambivalence of the Trickster Concept." *Journal of Analytical Psychology,* 3 (1958), 21–29.

Leach, Edmund. *Claude Lévi-Strauss.* New York: Viking, 1970.

Leach, Edmund. *Rethinking Anthropology*. London: Athlone, 1961.

———. "Pulleyar and the Lord Buddha: An Aspect of Religious Syncretism in Ceylon." *Psychoanalysis and the Psychoanalytic Review*, 49 (1962), 80–102.

Lévi-Strauss, Claude. *The Raw and the Cooked: Introduction to a Science of Mythology*, trans. John and Doreen Weightman. New York: Harper and Row, 1969.

———. *The Savage Mind*. Chicago: University of Chicago Press, 1966.

———. *Structural Anthropology*, trans. Claire Jacobson. New York: Basic Books, 1963.

Lifton, Robert J. *Boundaries: Psychological Man in Revolution*. New York: Random House, 1969.

Metman, Philip. "The Trickster in Schizophrenia." *Journal of Analytical Psychology*, 3 (1958), 5–21.

Piaget, Jean. *Structuralism*, trans. Chaninah Maschler. New York: Harper and Row, 1971.

Radin, Paul. *The Trickster: A Study in American Indian Mythology*. 1956; rpt. New York: Schocken, 1972.

Rooth, Birgitta Anna. *Loki in Scandinavian Mythology*. Lund: C.W.K. Gleerups, 1961.

Stonequist, Everett V. *The Marginal Man: A Study in Personality and Culture Conflict*. New York: Scribner's, 1937.

Turner, Victor W. *The Forest of Symbols: Aspects of Ndembu Ritual*. Ithaca: Cornell University Press, 1967.

———. "Myth and Symbol." *International Encyclopedia of the Social Sciences*. New York: Macmillan, 1968.

———. *The Ritual Process: Structure and Anti-Structure*. Chicago: Aldine, 1969.

Van Gennep, Arnold. *The Rites of Passage*, trans. Monika B. Vizedon and Gabrielle L. Cafee. 1908; rpt. Chicago: University of Chicago Press, 1960.

Welsford, Enid. *The Fool: His Social and Literary History*. London: Faber and Faber, 1935.

Wescott, Joan. "The Sculpture and Myths of Eshu-Elegba, the Yoruba Trickster: Definition and Interpretation in Yoruba Iconography." *Africa*, 32 (1962), 336–54.

Index

Titles of scholars' and critics' works are supplied only when they have a major bearing on this study.

Library of Congress Cataloging in Publication Data

Wadlington, Warwick, 1938-
    The confidence game in American literature.

    Bibliography: p.
    Includes index.
    1. American fiction—History and criticism.
2. Trickster in literature.   3. Deception in literature.
I. Title.
PS374.T7W3   813'.009   75-3480
ISBN 0-691-06294-3